Social Work
From theory to practice
Second edition

Social Work: From theory to practice uses an integrated approach to explore a variety of social theories through social work's unique interpretive lens. Systems, psychodynamic and person-centred theories, and cognitive-behavioural, narrative and strengths-based practices, are addressed specifically, and students are shown how to apply these in human service settings. These theories are supported by case studies written by experienced practitioners, providing an in-depth exploration of the use of theory in practice.

This second edition includes new material on mindfulness, and mind, body and spirit social work, as well as enhanced content relating to Indigenous social work.

Social Work: From theory to practice is an accessible and engaging text, which clearly explains the theories that underpin social work in practice.

Marie Connolly is Professor and Head of Social Work at the University of Melbourne.

Louise Harms is Associate Professor and Deputy Head of Social Work at the University of Melbourne.

Social Work
From theory to practice
Second edition

Marie Connolly   Louise Harms

CAMBRIDGE
UNIVERSITY PRESS

CAMBRIDGE
UNIVERSITY PRESS

477 Williamstown Road, Port Melbourne, VIC 3207, Australia

Cambridge University Press is part of the University of Cambridge.

It furthers the University's mission by disseminating knowledge in the pursuit of education, learning and research at the highest international levels of excellence.

www.cambridge.org
Information on this title: www.cambridge.org/9781107458635

First published 2011
Reprinted 2012 (twice), 2013
Second edition 2015
Reprinted 2016

Cover designed by Tanya De Silva-McKay
Typeset by Integra Software Services Pvt Ltd
Printed in Singapore by C.O.S. Printers Pte Ltd

A catalogue record for this publication is available from the British Library

A Cataloguing-in-Publication entry is available from the catalogue of the National Library of Australia at www.nla.gov.au

ISBN 978-1-107-45863-5 Paperback

Reproduction and communication for educational purposes

The Australian *Copyright Act 1968* (the Act) allows a maximum of one chapter or 10% of the pages of this work, whichever is the greater, to be reproduced and/or communicated by any educational institution for its educational purposes provided that the educational institution (or the body that administers it) has given a remuneration notice to Copyright Agency Limited (CAL) under the Act.

For details of the CAL licence for educational institutions contact:

Copyright Agency Limited
Level 15, 233 Castlereagh Street
Sydney NSW 2000
Telephone: (02) 9394 7600
Facsimile: (02) 9394 7601
Email: info@copyright.com.au

Cambridge University Press has no responsibility for the persistence or accuracy of URLs for external or third-party internet websites referred to in this publication and does not guarantee that any content on such websites is, or will remain, accurate or appropriate.

Please be aware that this publication may contain several variations of Aboriginal and Torres Strait Islander terms and spellings; no disrespect is intended. Please note that the terms 'Indigenous Australians', 'Aboriginal people' and 'Aboriginal and Torres Strait Islander peoples' may be used interchangeably in this publication.

Dedicated to

George Hook and Jane Sullivan

Foreword

We read a lot about social work and theorising, and we are taught that theory is crucial to social work. Yet applying *theory* in practice is not always as easy as it sounds, particularly for new practitioners. In this expanded examination of social work theory and practice, every chapter is replete with descriptions of theory, supported by rich case examples that show how theories connect to the life challenges faced by real people. The conceptual *theory into practice framework* is the bridge used by Connolly and Harms to connect the explanations about how and why life challenges happen with the practice actions of social workers as they work with individuals, families, groups and communities.

A number of years ago, as a student in a social work theory course, I remember thinking, 'I don't get this'. It was also clear from the discussions that followed that my classmates felt the same way. We struggled to understand how one applied theory to practice. I can remember wondering, from a Pasifika point of view, what relevance the theories had to my world. As we progressed through our social work degree and experienced the fieldwork practicum, our ability to connect theory with practice remained tenuous. Students of social work will be relieved to hear that, after a number of years of practice, the connections became clearer. Fast-forward a few years and I found myself teaching social work theory to students at the University of Canterbury in Aotearoa New Zealand's South Island. I recognised the same hesitating attempts to understand the theory/practice interface and the confusion that I knew very well from my own student experience. Thankfully, however, I had the first edition of *Social Work: From Theory to Practice* to help me. I finally had a textbook that enabled us to meaningfully engage with theory and clarified its relationship with the practice of social work. It helped me to purposefully engage students and bring theory to life, which is why I am so pleased to be writing the foreword to this second edition.

Both clients and social workers come to social work with diverse cultural backgrounds and world-views. Perceptions about the relevance or irrelevance of theory to lived realities can impede understanding and knowledge-building. The inclusion of a Prelude by Shawana Andrews focusing on Indigenous and decolonised social work practice is an exciting addition to the text. It brings important contexts to social work and highlights the commitment that Connolly and Harms have to presenting content about different ways of knowing. The Prelude illustrates how non-dominant explanations of the world, and the issues faced by families and communities are better understood in the knowledge that social work has traditionally been dominated by non-Indigenous views of the world. Insights from the Prelude are important to the chapters that follow – each of which is critically illuminated by a cultural lens, interpreting theories and exploring cultural fit.

The book provides a systematic way of developing an understanding of theory and social work practice. But perhaps even more importantly, it clarifies the social work contribution to theory development and application. Students sometimes find it difficult to articulate the role and contribution brought to practice by the social work profession – the particular disciplinary character that we might say is uniquely social work. As Connolly and Harms note, the practice theories discussed in this book are not the sole purview of social work. Other disciplines use client-centred practices, cognitive behavioural theories and narrative ways of working. So what makes these theories *social work* theories? It is the infusion of the social work interpretive lenses articulated in *Social Work: From Theory to Practice*, that make them social work practice theories. The lenses provide the disciplinary character that distinguishes social work practice from other disciplinary applications. This places the social work disciplinary stamp on practice – the recognisable commitment to relationship-based practice, critical reflection, social justice and client-led change. Students using this book will come away with a robust understanding of this and the systemic disciplinary foundation they bring to practice.

Being able to articulate the connection between theory and practice is fundamental to social work. On a daily basis, social workers have to make sound professional judgements based on thoughtful consideration of the information they have before them and of the theoretical knowledge that informs the work. As a social work educator, I am pleased to be able to use a book that helps me to engage students in ways that support them to be confident, reflective and responsive practitioners.

Yvonne Crichton-Hill
Department of Human Services and Social Work
University of Canterbury, New Zealand

Contents

Figures
and tables

Figures

Tables

Preface to the second edition

As social workers, we continually build understandings of practice that are theoretically and experientially informed. Despite occasional disciplinary uncertainty about whether we actually have a theoretical knowledge base underpinning our practice, the social work profession enjoys a long tradition of theorising. Writers have drawn upon a range of important perspectives, and social workers across a range of settings have used them to inform work with clients. Even though many of the theories used by social workers did not originate within the discipline, in applying a social work interpretive lens, we will argue that they have become distinctly social work practice theories. How they become social work practice theories is an important focus of this book.

Social work is fundamentally concerned with both people and their interactions with their environments, so it involves bringing together theories of the inner and outer worlds in which we live. Some social workers will be drawn to inner-world theories – such as psychodynamic approaches – that focus on individual and familial systems. Others will prefer outer-world theories that influence structural inequalities and disadvantage. Whether social workers are drawn to inner or outer world theories, our unique disciplinary lens creates theoretical responses that reinforce key disciplinary concerns so that theories are responsive to the needs of the people we work with and address broader social justice issues.

While social workers draw upon a range of theoretical perspectives, in this book our focus is on practice theories – theories that have both explanatory power that helps us to gain insight into the causes of distress, and practical direction and technique. We will use an integrated framework, adapted from Connolly and Healy (2013), to illustrate the way in which theory translates into practice, where theoretical explanations logically suggest practice approaches, then a set of techniques (see Figure 1.2 in Chapter 1). This process of unfolding from theory to practice is important, because it illustrates internal logic and theoretical consistency, and highlights in a relatively straightforward way how theories differ from one another. For this reason, we will use the framework consistently as we explore each of the theoretical perspectives presented in this book.

In talking to social work students and practitioners over a number of years, we have come to appreciate many of the challenges faced in translating theory into practice. We nevertheless see theories as important conceptual tools that can help us to navigate our way through complex human troubles. So, in addition to providing the theory/practice integrated framework explaining the unfolding of theory into practice, we have also invited experienced practitioners to reflect upon how they have used theory in their own work. These case studies, which are scattered through the chapters that follow, provide rich examples of ways in which theory is translated into practice across a range of contemporary practice settings.

In bringing together this second edition, we are delighted to have our colleagues Yvonne Crichton-Hill from the University of Canterbury write the Foreword and Shawana Andrews from the University of Melbourne write a Prelude to this edition. These are important contributions, which speak from different cultural perspectives about the ways in which social work practice can be more responsive to cultural need. Māori and Pasifika people in Aotearoa New Zealand and Aboriginal and Torres Strait Islander peoples in Australia continue to confront disadvantage and inequity, often finding themselves at the front-end of service delivery. Yvonne and Shawana share their ideas with us, providing important insights into how we might use social work theory – and how we might strive to be more culturally responsive in practice.

In this book, we capture key international perspectives in the development of social work theory and some of the unique cultural practices of Australia and Aotearoa New Zealand. Social work can be seen as a global endeavour, in that there is coherence in terms of disciplinary vision, values and concerns. Yet it is also intensely local in its application, responding necessarily to unique cultural contexts. Attention to culture and diversity is critically important when thinking about the application of theory in practice. In the chapters that follow, we invite the challenging of theoretical constructs in ways that respond to cultural context. Theories can be used positively to increase understanding and to help people work through difficulties in their lives. They can also be used to impose professional ideas in ways that are prejudicial to the interests of clients or lack synchronicity with their concerns.

In Chapter 1, we look specifically at the ways in which social work's interpretive lens helps us to interrogate theory so that it responds to the concerns of the people with whom we work. In fact, we look at four interpretive lenses, each of which reflects important disciplinary concerns: the *relational lens*, which highlights the importance of relationship-based practice; the *social justice lens*, which reinforces core disciplinary concerns relating to social reform; the *reflective lens*, which interrogates the power of cultural thinking and the ways in which culture shapes professional responses; and the *lens of change*, which informs the ways in which we understand the nature of change in human systems. As we explore the different theoretical perspectives, we come back to these lenses as important disciplinary influences that shape the application of theoretical ideas in practice. In Chapter 1, we also scaffold ideas that support the understanding of theory: what a theory is and what has influenced theory development over time. Then, in Chapter 2, we look at the ways in which models of practice have emerged from theoretical ideas. Social work has pioneered the development of models and frameworks that help to bridge theoretical ideas and intervention strategies within daily practice. One of the most enduringly influential frameworks developed by social work theorists has been Reid and Epstein's (1972) landmark task-centred casework model. We also look at models that explore dimensions of culture, providing important knowledge that can be incorporated into assessment processes and intervention practices. We argue that when theory, knowledge and practice come together in this way, it builds the fabric of a rich and continually evolving intellectual tradition within social work.

We then begin an exploration of key theoretical perspectives that have informed social work thinking and practice over time. Chapter 3 begins with an examination of systems theory, arguably one of the most influential sets of ideas to shape social work practice. Drawing upon the work of key writers, we explore the ways in which systems theories help us to think about interactions between people and their social and physical environments, how they help us to understand change and the range of ecosystem interventions. In Chapters 4, 5, 6 and 7, we draw upon the work of Connolly and Healy (2013) and group theories metaphorically in ways that we hope will be memorable. Our metaphorical distinctions are intended to capture the essential character of each group; hence onion-peeling theories in Chapter 4 describe theories that seek to peel back the layers of experience so that people can gain insight into what prevents them from moving forward in their lives. These inner world theories include psychodynamic approaches and person-centred practices. In Chapter 5, we use the faulty-engine metaphor to describe behaviourism and cognitive-behaviourism. Challenging the perceived limitations of insight-focused theories, these theories bring with them ideas and techniques that they thought would shift practice attention to the present and to more concrete evidence of change. The most evaluated and empirically supported of social work theories, the faulty-engine group, actively focuses on changing thoughts and behaviours in the here and now. Despite their history of success, they have struggled to gain traction in mainstream practice. In Chapter 5, we also look at mindfulness approaches, which are increasingly being used by practitioners in a range of practice settings.

Chapter 6 describes our story-telling theories, a group of theoretical approaches that explore narratives of strength and resilience in ways that can influence how we think, feel and act. Most fully articulated in narrative ways of working, story-telling theories are critically interested in the ways in which stories can be reinterpreted to enable more positive and rewarding life outcomes. Building on notions of strengths-based practice, they focus on externalising problems and finding narrative solutions that lead to a greater sense of well-being and freedom. Originating from post-structural and social constructionist traditions, these story-telling approaches also resonate with the last of our metaphorical distinctions, mountain-moving theories, presented in Chapter 7. This group of perspectives, which includes human rights-based approaches, seeks to eliminate disadvantage and empower people to realise their hopes for themselves, their families and their communities. These theories provide social work with an important critical edge, connecting the personal with the political and shifting focus from individual blame to collective solutions across social, economic and political domains. Social work theories evolve to respond to contemporary issues. Also in Chapter 7, we discuss the development of green social work approaches, which challenge us to address issues of environmental vulnerability and sustainability.

In our concluding chapter, we look at how the integration of theory and practice is an ongoing professional process for social workers. Integrating theory and practice in ways that respond to the unique needs of social work clients is a complex process, both intellectually and practically. In Chapter 8, we return to our earlier discussion of the disciplinary lenses that social work brings to practice and the ways in which they can help us to critically reflect on how we perceive our professional role and how we give effect to it in practice. Considering the circular process of reflection and reflexive practice, we look at both the dynamics of power and critical thought. We examine models of supervision as an important means of supporting good practice, providing a supportive professional space where we can critically reflect on practice thinking and action, and better understand the various domains of practice and how we can be most effective in our professional responses.

In presenting these theoretical perspectives, we seek to capture the essence of what makes the application of practice theory a uniquely social work intervention. In doing so, we hope we have demonstrated at least some of the vibrancy of social work thinking and the rich disciplinary tapestry that represents contemporary social work theorising.

Marie Connolly and Louise Harms

About the authors

Marie Connolly is Professor and Head of Social Work at the University of Melbourne. She was formerly Chief Social Worker, a senior executive within the New Zealand government. Prior to this, she was Associate Professor at the University of Canterbury and founding Director of the Te Awatea Violence Research Centre. She has a social work background in child protection.

Louise Harms is Associate Professor and Deputy Head of Social Work at the University of Melbourne. She has taught and researched there for many years, after having worked in medical social work and the university's student and staff counselling service.

Acknowledgements

As we have written this book, we have drawn upon our experiences of working with social workers in practice and social work students undertaking their studies with us. Their insights have been invaluable as we have worked together on how theory can be translated into practice, and ways of overcoming challenges and barriers to theoretically informed practice. In particular, we would like to thank social workers at Western Health in Melbourne upon whom we tested the relevance to contemporary practice of the theoretical frameworks explored in this book.

We would also like to acknowledge and thank the practitioners who contributed case studies to the second edition: Sarah Batty, Samantha Clavant, Jim van Rensburg, Michelle Spinks and Judy Wookey. Their important contributions bring to life the application of theory in practice. Thanks also to the staff of the Chief Social Worker's Office of the New Zealand Government, who proposed the title of 'mountain-moving' theories. We had spent ages trying to think of a suitable metaphor, and their creative suggestion put an end to our agonising search.

Special thanks are due to Nina Sharpe, our Cambridge University Press publisher, for her patience and support throughout the writing process. We are also grateful to the University of Melbourne for its ongoing support of scholarship, and to our colleagues at the School of Health Sciences for their encouragement.

Finally, our most grateful thanks go to George Hook and Jane Sullivan, to whom we dedicate this second edition.

The publisher and authors would like to thank the following sources for permission to reproduce material:
Figure 2.7: from *Social Work Now*, April 2011, p. 24. Reproduced with permission of Ministry of Social Work, New Zealand; **2.8, 4.2, 4.3, 5.1, 5.2, 6.1, 7.1, 8.1:** reproduced by permission of Oxford University Press Australia, from *Social Work: Contexts and Practice* (3rd edn), edited by M. Connolly and L. Harms, 2013. © Oxford University Press, www.oup.com.au; **7.2:** From Sherry R. Arnstein, 'A Ladder of Citizen Participation', *Journal of American Planning Association* 35(4): 216–24. Reproduced with permission of Taylor & Francis.

Every effort has been made to trace and acknowledge copyright. The publisher apologises for any accidental infringement and welcomes information that would rectify this situation.

Prelude

REIMAGINING SOCIAL WORK FROM AN ABORIGINAL THEORETICAL PERSPECTIVE

I am not an Aboriginal, or indeed Indigenous. I am ... [a] first nation's person. A sovereign person from this country.

Rosalie Kunoth-Monks (2014)

Notions of professional social work knowledge, theory and practice rest uneasily within the context of the interests, aspirations and sovereignty of first nations peoples. It has long been so, and it remains a challenge in contemporary social work. This new edition of *Social Work: From Theory to Practice* provides us with an opportunity to explore the cultural components of social work theory, and to use these insights to support and encourage practice that is responsive to cultural needs.

It is often said that the whole is greater than the sum of its parts, and so it is within a holistic framework of social justice and self-determination that Aboriginal[1] health and well-being must be approached. This is a perspective that encompasses the well-being of the collective, provides recognition of the Aboriginal world-view and validates the cultural memory of an ancient oral tradition filled with stories and connections to country. It is through reconciliatory and decolonised practices that these elements can be framed, and from which equitable and socially just outcomes for Aboriginal communities can be achieved.

Professor Taiaiake Alfred (2013), in his 2013 Narrm Oration,[2] maintains that the fundamental objective of historical colonisation was possessing land, and that the result was the *dis*possession of land from Aboriginal people. Connecting and *re*connecting with country must therefore be both the main objective in addressing contemporary colonisation and the impetus for achieving improvement in health, education, employment and other areas in which the *effects* of colonisation are so stark (Alfred 2013). Taking this as the position from which to discuss social work theories, practice frameworks and knowledge as they relate to Aboriginal people provides a foundation for

self-reflection and construction, revision of social discourse and consideration of social work values.

Aboriginal by definition, world-view or understanding

All too often, institutions and those who work in them are bound by their
administrative processes, which operate to label, catalogue, order and identify.
The Aboriginal community in Australia – which, since European invasion,
has experienced some of the most profound and de-humanising labelling –
contends on a daily basis with the notion that its indigeneity is wholly represented by the tick in the 'yes' box next to 'ATSI'[3] on the registration form
its members are handed. Whether in the health sector, the justice system, the
workforce or the education system, the government's processes of identifying
Aboriginal status have contributed to a distinct disparaging of the concept of
'indigeneity' and what it means to be an Aboriginal person.

While identification in any public system of service delivery is mandatory
and works towards the provision of Aboriginal-specific services, and targeted
funding and policy development, it also necessitates a definition of 'Aboriginal',
and has served to fuel a very complacent attitude across a number of sectors for
the purpose of identification. The idea that we can frame 'Aboriginal' using a
three-pronged government definition[4] is naïve; furthermore, the concept that
by the very nature of identifying Aboriginal people we have improved our service delivery does a significant injustice to the Aboriginal community. While
the data will do an accurate job in informing funding and policy at a broader
level, how does this personal information inform and improve the human service provided to the Aboriginal community? Does it support those who work
within the community to engage in decolonised practice? What does social
work practice look like in this context?

Reflection

Patients are identified within the system but we usually only know if they
are Aboriginal or Torres Strait Islander
if the Aboriginal Liaison Officer or
the patients themselves tell us. This
helps us to know what services to
engage but it doesn't really change
the way we work because we practise service equality and treat all our
patients equally.

Hospital social worker

Aboriginal world-view

If you listen deeply and pay close enough attention you will hear the songs and whispers of the land's people – those hard-to-hear voices that speak of the ancestors and which are framed by an Aboriginal world-view.

The concept of a world-view may be seen as a 'social lens' through which we view the world, and that develops and evolves across a lifetime through our social interactions with one another. Hart (2010: 2) describes world-views as 'cognitive, perceptual, and affective maps that people continuously use to make sense of the social landscape', while Kovach (2010: 40) makes reference to the story-telling that maintains Aboriginal world-views, rendering them 'relational at [their] core'. Aboriginal expression is supported by many generations of keepers and protectors of knowledge. It is knowledge that Aboriginal people, receptive to the infinite resources that the land is able to offer, have been able to harness, manipulate and build upon for 60 000 years. The Aboriginal world-view is conveyed by an oral tradition of sharing knowledge through story, song and dance, and is subsequently communicated and sustained down through successive generations.

As the keepers of knowledge about medicinal plants, seed stocks and seasonal growth, a group of women travel the paths of their ancestors to gather stores. They walk in single file so as not to damage the delicate biodiversity, each step taken placed in that of those ahead of them, securing the sustainability of the environment for generations to come.

This practice has been taught and learnt by grandmother, mother, aunt and daughter, and frames their understanding of dependence and the survival of not only themselves but their ancestors, descendants, culture and environment. As a common factor among Aboriginal people all over the world, the relationship with the land and its resources situates connectedness, reciprocity and accountability as central to the Aboriginal world-view, and therefore to our indigeneity (Smith 2003; Kovach 2010).

Reflection

The women keep walking behind me, in single file, down the corridor. How can I explain to them that they don't need to follow me when we walk together? Why don't they walk next to me so we can chat?

Hospital social worker

Bishop et al. (2002: 611) state that 'understanding worldviews of both the targeted community and ourselves is imperative if we are going to do more good than harm'. The social work profession's relationship with Aboriginal communities is a fraught one. Burdened with its history of colonising and dispossessing practices, endorsement of and participation in cultural genocide through child-removal policies and its use of Western-framed human behaviour and social systems theories to define Aboriginal experiences, the complexities of social work practice with Aboriginal communities are significant (Briskman 2014). Social work practice is, however, strengthening in its burgeoning shifts in thinking and understanding of a decolonised practice, as articulated by the Australian Association of Social Workers (AASW) in its introduction of 'Indigenous ways of knowing, being and doing' as one of four core curriculum content areas to be included in all AASW-accredited social work programs (AASW 2014: 20). Bessarab and colleagues (2014) have subsequently used this as the impetus for their teaching and learning framework that specifically situates social work practitioners' and students' understanding of Aboriginal world-views as central to effective engagement with Aboriginal communities.

Reconciliatory practice frameworks and knowledges

When you step into an Aboriginal community-controlled organisation, you step into an environment that is, by its very nature, an expression of self-determination. Born of the Black Power era of the 1960s, many Aboriginal community-controlled organisations are the culmination of the Aboriginal political movement that sought to achieve the collective rights that Hemingway (2012) maintains 'tested the liberal democratic principles upon which Australian citizenship is based'. Organisations such as the Victorian Aboriginal Health Service provide comprehensive primary health care to their Aboriginal communities, reflective of each community's collective health needs and priorities, and consistent with the National Aboriginal Community Controlled Health Organisation's (NACCHO 2014) definition of health, which refers to:

> not just the physical well-being of an individual but refers to the social, emotional and cultural well-being of the whole Community in which each individual is able to achieve their full potential as a human being thereby bringing about the total well-being of their Community. (NACCHO 2014)

While not all social workers will work within an Aboriginal community-controlled organisation, such services provide a practical demonstration of the culturally safe practice frameworks that are used effectively by social workers. Such self-determining articulation within Aboriginal communities reflects a history of Aboriginal resistance and protest against colonial control, despite the fact that control over Aboriginal health continues to rest with the government (Briskman 2014).

> William Barak, traditionally known as Beruk, was taught the ways of traditional practice by his Uncle Billibellary and, in a similar style to his Elder, provided leadership for his people with a foresight that challenged the colonial intentions. In 1863, when the Wurundjeri people had been dispossessed of their country and placed on government-run missions, dying of starvation, introduced disease and massacres, William Barak and his cousin, Simon Wonga (Billibellary's son), among others, recognised the inevitabilities that lay ahead. In response, they initiated, through negotiation of the political arena, the establishment of Coranderrk, a self-sufficient Aboriginal reserve near Healesville that soon became a thriving community and a very successful enterprise selling wheat, hops and vegetables. Through his work to establish Coranderrk, and by challenging the authorities of the time for it to remain Aboriginal community-controlled in 1881, William Barak demonstrated the self-determination and fighting spirit of a true visionary. (Andrews, Murray & Torrens 2012: 9)

Decolonised practice

Colonisation and colonial constructs and theories are structures that are created within our contemporary lives through social, political, economic and cultural processes that are defined by the dominant discourse (Alfred 2013). The parallel standpoints that are generated by this, emphasised by colonial power relations, highlight a fundamental aperture between Aboriginal and non-Aboriginal world-views. Briskman (2014: 88) describes this as a 'disjuncture' between competing value systems of the social work profession itself, organisations within which social work practice takes place and Aboriginal communities. She suggests that as values underpin the core of social work's ideology, consideration of their application and how they differ from those of Aboriginal people is critical. Similarly, Nakata (2007) argues for the recognition of the complexity of the space in which Aboriginal people now live – the cultural interface – and proposes an alternative Aboriginal theoretical standpoint to account for Aboriginal experience of this space. Differing value systems and an Aboriginal standpoint that encompasses a knowledge system built far outside that of the governing Western knowledge framework, uniquely frame the needs of Aboriginal people within a praxis of being, and command a decolonised lens through which practice must be defined and articulated.

Critical reflection

Decolonised practice requires a critical reflective approach that fosters a mindful and critical awareness of the cultural self and the value of cultural and professional humility. Defined by Fook and Gardner (2007: 14) as a process for 'unearthing individually held social assumptions in order to make changes in the social world', critical reflection primarily focuses on the *method* of working rather than the outcome. It necessitates a way of working that requires an introspective analysis of where practitioners position themselves in relation to the experiences of Aboriginal people. Reflective practice challenges the notion of self and the knowledge that informs it – in other words, how some people come to understand the world and make meaning from it may not be the same way Aboriginal people come to know the world (Nakata 2007). Briskman's (2014) disjuncture and Nakata's (2007) cultural interface lie central to critical reflective practice in that they are spaces that hold the racial 'other', the perpetuation of power and privilege and colonial constructs.

> The consciousness of self is not the closing of a door to communication. Philosophic thought teaches us, on the contrary, that it is its guarantee. (Fanon 1968: 247)

Burchall and Green (2014), in their work against violence towards women in Central Australia, discuss the role of social work in this context, and contend that 'an enduring collusion with colonisation remains invisible and has not undergone rigorous critical reflection'. A fundamental component of critical reflective social work practice in Australia is the acknowledgement of the profession's agency in colonisation and the social worker's own participation in the dominant culture that, by its very nature, perpetuates the power structures that maintain white privilege and Aboriginal marginalisation. Burchall and Green (2014) reframe the discourse and promote a 'gendered *and* raced' approach to men's violence towards women in the remote communities of Central Australia. Such an approach does three things: it contests the *a priori* Western feminist discourse; it highlights the multidimensional facets of Aboriginal oppression; and it raises unique challenges for social workers with respect to both positioning and assumptions.

Oral tradition, identity and yarning

Aboriginal oral tradition and the encompassed narrative and story-telling underpin the relational aspect of Aboriginal world-views (Kovach 2010), and form what Jan Assman (1995) defines as *cultural memory*. Drawing on Maurice Halbwachs' mid-nineteenth century theory of collective memory, Assman describes cultural memory as a social archive maintained through generations by cultural practices (dance, story, rite, ceremony, song) that underpin the unity of the group, referred to as 'figures of memory' (1995: 129). Distinguished from 'communicative memory' by its distance from the everyday, Assman differentiates cultural memory by its reconstructive value, and contends that 'it always relates its knowledge to an actual and contemporary situation' (1995: 120). We can see the significance of this when we consider the experiences of Indigenous peoples the world over, whose oral histories and cultural memories have been damaged and interrupted by colonisation but who maintain a collective consciousness of unity that has been reframed to reflect their contemporary situation (Assman 1995).

Cultural memory is a 'repository for knowledge' and identity, and is what facilitates the positioning of indigeneity in contemporary societies (Leiden University Institute for History 2014). It challenges the colonial essentialism that dichotomises indigeneity, which Edmunds (2012: 26) describes as either 'traditional' or 'urban' (and therefore 'maintained' or 'lost'), and Paradies (2006) says is either 'exclusively Indigenous or exclusively non-Indigenous' and perniciously underpinned by an 'intense questioning of authenticity'. The discourse and narrative defining what it is to be 'Indigenous' or 'Aboriginal' have largely been framed by non-Aboriginal people, and are often historically immersed and built around a deficit-based representation of the 'other' – the dying race, the noble savage, the ill-fated, the protected, the at-risk ... the colonised. Recent re-authoring of indigeneity has seen Aboriginal voices reframing the narrative, which as much frees Aboriginal people from the colonial 'gaze' as it does non-Aboriginal people from the coloniser's vice. Reconnecting with indigeneity through 'figures of memory' (Assman 1995: 129), such as song, dance and ceremony, seeks to express a reconstructed story, reconciling that within Aboriginal cultural memory and the contemporary Aboriginal experience.

> Reframing occurs in ... contexts where Indigenous people resist being
> boxed and labelled according to categories which do not fit. This is
> particularly pertinent in relation to various development programmes,
> government and non-government. In the case of Māori, for example, a
> Māori language initiative for young children from birth to school age –
> known as Te Kohanga Reo, or Māori language nests – constantly has to
> explain why it is not a child-care centre but a language and culture ini-
> tiative for young children. The problem of definition is important in this
> case because it affects funding, but the constant need to justify difference
> is experienced by many other communities whose initiatives are about
> changing things on a holistic basis rather than endorsing the individual-
> ized programme emphasis of government models. The need to reframe is
> about retaining strengths of a vision and the participation of a whole com-
> munity. (Smith 2003: 153)

In this sense, social work approaches to healing require an understanding of
positioning (both personal and professional), of Aboriginal experiences of the
dominant discourse and what that discourse is, and of the process of reframing
representations of alterity. Aboriginal story-telling and yarning between Elders,
adults and children provide the foundation for connectedness, reciprocity and
accountability, which position people in relation both to one another, and to the
land and the spiritual world. Smith (2003: 144) says that the important thing
about individuals' stories is that 'they contribute to a collective story in which
every Indigenous person has a place'.

Narrative approaches hold a certain congruence with the nature of
Aboriginal yarning, described by Bessarab (2012) as a 'culturally safe' form
of conversation. Story-telling is a useful framework for social work practice
as it enables the deconstruction and reconstruction of a story, uncovering its
layers of meaning and reframing them to be ones that validate and legitimise
culture, foster pride and confidence in the cultural self and can thereby lead to
healing (Raphael and Swan 1998). Denborough and colleagues (2006) describe
the narrative ideas that were used to simultaneously engage two communities
experiencing the effects of suicide and facilitate the sharing of stories between
them. Their article highlights Aboriginal connectedness and the rediscovery of
strength and cultural knowledge through yarning.

Of particular relevance for non-Aboriginal social workers, however, is the
importance of understanding who the keepers of stories are and acknowledging that not all Aboriginal knowledges within stories can be shared. In her
2014 Narrm Oration, Professor Linda Tuhiwai Smith (Smith 2014) begins by

defining the many different types of Aboriginal knowledges and proposes the following definition:

> It is about the understanding of the human person and communities, and their relationships to all other non-human, non-sentient agents. It is about concepts of time and space that connect earth to earth's universe and beyond, and that connects humans to ideas a million times greater than the idea of humankind. It is about imagination inspired by experience over the generations.
>
> It has been honed, tested, shaped by experience, by our own social controversies, by traumatic crises, by the resilience of our ancestors. Indigenous knowledges are philosophies, systems, applications, laws, values and practices created by diverse Indigenous peoples as a coherent way of living in the world. It is produced by Indigenous peoples and continues to be created.

From this we understand that stories and yarns will include many different forms of Aboriginal knowledges, much of which can be shared, but some of which can not. There are many questions and uncertainties that will arise for practitioners, and fear, doubt and anxiety will all contribute to a reflective process of decolonised practice. Indeed, Smith (2014) goes on to pose the question of who the experts are when it comes to Aboriginal knowledge and cites aunties, grandmothers, Elders, hunters and artists, among other community people, some of whom are the very people many social workers will cross paths with. Recognising this expertise and the knowledges they bring to the storytelling requires an approach of 'informed not-knowing' and thereby acknowledges the dynamics of power and privilege (Mandell 2007: 7).

Deep listening

The dominant discourse about Aboriginal people and the effects of colonisation are often framed as the 'Aboriginal problem'; this tends to be narrated outside of Aboriginal communities (Alfred 2013). The call from Aboriginal communities for a self-determining path to health and well-being continues to fall upon the deaf ears of those who generate and subscribe to the discourse. Listening to Aboriginal communities and enabling the time and space for thought and introspection are the strategies being requested of governments, government organisations, service providers, academics, clinicians and many others.

Deep listening is defined as an intuitive awareness and presence that requires 'listening with the heart' (Bennett 2010). Verbal communication only partly involves deep listening, with silence and unspoken interaction used comfortably and non-threateningly. Miriam-Rose Ungunmerr-Baumann (2002: np.) describes deep listening, known as *dadirri* in her language:

> As we grow older, we ourselves become the story-tellers. We pass on to the young ones all they must know. The stories and songs sink quietly into our minds and we hold them deep inside. In the ceremonies we celebrate the awareness of our lives as sacred.
>
> The contemplative way of *dadirri* spreads over our whole life. It renews us and brings us peace. It makes us feel whole again . . .
>
> In our Aboriginal way, we learnt to listen from our earliest days. We could not live good and useful lives unless we listened. This was the normal way for us to learn – not by asking questions. We learnt by watching and listening, waiting and then acting. Our people have passed on this way of listening for over 40 000 years . . .
>
> There is no need to reflect too much and to do a lot of thinking. It is just being aware.
>
> My people are not threatened by silence. They are completely at home in it. They have lived for thousands of years with Nature's quietness. My people today, recognise and experience in this quietness, the great Life-Giving Spirit . . .

From these words, we can revisit those of Kovach (2010: 40), who describes Aboriginal world-views as 'relational at [their] core', making reference not only to interpersonal relationships but also to relationships with the land and the spiritual world. Awareness of the world around us and our place within it, with accountability and reciprocity central to the interaction, frames the survival that only 60 000 years of history could foster.

Reflection

I went into the Emergency Department to see an Aboriginal family. When I asked the grandmother about the incident, how it happened, she started telling me about *her* grandmother. About how she used to sing. I couldn't see the point initially but I sat down . . . what she revealed to me was a story of generational heartache, child removal and trauma, but one that also spoke of survival, strength and cultural resilience. At the end she sat in silence, as did I, until the doctor arrived. I've never had a response to a basic question quite like that and it has changed the way I practise. I heard what she said, but I also heard what she didn't say. I realised that *how* the incident had happened didn't really matter and that my 'social worky' way of going about my day, working to get tangible outcomes for people, didn't really allow me to just *be* with people, and for some, such as this grandmother, that was all they needed.

Hospital social worker

Emancipatory approaches and frameworks

To articulate the experience of Indigenous peoples across the globe and deter-mine the nature of how, when and why social work plays a role in Indigenous communities, we must look to emancipatory possibilities, which can often lie beyond the frame of the discipline. Briskman (2014: 93) argues that social workers must use an approach that 'places social justice to the forefront and engages in challenges to the welfare system' without which therapeutic, indi-vidualised practice will be futile. The emancipatory nature of concepts and theoretical frameworks such as intersectionality and critical race theory is sig-nificant to the legitimacy and validation of Aboriginal agency, recognising the multifaceted nature of oppression. Supporting these are Edward Said (1978) and Michel Foucault's (1979) concepts of discourse, power and knowledge, and Western representations of the 'other' that offer a framework through which to situate the social work profession within an acknowledged broader colonial context. Similarly, Frantz Fanon's (1968) work in *Wretched of the Earth* defends the rights of colonised people and reflects upon strengths-based thinking about the deepening of the condition of culture, of its fruitfulness and its continuous renewal.

In all of these approaches and frameworks is found an innate and funda-mental alliance with human rights that can be challenging to social work. They have been politically generated and therefore promote a political stance that fosters activism (Briskman 2014). Looking to our local history, we can usually find stories of political activism, contextualised by an early experience of dis-possession, which are pertinent to framing contemporary social work practice with Aboriginal communities.

Aboriginal people have fought for their land and their rights since the time of European arrival. Residents of Coranderrk Aboriginal Station sent depu-tations to the Victorian government during the 1870s–1880s, protesting against their lack of rights and the threatened closure of the settlement.

Located 50 km north-east of Melbourne, Coranderrk was established in 1863 as part of the 'protectorate' for these original inhabitants. But increas-ing pressure came from neighbouring farmers wanting the fertile land. From 1886, the government sought to integrate 'half-castes' into white society.

Activist William Barak and others sent this petition on behalf of the Aboriginal people of Coranderrk to the Victorian Government in 1886:

> Could we get our freedom to go away Shearing and Harvesting and to come home when we wish and also to go for the good of our Health when we need it ...
>
> We should be free like the White Population. There is only few Blacks now rem[a]ining in Victoria, we are all dying away now and we Blacks of Aboriginal Blood, wish to have now freedom for all our life time ...
>
> Why does the Board seek in these latter days more stronger authority over us Aborigines than it has yet been?
>
> Regardless of the residents' protests, Coranderrk was scaled back. It continued as an Aboriginal reserve until 1924, when the remaining community was relocated to Lake Tyers in Gippsland. Healesville Sanctuary now occupies part of the original Coranderrk reserve. (Melbourne Museum 2014)

Much of what I have raised in this discussion has been about deconstructing knowledge and decolonising thinking. This inevitably involves a process of reflective self-analysis and critical thinking that will place many social workers outside of their comfort zones, but that is the point! This book reinforces strongly the importance of social work's interpretive lenses. In the context of social work practice with Indigenous peoples, both our social justice lens and our reflective lens are of critical importance. If we go back to where we began, and consider Professor Alfred's (2013) premise that to achieve collective healing in Aboriginal communities requires addressing contemporary colonisation and its effects through reconnection with country, then social work can clearly play a role. Its effectiveness and relevance to Aboriginal communities, however, will rely upon a professional recalibration of values and a consideration of its own position in relation to the experiences of Aboriginal communities.

Shawana Andrews
University of Melbourne

Useful resources

Australian Indigenous Health InfoNet: http://www.healthinfonet.ecu.edu.au.

Briskman, L. 2014. *Social Work with Indigenous Communities: A Human Rights Approach*, 2nd edn. Sydney: Federation Press.

Eckerman, A., Dowd, T., Chong, E., Nixon, L., Gray, R. & Johnson, S. 2010. *Binan Goonj: Bridging Cultures in Aboriginal Health*. Sydney: Elselvier.

Perkins, R. & Dale, D. 2008. *First Australians* [video]. SBS/Blackfella Films.

Notes

1 The term 'Aboriginal' has been used throughout this chapter in reference to Aboriginal and Torres Strait Islander peoples of Australia and to first nations people globally.

2 The Narrm Oration, presented by Murrup Barak, Melbourne Institute for Indigenous Development at the University of Melbourne and Rio Tinto Australia, is held annually and profiles leading Indigenous thinkers from across the globe to enrich our ideas about possible futures for Indigenous Australians.

3 An acronym for Aboriginal and/or Torres Strait Islander.

4 An Aboriginal or Torres Strait Islander is a person of Aboriginal or Torres Strait Islander descent who identifies as an Aboriginal or Torres Strait Islander and is accepted as such by the community in which they live (Parliament of Australia 2014).

1 Social work knowledge, theory and practice

Social workers practise across a wide range of settings, with all kinds of different people who have diverse cultural experiences. Some work primarily with individuals, whereas others work with families or groups of people in therapeutic or community contexts. Some social workers focus on community advocacy, community action and social change. In such diverse practice contexts, the notion of theoretically informed practice can seem complicated. Yet social workers do draw upon a range of theoretical perspectives in their work, using theory to help understand and make sense of what is, in reality, a complex human world. Many theories used by social workers can also be found influencing the practices of allied professionals: counsellors, psychologists and others working within the human services. Theories explored in this book are not the sole purview of the social work profession, nor can they be claimed as necessarily emerging from within a social work paradigm. Professional interpretations of knowledge and theory overlap and interweave (Trevithick 2012). We would nevertheless argue that theory applied in social work has a disciplinary character that distinguishes it from the application of the same theories across allied disciplines. This is because knowledge and theory in practice are critically influenced by disciplinary attachments and the underpinning values and nature of the profession itself.

Social work's interpretive lens

In the following chapters, we explore a range of practice theories that have been influential in social work. First, however, we will tease out the disciplinary nature of social work's interpretive lens to see how it influences the application of knowledge and theory, what we understand theory to be, and how contemporary debates have influenced the application of theory over time. We propose that the social work interpretive lens is enriched by four additional lenses that together influence the ways in which we apply theory in practice: the relational lens; the social justice lens; the reflective lens; and the lens of change.

The relational lens

According to Howe (2009), relationship-based practice has been an integral part of social work since its inception, and some writers have argued that it represents a critical component of effective social work (Teater 2010). In the Prelude to this edition, Shawana Andrews provides a lovely example of relational practice when the hospital social worker sits and listens to an Aboriginal woman talking about her own grandmother and events of the past. This is an example of relational practice based on engagement through listening and silence. Although the relational aspect of social work has been foundational in social work thinking and practice, it has nevertheless not been without criticism:

> Relationship-based social work has often been treated unkindly by radical and structural theorists. Traditional and radical theories have argued that relationship-based practices are at best a plaster on the deep wound of oppression and at worst a capitalist trick to keep the poor and disadvantaged quiet and in their place. (Howe 2009: 156)

This division between practices that are perceived to maintain inequality versus practices that support empowerment and social change runs deep in social work history. Recent writers have noted a dichotomy between the approaches of social work pioneers Mary Richmond and Jane Addams (Mendes 2009). Richmond maintained that the social work relationship was a critical component of successful client change, and her work was influential in shifting practice from charitable visiting to more scientific professional responses (Miehls 2011). Some writers have argued that Richmond sought to marry social action and casework approaches (Howe 2009); however, others criticise her focus on individual casework as moralistic, with too great a focus on human deficits. Mendes (2009) sees Richmond's approach as being in stark contrast to the social action approach adopted by Jane Addams, a contemporary of Richmond. Addams, who was acutely aware of the impact of economic disadvantage, worked towards reforming the social environment that created disadvantage – for example, income and the minimum wage, as well as factory and housing conditions. It is important to remember that Richmond and Addams practised in the early twentieth century, and a good deal has happened since then. Given how influenced we are by time and place, judging historical action through a contemporary lens is always a complex endeavour. Yet thinking about how practice seems at the time and then viewing it in retrospect can be illuminating. Take, for example, this reflection from an experienced social worker in a very senior non-government role. Clearly, when we are in the thick of practice, it is not always easy to see the bigger picture.

Reflection: The relational lens

I was sitting in a meeting with a group of non-government chief executives, listening to an analysis of child welfare practices over time. The presenter talked about the way in which practices during the 1990s had become more forensic, more focused on investigations and less focused on helping families find solutions. She talked about how the practice literature was risk-saturated, critically influencing the way in which child protection work developed over the decade.

It suddenly hit me – I was working in child protection at that time. We had all been deeply committed to working positively with families, yet there was no doubt that we had indeed become more forensic. We started to believe that it was investigations that were important, not supporting families to change. Somehow we had let this happen. I can see this now, but it wasn't clear to me at the time.

CEO working within the non-government sector

There are dangers in perceiving practice through a singular lens. Limiting social work to processes of individual change, whether mediated through the mechanism of a relationship or not, can slip into practice that is deficit focused and blames people for the very predicaments in which they find themselves. This is something we will discuss further in Chapter 7. This is when viewing practice through a critical social work lens is of significant importance. In social work, we are not only influenced by notions of relationship but also have a long-standing commitment to social justice and social change (Briskman 2014). Social work is not only concerned with helping people; it is also fundamentally concerned with changing systems that contribute to disadvantage and oppression.

The social justice lens

In many respects, the work of Addams epitomises social work's commitment to social justice. Social justice 'provided a thread of historical continuity' that influenced the development of progressive paradigms, including radical, feminist, anti-racist and more recent anti-oppressive social work practices (Dominelli 2002: 4), perspectives that will be discussed more fully in Chapter 7. When systems are considered unjust, social work advocates change, at least according to more radical theorists. During the 1970s – a formative time in the development of the social work profession – social work's commitment to social justice was exposed to critical scrutiny as writers saw the profession maintaining conditions of oppression rather than ameliorating them (Skenridge & Lennie 1978). Indeed, Pemberton and Locke (1971: 101) went so far as to accuse social work of duplicitous intent: 'The social worker is a double-agent; while claiming to be working on behalf of the client he [sic] is really an agent of socio-political control, bolstering the existing social order by reinforcing and interpreting moral, social and political rules.'

Although social work practices cross a range of practice domains, the field's positioning within statutory settings – for example, child protection, mental health and criminal justice – illuminates well the tension inherent in providing the professional functions of both care and control. In these settings in particular, social workers can exercise considerable power over personal liberty and freedom. Children who are assessed as needing care can be removed from their parents. People assessed as being mentally ill can be involuntarily confined. Social workers can recommend that people who offend against the law be sent to corrective facilities rather than serving community sentences. These powers rest uncomfortably alongside professional values of social justice, anti-oppression and anti-discrimination – even more so when the clients themselves have suffered unfair treatment and discrimination throughout their lives. As Beddoe and Maidment (2009) note, social justice is not necessarily at the forefront of service delivery concern. Indeed, an increased focus on the need to reduce risk has created a contemporary practice environment in which social workers may think twice in their management of risky situations. A risk of community opprobrium may cause a worker to recommend residential options for a young person who offends as opposed to placement in a community setting, even when it is considered a more appropriate rehabilitative option. Fear of blame should things go wrong in child protection may influence a worker's willingness to consider family placement options for a child and result in premature removal from the parent (Connolly & Doolan 2007). Yet, as we can see from the following reflection, social justice and emancipatory practice can also exist even within the most constrained of statutory environments.

Reflection: The social justice lens

Through the course of my work, I was fortunate to be invited to a meeting in a maximum security prison that offered a sex offender treatment program. The meetings were held regularly, and all the men in the program attended, along with the therapists, a few of the guards and some outsiders with links to the program. There were upwards of 60 men in treatment so the room was quite full.

The chairs were positioned in a large circle. Two of the men in the program chaired the meeting, encouraging discussion about issues and concerns. People had their say in a context of shared support and challenge. I was so impressed by the way in which the meeting provided for participation and the fact that the men's concerns were responded to with dignity and respect. To me, it was a demonstration of rights-based ideals in action.

Senior government official

Over generations of social work practice, the thread of social justice has continued to provide a critical challenge, reminding us of the profession's fundamental commitment to social action. Despite the changing context of contemporary practice, in the same way Jane Addams advocated social change in the early twentieth century, social work writers and practitioners have continued to endorse a social justice agenda. Social justice continues to feature predominantly in social work codes of ethical practice, thus challenging social workers to find ways of giving effect to emancipatory practice no matter where they may work and regardless of the limitations of their organisational context. Identifying social justice as a key theme across practice domains, Harms and Connolly (2013b: 453) note that: 'While social workers may debate, both individually and collectively, aspects of the ethical value-base of our practice, it is important that we unify around the core values of securing social justice, supporting client autonomy, and promoting social well-being no matter where we may work across the service continuum.'

The social justice lens also has an essential historical and contemporary perspective in the context of supporting the rights and aspirations of first nations peoples. Indigenous peoples of Australia and Aotearoa New Zealand have experienced a devastating cultural dislocation through processes of colonisation, a legacy that creates continued disadvantage (Gilbert 2013; Ruwhiu 2013; Andrews in Prelude to this book). Social work acknowledges the impact of this on the cultural fabric of Indigenous communities, and is committed to developing deeper understandings and more responsive ways of supporting cultural narratives, empowerment and Indigenous self-determination. This involves not imposing theories and models that lack cultural fit, and working with people to explore ways in which their needs and aspirations can be met.

The social justice lens intersects with the relational lens, providing a critical edge to social work practice. Embraced as an essential interpretive lens, a focus on social justice challenges individualistic responses that can negatively merge with notions of individual culpability, blame and stigmatisation. An equally critical interpretive lens that intersects with social justice and relationship practice is the reflective lens.

The reflective lens

Cultural thinking shapes the way we feel, think and act. Over decades of practice, social work has appreciated the power of cultural thinking and the ways in which culture shapes professional responses. Whether culture is considered in the context of ethnicity or other cultural identities – gender, sexuality, religiosity, ability – it is vitally important to the way we understand the world and the people within it. Our own thinking may include these multiple cultural interpretations. Our views about the world are also likely to be influenced by the cultural interpretations of our childhood – the influence of family and the way in which we were raised, our education and the influence of our peers. These all contribute to the ways in which we understand and appreciate the world of another. Reflecting upon the ways in which personal and professional cultural thinking influences what we do and how we think has become a hallmark of good social work practice.

While appreciation of the personal self and its potential to affect the way a social worker practises is now well understood, the influence of professional ideologies and the professional self has received less attention; however, it is every bit as important. This is where the notion of 'institutional attachments' (Wacquant 1998: 226) is relevant. The professional self, infused with explanatory theories, professional attitudes and beliefs (reflected in practice standards and codes of ethical practice), also creates cultural understandings and professional ways of thinking that can affect practice. If a worker holds strong beliefs about an issue or concern, or is uncritically attached to institutional mandates, this may unwittingly restrict the worker's ability to consider alternative explanations. In this reflection, a traditional feminist interpretation of relationships of dominance and subordination contrasts starkly with an alternative response that attributes greater importance to cultural dimensions and imperatives. Such differences in professional cultural thinking can run very deep, and may influence our capacity to 'change lens':

Our own world suddenly becomes self-evident, so unproblematically 'the way it is', that the other's world can seem blatantly incoherent ... Instead of inviting mutual inquiry into our ways of world making, we defend our world, even impose it on others. (McKee 2003: 3)

Reflection: The reflective lens

I recall being at a conference on violence and families. It was quite a long time ago now – probably 1990 – but I remember it vividly as it was the first time I'd seen open hostility in response to a presentation. An Asian academic was presenting on domestic violence in Asian families. She talked about the status of men as the head of the family and how 'saving face' for men was important when working with domestic violence. She explored the ways in which women could use this to reduce the violence that was directed towards them. The response from a small group of Anglo women was quick and angry. She was accused of shifting responsibility for male violence onto women, and of accommodating and supporting, gender inequality within the family. The presenter tried to explain how important it was to work with cultural strengths, but it fell on deaf ears. It was one of the clearest examples of cultural miscommunication I think I have ever seen.

Social work academic

The social work profession has paid considerable attention to the ways in which cultural thinking influences practice and how practitioners can develop reflexive responsiveness. Writers have argued for the importance of self-reflection, greater awareness of the influence of personal and professional values, and the development strategies that support reflective and reflexive practice – something to which we will return in Chapter 8. The discipline's commitment to supervision is an example of this commitment to critical reflectiveness in practice. As a safe forum for exploring practice issues, the commitment to supervision has remained strong in spite of what Phillipson (2002: 244) describes as 'seismic upheavals' in social work. Supervision provides an important reflective opportunity to explore understandings of both the personal and professional self in practice:

> Such a capacity for containment, empathy, reflection and their encouragement of analysis in depth can help us to cope with the pain, violence and anxiety we may encounter. It can also help us to become more able to take responsibility for our own work, to make our own judgements and then improve them ... supervision is time for exploration, reflection, learning and problem-solving. (Lishman 2002: 104)

This acknowledgement of the complex dynamics of practice and the need to support practitioners as they navigate their way through cultural landscapes has provided an important focus in the training and practice of social work. It adds a unique dimension to relationship-building in practice and our interpretation of social justice and human rights.

These first three interpretive prisms – relationship, social justice and reflection – have all featured prominently in social work literature and practice. Despite waxing and waning, they have remained constant and frequently appear in some shape or form in social work codes of ethical practice, each influencing the ways in which we interpret social work theory and perspectives. Our last interpretive lens, although implicitly important, has received less attention in terms of its power to influence the ways in which we think about practising in social work.

The lens of change

Many books have been written about how to both understand and change people. There has been less emphasis on the nature of change itself and the importance of this understanding to what we do. In our view, social work interpretation of what is considered necessary to create change in human systems nevertheless provides a unique disciplinary influence. It influences our appreciation of theory and method, and it also influences the application of theory and method in practice. Our interpretation of change influences the theoretical choices we make and provides a particular dimension to theory development. Although we would argue that the lens of change provides a unique contemporary social work interpretive perspective, insights with respect to its development have been drawn from a broad range of multidisciplinary thinking.

Two early influences with respect to our understanding of change can be found in the theorising of systems and systems thinking. We discuss the evolution of ecosystems theory in greater depth in Chapter 3. Here we focus specifically on how it has influenced the way we think about change. In a nutshell, a systems approach pays attention to the 'here and now' interactive processes within complex systems (Connolly & Healy 2013: 21). Change happens in the context of this interactive dynamic, and social workers have the potential to influence that change. The nature of change has been explored further in the context of understanding family systems theory. Here, the way in which one family member thinks, feels and behaves affects everyone else in the family – an insight that is captured in the following reflection.

Reflection: The lens of change

I was sitting in a lecture on family therapy. The lecturer was talking about family systems, homeostasis and what happens when balance is disrupted. The lecturer held what looked like a child's hanging mobile in front of us – a set of funny little family members hanging on strings. She held it out very carefully and asked us what would happen if she were to pull on one of the little figures. There was a murmur around the room and I wasn't quite sure what she meant. Then she pulled on one, and the rest jumped up and down with the impact. What happened to one person impacted on them all. Suddenly it made sense to me. The phrase I'd read in the literature also started to make sense: 'The whole is greater than the sum of its parts.'

Social work student

Friedman and Neuman Allen (2011: 9) also describe how broader systems influence interactional dynamics within the family:

> Within the context of a family there may be forces affecting the parental subsystem that trickle down to affect the children without the children even being aware of them. For example, if a parent is experiencing stress at work and displaces his or her frustration at home by yelling at the children, one may see how events outside the child's immediate environment may exert a pronounced effect on the child's development.

Ideas emerging from Brief Family Therapy and the work of Watzlawick, Weakland and Fisch (1974) have also been influential. These writers introduced the notion of first- and second-order change. First-order change is one that 'occurs within a given system which itself remains unchanged', while second-order change produces a change in the system itself (1974: 10). These ideas have been influential in social work thinking, and have shaped interpretations about the way change occurs both within and outside the immediate family. They provide a broad interpretive framework that enriches our application of theory in practice. In more recent years, two further perspectives have influenced the ways in which we think about change and how we approach theories of practice: the strengths perspective and social constructivism.

Although, in contemporary practice, the notion of building on strengths is not a new idea – it has featured in a variety of ways across a range of perspectives – it emerged first and most powerfully in the social work literature, particularly through the work of Dennis Saleebey (1992) and Charles Rapp (1998). Following these seminal works, other disciplines began to engage with strengths-based ideas – for example, positive psychology was introduced towards the end of the decade. Strengths-based ideas captured the imagination of social workers, who were keen to shift from a negative focus on problems and deficits to one exploring possibilities and solutions. From Kondrat's (2010: 39) perspective, it was developed 'to bring the practice of social work back to its foundation of valuing and collaborating with the client'. We will talk further about narratives of strengths and resilience in Chapter 6, but what is important to this discussion is the core strengths-based principle relating to change: that all people have the capacity to grow and change. This process of change is achieved through collaboration, supported by the belief that people are experts in their own lives and that they have an innate ability to change their lives for the better. This positions the social work role as one of professional supporter and facilitator of change. Strongly associated with the strengths-based approach is the concept of social constructivism, which brings with it another set of ideas that have influenced the social work lens of change.

In essence, social constructivism is based on the notion that reality is constructed by equal measures of individual and social factors (Teater 2010). Human experience is defined and constructed by various discourses that can enhance or limit a person's ability to live a full and rewarding life. Like the strengths-based approach, control over change rests with the client: if realities are constructed, then they can be deconstructed. Howe (2009: 89) reports messages from social work clients:

> What they say is that in conversation with warm, interested and empathic social workers they value the change to control the meaning of their own experience and the meaning that others give to that experience . . . when they recover feelings of personal control [they] begin to hope.

While there will always be ideas and experience that influence knowledge and practice, in this discussion we have identified what we consider to be four critical influences with respect to the interpretive lens of social work. When a social work writer discusses a theory, it is likely that they will filter their ideas through the specifics of the social work disciplinary lens, creating theoretical appreciations and applications that are different from those of someone outside the profession. See, for example, Sharon Berlin's (2002) important discussion of clinical social work within the context of a cognitive-integrative approach. While Berlin specifically focuses on cognitive theory, there is no mistaking her disciplinary background as she incorporates key social work ideas: the person in environment; human agency; socially derived meanings; culture and change. The result is a book that is fundamentally different from other cognitive theoretical treatments that have emerged from professions outside the discipline of social work (e.g. see Kazantzis, Reinecke & Freeman 2010, writing from a psychology perspective). This is not to say that one disciplinary approach is superior or inferior to another; it is just that they differ in important ways. Although we have discussed influencing lenses individually in this chapter, it is more helpful to consider them in the context of a set of related ideas that intersect and interact with each other (see Figure 1.1). We would argue that, together, they have the potential to provide a unique social work perspective that shapes our understanding and application of theory in practice.

FIGURE
1.1:   *The intersecting interpretive lenses of social work*

Throughout this book, we will highlight the ways in which these social work interpretive lenses influence the particular application of theory, and illustrate how their application creates practice that is characteristically social work in nature. But before we move on to looking at specific theoretical frameworks, it is important to tease out what we mean by 'theory' and the nature of different theoretical types, then take some time to explore which ideas have influenced the application of theory in practice.

Theory and practice

In the practice literature a confusing array of terms is used to describe the knowledge base underpinning practice. Writers use 'theory', 'perspective', 'models' and 'frameworks', to name just a few, and sometimes these are used interchangeably. They do, in fact, represent different but connected collections of ideas, so it is very easy to see how they can become confused.

Theories, perspectives, models and frameworks

Previously, we have argued that practice theories are used to explain the nature of people's troubles and the nature of change (Harms & Connolly 2013a). They represent a systematic ordering of ideas, drawn from a range of sources that help us to understand a person's circumstances and how we might helpfully intervene. Sheldon (1995: 8) suggests that humans are unable to avoid theorising:

> It is psychologically impossible not to have theories about things. It is impossible at a basic perceptual level, at a cognitive and at an emotional level. The search for meaning, as a basis for predicting behavioural success and avoiding danger, appears to have been 'wired' into our brains . . .

The changing nature of knowledge development means that theories change as new information influences how we understand things or disproves our hypotheses altogether. Theoretical explanations are therefore fluid, changing and shifting as new knowledge comes to hand (Trevithick 2012). In addition, different theories may explain the same issue or problem in quite different ways, which suggests that there is more than one way of validly explaining a phenomenon.

A set of criteria can be useful in determining the strength of a theory:

- *Predictive accuracy, empirical adequacy* and *scope* concern whether the theory can account for existing findings and the range of phenomena requiring explanation.
- *Internal coherence* refers to whether a theory contains contradictions or logical gaps.
- *External consistency* is concerned with whether the theory in question is consistent with other background theories that are currently accepted.
- *Unifying power* relates to whether existing theory is drawn together in an innovative way and whether the theory can account for phenomena from related domains – for example, does it unify aspects of a domain of research that were previously viewed as separate?
- *Fertility* or *heuristic value* refers to a theory's ability to lead to new predictions and open up new avenues of inquiry. In a practice setting, this may also include a theory's capacity to lead to new and effective interventions.

- *Simplicity*, as the name suggests, refers to a theory that makes the fewest theoretical assumptions.
- *Explanatory depth* refers to the theory's ability to describe deep underlying causes and processes (Connolly, Crichton-Hill & Ward 2006: 113).

While setting the bar high in terms of interrogating and defining social work practice theories, having a set of criteria does help to distinguish differences between practice approaches that meet the expectations of a theory (for example, cognitive-behavioural theory) and those that do not, or have yet to be tested through research, generally placing them in a different category of knowledge where they may be referred to as perspectives (for example, the strengths perspective) or discourses (for example, postmodernist discourses). The notion of knowledge having scientific validity has created considerable social work debate, particularly in the context of evidence-based practice expectations and postmodernist critiques – something to which we will return later in the chapter.

Models, theories and frameworks are different again. This is where the literature becomes really confusing, as the terms are used interchangeably with other similar terms, such as 'approaches'. Helpfully, Howe distinguishes models from theories on the basis of descriptive versus explanatory functions:

> Models, acting as analogies, can be used to order, define, [and] describe phenomena. They do not explain the things seen, but they do begin to impose some low level order on what is otherwise a jumble of information. Models act as bricks in theory building. (Howe, cited in Trevithick 2012: 78)

Frameworks seem to have similar characteristics to Howe's articulation of a model and, according to the *Shorter Oxford English Dictionary*, they also have similar characteristics: a model represents 'a structure; design, pattern or structural type', whereas a framework represents 'a structure made of parts; a skeleton'. That is good enough for us, and we will use *model* and *framework* interchangeably when we discuss them in greater depth in Chapter 2.

Types of theory

Social workers use a range of theories to inform their practice (Connolly & Healy 2013). For example, theories of deviance explore social norms and what happens when these are transgressed. Theories of moral reasoning help us to understand how we make decisions that are ethically strong. As we noted earlier, feminist theory provides us with important understandings with respect to the nature of gender dynamics and the relationships of dominance and subordination, while attachment theory helps us to understand the relational aspects of human experience and its impact on human development. Theories also create new areas for research and further theorising, as synergies across theoretical perspectives develop:

> Contemporary literature from the broad fields of infant research, child development theory, contemporary attachment theory, trauma theory, cognitive neuroscience, relational theory, and psychodynamic clinical theory is converging in a synergistic and interesting manner that supports the notions that human beings are resilient and that change is possible across the life cycle ...
> (Miehls 2011: 81)

These theories provide important knowledge for practice, and help to build a picture of human existence, experience and behaviour. While we may touch on some of these broader explanatory theories in the following chapters, in this book we nevertheless focus our attention predominantly on *practice theories*. Practice theories help us to navigate our way through complex human troubles. They differ from these broader explanatory theories in that they embrace both causal explanations and practice responses. This focus on causal explanation (causality) and practice response (method) provides us with a framework, adapted from Connolly and Healy (2013), that we use consistently in the following chapters, illustrating the way in which practice theory unfolds into practice (see Figure 1.2). The theoretical explanation clarifies why difficulties have occurred, which in turn informs the practice approach and essential characteristics of the method. Completing the unfolding of theory into practice, the framework then suggests a repertoire of techniques that are consistent with both the theoretical explanation and the practice approach.

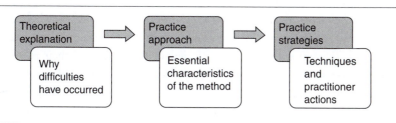

FIGURE 1.2: *The unfolding of theory into practice*

The framework's suggestion of a linear process in terms of moving from theoretical understanding to method and action is useful conceptually, as it illustrates an internal logic and helps us to see the broader integration of theory and practice. Practice is, however, a lively and dynamic process that rarely behaves in a linear and orderly fashion. Although some social workers will indeed remain consistently dedicated to a particular theoretical approach, applying its theory, method and technique, many will pick and choose theoretical ideas that are useful in any given situation. This is known as practising eclectically, a notion that we will now discuss in the context of contested debates in the application of theory in social work.

Ideas that have influenced the application of theory in practice

A range of ideas have influenced the application of theory in practice. Views about the value of theory as an organising construct for practice and whether a single theory can hope to respond to the complexity of human need have been the subject of considerable dispute over many years of social work theorising. This is captured in debates about eclectic versus purist approaches to theory.

Eclectic practice versus a purist approach to theory

Because practice theories provide a more or less complete picture of an intervention approach, they are rather like a blueprint for practice: they guide theoretical understanding, choice of practice approach and action. Understanding the theoretical basics can help a worker to get back on track if they lose their way, and there is a degree of comfort in this. Often clients present with multiple issues in their lives, and it is easy for a social worker to become overwhelmed by the enormity of their task. Workers are often drawn to theoretical approaches that are consistent with their general view of the world and their particular practice orientation. If a worker develops expertise in a particular theoretical approach and applies it consistently, this is known as a *purist* approach to theory application (Connolly & Healy 2013). The theory is used regardless of the nature of the presenting issues, and the theoretical blueprint provides relatively clear direction and structure for the intervention. The worker is able to articulate the rationale for the practice approach and can clarify this for the client, a transparency that can also help to motivate the client towards change. In a practice space where things are rarely certain, adopting a purist approach to practice can give both client and worker confidence that things are on track and moving forward, and that the worker has the expertise to help.

The idea that one theory is able to respond to a diverse client population is a key challenge for the purist approach. Basic theoretical tenets may be discordant with the client's concerns, and while the theory may fit the worker's orientation and world-view, it might not resonate with the person at the other end of the service. For example, a person seeking help may be pragmatic in style and want some advice on quick solutions to their problems. A worker adopting a theoretical framework that privileges insight-focused theory (see Chapter 4) with an aim of unearthing deep personal issues might not provide a good fit. Even worse, when working with couples, a theoretical approach might suit one person but not the other, thus leaving an impression that the worker is taking sides. So using a purist approach can be problematic and result in some social workers considering a more eclectic approach to the application of theory.

Eclectic practice refers to an approach that does not specifically favour one theory but rather uses theory flexibly as it is considered useful in any given situation. When a theory, or mix of theoretical ideas, seems useful to the client's presenting issues, then no approach is excluded and workers use techniques from different theoretical frameworks that may be considered helpful. To some extent, this resolves the problem of a lack of theoretical fit with a client, but it does nevertheless present its own set of challenges. Without a good knowledge of a range of theories, it is not necessarily obvious which theories fit comfortably together. Theories might have fundamentally different assumptions or they might try to do quite different things. This can cause confusion for both worker and client if one approach undermines the other. For example, if one theory focuses on the here and now while another delves into things past, all the benefits of immediacy could be lost even though immediacy may be critical to the way the theory facilitates positive change. Workers practising eclectically may also lack the in-depth theoretical knowledge needed to make safe use of the techniques. Superficial use of a variety of approaches could undermine good practice. Whereas the purist approach offers a relatively clear blueprint, working eclectically has minimal structure and it can be easy to get lost along the practice route.

Whether social workers take a purist or eclectic approach to theory is likely to depend upon whether they are inclined towards a more or less structured approach, and whether they agree that a more structured theoretical approach can provide a complete picture from explanation to technique. According to Trevithick (2012), debate relating to the value of theory in practice has also been influenced by whether social work is considered as a scientific endeavour or a humanistic pursuit. This has been a critical question in contemporary postmodern critiques, where more holistic and contextual responses have been privileged over more rule-bound practice approaches (Fook 2002).

Postmodern critiques

Largely influenced by the sociological writings of such theorists as Michel Foucault, postmodern critiques have challenged the primacy of science and scientific knowledge (Briskman, Pease & Allan 2009). Understanding the world through scientific endeavour and the search for scientific truth was anathema to Foucault:

> In Foucault's world, there are no deep, unifying patterns of meaning. There are no grand theories … no utopia, no social progress or golden road to the best of all possible worlds … there is no all-encompassing explanation of class, power, gender, change and conflict … The postmodern world is more fluid, more open to interpretation, more tolerant of diversity, more self-made, and less certain. (Howe 2009: 131–2)

Prevailing postmodernist notions that there are no objective standards, no scientific absolutism and no privileging of knowledge swept into contemporary social work thinking like a theoretical whirlwind. No longer could things be taken for granted. Modernity's promise of certainty was disintegrating as difference and diversity was increasingly embraced and celebrated. This was a new way of thinking that would find its way into new practice approaches (see Chapter 6). Privileging professional knowledge and power was a key component of the postmodernist critique:

> The idea of a connection between knowledge and power is a postmodern one, in that it is argued that whatever group controls the way things are seen in some ways also has the power to control the way things are … Professionals therefore stand to lose quite a bit of power if alternative perspectives are accepted, so a challenge to the exclusive knowledge of professionals is a direct challenge to their power base. (Fook 2002: 37)

Professional power to define according to professional concepts of normality and the perceived value-laden professional language within social work all came under fire within the postmodernist critique. New practice models took all this very seriously, and worked on ways in which power imbalances could be ameliorated, thus creating a much stronger emphasis on the client-as-expert and promoting greater transparency in practice.

Overall, theoretical ideas move in and out of favour, and are generally influenced by critique along the way. Postmodernism has contributed richness to critical social work perspectives, yet it also offers challenges. Inevitably, like all new ways of thinking, postmodernism has had its share of critical scrutiny. According to Beckett (2006: 79):

> simplistic or lazy application of these ideas can end up as a facile notion that there is no such thing as external reality and that, simply by changing the words for things, we can change the world. This can result in a kind of Orwellian 'doublespeak' in which words like 'needs-led assessment' or 'partnership' or 'empowerment' or 'anti-oppressive practice' can end up describing processes that seem almost opposite to what we imagine these words to mean.

Throughout history, social work theorising has been riddled with binary positioning, the modernist versus postmodernist being just one of the more recent. A further take on this philosophical dichotomy has been the debate surrounding the importance of evidence-based practice. Critical ideas about the place of evidence and the privileging of professional knowledge have been at the heart of the debate.

Evidence-based practice

As practice evolves, it is inevitably subjected to critical scrutiny. Whether practice effectively responds to the needs of social work clients is not a new question (Plath 2009). Indeed, the effectiveness challenge has concerned social work since the beginnings of practice (see Gibbons 2001 for a summarised history of research into effectiveness). What is perhaps different in the evidence-based practice development is the way in which it has influenced funding and policy decision-making, particularly in some countries. This has been most obvious in the United States, where it has created a hierarchy of services that are considered worthy of support. Some writers have suggested that this represents a way of advancing neo-liberal ideas, a 're-emergence of the scientific aspirations of social work, indicating the extent to which it was … a quintessentially modernist project' (Gray & McDonald 2006: 8). Other writers have examined the assumptions and principles underpinning evidence-based practice and, finding them to be contested, complex and interpretive in nature, have argued the need for caution with respect to implementation (Plath 2009). At the same time, evidence-based practice has been described as 'a method for making practice decisions requiring lifelong learning ... intended to help clinicians use research knowledge to select the optimal treatment for their clients' needs' (Drisko 2011: 732).

Briefly, evidence-based practice has been drawn from medicine, and is captured in this often-quoted interpretation from Sackett and colleagues (1996: 71–2):

> [Evidence-based practice is] the conscientious, explicit, and judicious use of current best evidence in making decisions about the care of individual(s). The practice of evidence-based medicine means integrating individual clinical expertise with the best available external clinical evidence from systematic research ... It involves tracking down the best external evidence with which to answer our clinical questions.

This interpretation privileges both practice expertise and research knowledge – something that is also identified in the model's sequential steps, beginning with an identification of the problem; the development of clinical questions emerging from this assessment; a search of the available research literature addressing the concern; an appraisal and evaluation of its applicability; identification of treatment response in collaboration with the patient; administering of the treatment and its evaluation (Drisko 2011). This privileging of practice expertise is not identified strongly in much of the evidence-based literature, however, and differing interpretations of what it represents have created ambivalence and scepticism in social work.

When considered in the context of social work theory development and application, ideas about evidence-based practice are important because they have the potential to influence which theories are considered relevant or useful in practice. From an evidence-based perspective, those theories that can be empirically supported would be given ascendency over those lacking a supportive research base. For example, this would position cognitive-behavioural theory, which has strong empirical support, over theoretical frameworks that lack an evidence base (see Chapter 5).

Whether or not it is agreed that evidence should support theory, an important contribution provided by the evidence-based practice debate is increased awareness of the ways in which research *can* inform theory and practice. It challenges us to consider what knowledge underpins our work, and requires us to be much clearer about what we mean when we use such terms as 'best practice' and 'what works' – both of which we use loosely in our social work language and literature. Most social work writers support the integration of research and practice in some shape or form, and a perceived rigidity in evidence-based practice ideas has been moderated in language and interpretation by the use of such terms as 'research-based knowledge' and 'research-informed practice' (Trevithick 2005: 56). These terms generally provide a broader interpretation of knowledge that is considered valuable to practice, and a stronger sense of the active and reciprocal relationship between research and practice.

So far in this chapter, we have talked about the various ideas that have influenced the application of social work theory to practice. These have largely related to contemporary critiques and ideological challenges that have shaped the ways in which we think about social work theory and practice. Although conceptual debates are important to the theoretical strengthening of the discipline, social work is nevertheless a practical endeavour typically undertaken within organisational settings. Within these formal structures, organisational concerns and priorities, along with shifting political sands that drive organisational practice, can have an important influence upon the application of theory. So we will now turn to practice within service settings and explore the organisational discourses that can provide legitimacy to theoretically informed practice.

Organisational contexts

While some social workers apply their skills in private practice, most social work is undertaken within organisations. Some social workers practise within government contexts, others in agencies across the service spectrum. Agency mandate, values and objectives largely determine the kind of social work that is practised within an organisation (Beddoe & Maidment 2009). He Waka Tapu,[1] a Māori health and well-being service in Aotearoa New Zealand, has a particular set of principles and values, which support services that are culturally safe and based on notions of empowerment. Its agency mandate supporting the needs and aspirations of Māori *whānau* drives practice in certain ways. Similarly, Aboriginal community-controlled services, such as the Victorian Aboriginal Child Care Agency (VACCA),[2] have a clearly articulated respect for cultural rights, promoting rights-based practice and reinforcing Aboriginal culture and self-determination. The value base of VACCA, and other Aboriginal-controlled organisations, asserts a particular world-view that is holistic and responsive to particular cultural needs.

Laws and policies critically impact upon operational practices (Healy 2005), although the influence of this is likely to be determined by the statutory or non-statutory nature of the work. Writers have noted the increasingly dominating role played by legal discourses in social work practice in recent years (e.g. see Sheehan 2013). A legislative focus on resolving problems procedurally does not always rest easily within an uncertain practice environment where social workers are committed to partnership and empowerment as they work through complex interpersonal dynamics. According to Sheehan (2013: 348), although social workers need to be knowledgeable about the law, they also need to be mindful 'of the increasing influence of legal interpretations and procedural standards in shaping ... practice'.

As we noted earlier in the chapter, in statutory services (such as child protection, mental health and criminal justice) social workers have formal powers that can significantly affect the lives of service users. Subtle and explicit pressure from external systems such as the media can be applied, and can influence the way in which practice is undertaken. Beddoe and Maidment (2009) discuss elements of this pressure in the context of social work and the *risk society*, whereby a preoccupation with risk dominates responses in the context of service delivery and results in more defensive practices. Public criticism of social work practices, largely exposed through high-profile media attention, has created an environment in which the management of risk itself takes up considerable effort and resources. According to Beddoe and Maidment (2009: 52), 'Practice becomes dominated by technicist approaches where risk assessment systems and checklists are put in place to minimise the risk of practitioners "missing something important".'

Biomedical discourses – elements of which we explored earlier in our discussion of evidence-based practice – have also been powerful in shaping social work in health and welfare (Healy 2005). Diagnostic labelling and prevailing notions of 'the expert' within medical contexts confer power and create hierarchies that can also affect the nature of the services provided. As Rapp (1998: 2) notes in his discussion of the dominance of deficits:

> In trying to cope with complex realities, human societies have created stark divisions between the good and the bad, the safe and the unsafe, the friend and the enemy. It is a curious fact that greater attention invariably is paid to the negative poles of the dichotomy ... This pull towards the negative aspects of life has given a peculiar shape to human endeavours and has ... created a profound tilt towards the pathological.

Organisational drivers can create a challenge to the development of theoretically informed practice. That said, applying theory can provide a sense of order and discipline, both to practice and to the analytical thinking that underpins it. Social work in these complex organisational environments has a key role to play in supporting service users to get what they need, when they need it. Confidently applying a social work disciplinary lens in these organisational contexts is important. Social work is concerned with facilitating systemic and holistic responses that privilege both relationship and social justice. It is also committed to collaborative ways of working that harness the strengths of people towards positive solutions in their lives and in their communities. These are valuable disciplinary perspectives that give character to social work interventions and specifically enhance theory in disciplinary ways. They emerge from a developed body of knowledge, research and theory that is essentially client centred (Webber & Nathan 2010: 256–7):

> Social workers are *the* professional grouping who possess the tradition, expertise and experience to challenge the creeping bureau-medicalisation of practice ... Social workers play a key role in representing the institution they work for *and* putting service users at the centre of their practice ensuring that their voice is heard. No other professional body carries this unique role.

Although it is not always easy to influence organisational systems, confidently and professionally articulating this social work knowledge base has the potential not only to strengthen social work practice but also to humanise social services.

Conclusion

There have been a range of challenges to the development of theoretically informed practice and the privileging of social work knowledge. Most often, research and theory development is undertaken by academics who themselves may be distanced from the realities of practice. Making knowledge, research and theory relevant and useful to the field is a key challenge as social work continues to develop as a discipline. Relevancy across cultural contexts is particularly important – a challenge that can nevertheless be overcome through meaningful partnerships stretching both field and academic boundaries. We consider theories to be indispensable tools for practitioners. They provide cultural resources that help us to professionally address human concerns so that people can move forward and live rewarding lives.

The relationship between social work research, theory and practice has always been subjected to critical appraisal, and this is a good thing. Practice theories need to be constantly interrogated for cultural fit, and the ways in which they do, or do not, respond to culturally diverse populations. Research also raises possibilities for practice, both by challenging the way we do things and by suggesting new ways of understanding and giving effect to practice. Theory offers us something in addition to this. Not everything in research is necessarily useful in practice, and it would be quite unrealistic to expect practitioners to be constantly assessing the value of research findings in any particular situation. Theory can be instrumental in explaining inconsistencies, tensions and contradictions that are found within the research literature (Jordan 2004) and in practice more generally. Theory also brings together empirical research findings and valued elements of social work – our interpretive lens – in accessible ways through the development of models and frameworks. Ultimately, this fusion of our interpretive lens, appreciation of culture and the theories that are adopted in practice has the potential to articulate a stronger social work discourse and a broader vision for social work.

In the chapters that follow, we look at models, frameworks and theories that social workers have found helpful in practice. We have grouped the theories metaphorically in a way that we hope will be memorable, and as we consider them we will look specifically at how our disciplinary lens makes them distinctly social work theories.

Useful resource

Connolly, M. & Harms, L. (eds) 2013. *Social Work: Contexts and Practice*, 3rd edn. Melbourne: Oxford University Press.

Notes

1 See http://www.hewakatapu.org.nz.
2 See http://www.vacca.org.

2 Frameworks, models and practice

To suggest that social work theory and empirical research necessarily inform and strengthen practice under-estimates the difficulties involved in bringing together conceptual and practical endeavours. Building linkages between theory, research and practice has been a long-standing challenge in social work. Busy practitioners have little opportunity to keep abreast of new research, and the higher-order nature of some theories and perspectives means that they lack the capacity for straightforward translation into practice. As a consequence, models of practice have emerged from theoretical ideas. These function as bridges between broader theoretical ideas and intervention strategies used in daily practice. For example, empowerment perspectives (see Chapter 7) do not provide a tractable practice pathway, yet the family group conference is a good example of a practice model that can trace its roots to the empowerment tradition (Connolly 1999). This is an example of a practice model that has emerged from theoretical concepts and ideas. When theory, knowledge and practice come together in this way, the result becomes part of a rich and continually evolving intellectual tradition within social work. Connolly and Healy (2013: 32) note the integrative potential of accessible frameworks for practitioners in their day-to-day work:

> Based on research findings, 'good practice' principles and natural justice for clients, practice frameworks provide clarity with respect to understanding the critical aspects of the social work task, and the means through which knowledge can influence intervention pathways.

Social work theorists have, in fact, pioneered the development of frameworks that use theoretical and empirical knowledge to inform practice. Perlman's (1957) problem-solving approach was an early pragmatic response to finding solutions in the context of casework practice. Breaking down problems into manageable steps was the hallmark of this approach, together with a strong belief that it is clients themselves who are best placed to solve their own problems (Howe 2009). Although Perlman remained dedicated to psychodynamic approaches and considered her approach a reform rather than a replacement for psychodynamic casework, her legacy can be found in contemporary solution-focused approaches. Her work also laid a pathway for Reid and Epstein's (1972) landmark task-centred casework model. Like the problem-solving approach, the task-centred model is not a theory but rather a practical response that uses theoretical ideas and empirical knowledge within an accessible format that can be used in day-to-day practice. So before we discuss social work practice theories, in this chapter we will begin by looking at some of these bridging frameworks and models. Reid and Epstein's (1972) task-centred casework – more recently referred to as task-centred practice – was innovative when it was introduced and has remained influential.

Task-centred practice

Research undertaken by Reid and Shyne (1969) was formative in the development of the task-centred casework model. This research, looking at casework effectiveness, examined longer-term interventions that ran their course, as well as interventions that were cut short after a limited number of sessions (Doel 2002). Interestingly, they found no difference in effectiveness between the two. This encouraged the proposal of more structured, time-limited, problem-focused interventions, which represented a direct challenge to the less-focused psychoanalytic perspectives that were so popular at the time (see Chapter 4). Reid and Epstein's book, *Task-centered Casework* (1972), brought together these ideas in a way that captured the hearts and minds of practitioners who were daily confronting the realities of responding to a range of complex needs. The task-centred model was easily understood and could be used across a range of practice settings. It provided a step-by-step framework that also allowed flexibility in the use of other approaches. For example, practitioners could use behavioural techniques within a task-centred framework. Nothing was excluded, as long as it did not compromise its time-limited and problem-resolution aims. Its emphasis on creating contexts within which clients solved their own problems was empowering, and the notion that human beings respond to deadlines was compelling in its simplicity. It was also based on scientific research, and was amenable itself to being researched in terms of its effectiveness.

Healy (2005: 113–15) identifies seven practice principles within the task-centred model:

- *Mutual clarity.* Clarity provides a strong basis for a good working relationship. Within this approach, it is important that the worker and the client develop the focus and process of the work they will undertake together. This is based on realistic expectations and a clear contract between them, including a collaborative review of effort and progress towards the goals that have been established. There are no hidden goals or agendas.
- *Small, realistic steps.* This provides a way of avoiding being overwhelmed by a multitude of problems. Achievable change is critical to the task-centred approach. Success is seen as positively reinforcing and important to the building of confidence that change is possible. One small positive change builds upon another.
- *Focus on the here and now.* Rather than delving into past history, the task-centred model focuses on problems in the present. Past events are relevant only if they directly affect the here-and-now problem-solving effort.
- *Collaborative relationship.* The client is the key to the change process. Their active participation and involvement in the problem-solving effort includes responsibility for the development, implementation and monitoring of the work.
- *Building resource and skill capacity.* Client action towards the alleviation of problems is of greatest importance and creating the capacity for action is central to the approach. Structural problems that may disadvantage a person or other deeper psychological problems, although not considered unimportant, are not within the scope of the approach. Rather, task-centred practice focuses on alleviating problems that are within the control of the person.
- *Planned brevity.* The approach is built upon the notion that short-term interventions are more likely to be effective. Time limits create deadlines to which people respond, and interventions are expected to be no longer than three months in duration.
- *Systematic and structured approach.* A standardised framework that has sequentially predetermined stages. While task-centred practice allows the flexibility to use other approaches, such as counselling, and promotes considerable discretion in determining the content of practice, this is nevertheless undertaken within the structured framework of the task-centred model.
- *Empirical focus.* The model is not only based on what has been identified scientifically to work in practice; it is also expected that practice will be subjected to scientific review and evaluation. Hence each stage of the intervention framework is also amenable to being evaluated systematically.

In addition to these practice principles, the task-centred model reinforces the importance of promoting problem-solving and reducing dependency behaviour (Beckett 2006), and building on strengths rather than focusing on deficits (Teater 2010).

The step-by-step approach of task-centred practice

As guided by the structured approach principle, the task-centred model proceeds through a series of three intervention phases (Doel 2002): exploring problems; agreeing on a goal; and planning and implementing tasks (see Figure 2.1).

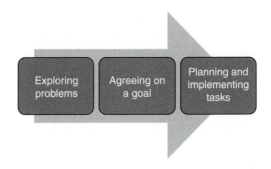

| Exploring problems | Agreeing on a goal | Planning and implementing tasks |

FIGURE
2.1: *Task-centred intervention steps*

Before proceeding through these steps, consistent with the social work interpretive lens, attention is paid to relationship. Engaging with the client and working in partnership is important to the success of the intervention:

> [G]ood practice hinges on being able to work in partnership. If people are not actively involved in the process of change, then they are less likely to take ownership for the problems and the steps towards a solution. This can create a degree of dependency on the worker, and thereby serves to disempower service users – giving less control over one's life and circumstances, undermining confidence and so on. The skills of working in partnership are therefore essential aspects of effective people work. (Thompson 2002: 179)

Understanding the context of the intervention and being clear about the limits to and boundaries of the client–worker relationship is considered to be very important within the task-centred model (Healy 2005). Reid and Epstein originally intended their model to be used with voluntary clients. The emphasis on collaborative decision-making and the ways in which this guides the identification of target problems and tasks in this context of clinical practice is somewhat different from situations where clients do not choose to be involved in services – for example, in child protection or criminal justice settings. Yet social workers within these fields do engage with the task-centred approach, so the first phase of the intervention needs to clarify the nature of the referral, and what this means for the work they will be undertaking together. The practice principles of mutual clarity and collaboration are important at any time, but particularly so when working with involuntary clients. It is important that the nature of the professional role, boundaries of power, agency mandate and limitations of confidentiality are understood, and that the involuntary nature of the client's position is respected. Establishing a good working relationship is important whichever practice model is used. In the task-centred model, it sets the groundwork for exploring the nature of the problems faced.

Exploring problems

Problem exploration is a critical component of the model. People are encouraged to talk about their problems in concrete terms, and to explore what they have done to try to resolve them. General statements are explored for their specific potential – 'feeling overwhelmed' is too general. Instead, what is needed is a clear identification of what is overwhelming: what are the activities and behaviours that are creating these feelings? A problem-scanning technique does as is term suggests – it scans the problematic areas, avoiding leaps to premature solutions. The worker starts where the client is (Healy 2005). During this phase, the worker may raise problem areas that they have noted. Exploratory questioning is used: How important is the problem? What effect is it having? What has been done so far to try to overcome it? What will need to change to enable the client to know whether they are getting on top of it? As Howe (2009: 79) notes: 'By the end of the problem exploration, both social worker and service user should have a clear, solid, explicit set of descriptions and characterizations of the major problems.'

The problems are then prioritised by the client on the basis of what is most important to them. This begins the process of managing the problems and encouraging problem-management skills. In the context of involuntary clients, an exploration of agency expectations and mandates is also important. In these situations, even though the client might not agree with the bottom lines of the agency, they are likely to influence the person's ability to get what they want, and therefore can legitimately be discussed as problem areas where change is important. Problems are identifiable. They are not an overwhelming mass of issues over which the client has no control. They can be broken down into manageable steps – small steps that build problem-solving capacity – and tackled, generating a sense of hope. Agreement is reached on which problems will be worked on first. Importantly, the work focuses upon the *problem*. The approach builds on strengths, and it is the worker's job to shift the focus from individual failure or deficit towards the management of circumstances and situation.

Reflection: Shifting from individual failure to tasks

In child protection, it is really hard to avoid the focus on the person's failure and seeing problems as somehow unchangeable. The way the task-centred approach keeps everyone focused on what can change also helps us to focus on what children need and what parents can do to look after their children well.

Social worker

Agreeing to a goal

Once there is agreement on what needs to change, tasks are identified to move towards identified goal(s). Goals are specific and achievable, and goal achievement can be described in behavioural terms. Again, the task-centred worker does not leap ahead with ready solutions – it is a process of collaboration in which the client is the key to successful change. The task is one of building problem-solving capacity, identifying step by step the tasks that are achievable and measurable. Building in time limits is an important aspect of this phase of the work. Deadlines provide motivation for change, positioning the work within a frame of action:

> For most people, *doing* things is more effective than thinking or talking about them. Changing the way you think and feel is often brought about by action. Task-centred work harnesses the user's potential for action, for doing things, not their proclivity to reflect and dwell. (Howe 2009: 80)

The identified problems, the agreed goals and tasks, and the time limits set to achieve the tasks provide the key components of the agreed contract. Recording these formally in ways that are accessible to the client is encouraged. It is useful to have them recorded when reviewing the goals and tasks.

Planning and implementing tasks

Sessions then unfold in which tasks are evaluated and future tasks are developed and put into place (Doel 2002). Gains are acknowledged, and if tasks are not completed it is a trigger for further exploration of their relevance to the client (Howe 2009). It may be that the particular task is premature – perhaps the person or couple is not yet ready to attend relationship counselling. Perhaps there are steps to go through to prepare them for the bigger step of formal help. Tasks are renegotiated – small steps are taken towards the goal. New goals are established, along with tasks and timelines for completion. It is important not to allow things to drift, as this can negatively affect motivation. The contract overall is time-limited, and in general the intervention is not expected to go beyond three months. Where long-term service agreements are in place – for example, custodial treatment – there is flexibility to renegotiate task-centred agreements, although task-centred practitioners are cautious about extending the intervention, since this may cause the intervention to drift (Healy 2005).

The method is incremental, and the end of the intervention is planned from the beginning (Doel 2002). The work builds towards closure, and the final session provides the opportunity to review the process overall – not only the completion of tasks and the achievement of goals but also perceptions about the process.

Task-centred practice made a big impression on the social work professional community when it was introduced, and it has continued to influence practice since. Its practical orientation, strengths-based focus and flexibility in terms of using other theories and perspectives concurrently have made it attractive to workers. Nevertheless, care needs to be taken when tasks are not achieved. It is easy for despondency to set in, followed by a loss of confidence in the possibilities of making headway (Trevithick 2012). Its use with involuntary clients can also create tensions when clients are not prepared to collaborate and/ or there is disagreement with respect to the nature of the problems and what needs to change. Agreements or contracts in the context of involuntary interventions can be inappropriately used against clients as evidence of lack of ability or motivation. Yet to do so goes against all the principles of client-centred practice. There are ethical and professional responsibilities when entering into an intervention that is built on trust, collaboration and respect. Good professional judgement is needed in deciding whether a model is appropriate for the particular practice setting.

The task-centred framework is a generic model that can be applied when appropriate across a range of practice settings. So, despite being clinically based, it has not been developed for any particular area of practice. It was more important to the original developers of the model that methods were based on empirical research. As practice has evolved, the notion of frameworks and models that are supported by a strong knowledge base has gained momentum (Healy 2005; Lonne et al. 2009). Gould's (2006) conceptual model, which incorporates four dimensions of knowledge that are important to practice, is a case in point. Focused on the specialist area of mental health, his model captures individual and collective concern, and reinforces the need be inclusive and draw upon both qualitative and quantitative measures to strengthen the knowledge base for practice. In recent years, practice frameworks have also been developed to support practice in specific fields – for example, child welfare (Connolly 2007) and criminal justice (Ward & Connolly 2008). These frameworks demonstrate the way in which knowledge can be incorporated into accessible tools for practice (Connolly & Smith 2010), serving to bridge the theory/research/practice divide.

Practice frameworks in child welfare

Maintaining currency with developing knowledge and research can be difficult in the busy social work practice environment. Practice frameworks provide one way of bringing together theory and research in accessible ways for field practitioners (Connolly & Healy 2013). Weaving together important practice values, knowledge and research in ways that can influence practice interventions can be a challenging endeavour. It requires attention to both higher-level principles and practical mechanisms for integrating theory and practice. It also requires a method that can bring these things together, synthesising information then translating the result into practice action. The Care and Protection Practice Framework, developed for child welfare practice in Aotearoa New Zealand, provides one example of this translation (Connolly 2007).

The first step in developing the framework was to identify the information that was important to child care and protection practice. The vast volume of literature dedicated to child welfare practice required a selective review of identified 'good' or 'best' practice initiatives, and what research suggests provides good outcomes for children and their families. As the analysis of the literature unfolded, three strands were identified as important: the need for child-centred practice within child protection; the need to be both family and culturally responsive; and the need to ensure that practice was informed by both a strengths and an evidence base. These three strands became critical perspectives within the developing framework, and were woven through the three identified phases of the child protection practice process: the important first phase of engagement and assessment; the need to seek responsive solutions that would keep the child safe; and the need to secure on-going safety and a feeling of belonging for the child. A basket metaphor became an effective way to illustrate this weaving together of key perspectives across the phases of the work (see Figure 2.2). One strand does not make a basket – it is the weaving together of all the strands that makes the basket strong. In practice, no one perspective is enough – practice needs to be child centred, family led and culturally responsive, and based on strengths and evidence. Within the framework, it is the weaving together of these perspectives that makes practice strong.

TABLE 2.1: *The Care and Protection Practice Framework*

SAFETY, SECURITY AND WELL-BEING				
		The phases of work		
		Engagement and assessment	**Seeking solutions**	**Securing safety and belongings**
Our principles and perspectives	Child centred	**Practice triggers** Are we engaging with the child?	**Practice triggers** Does the child have an advocate?	**Practice triggers** Does the child have family mementos?
	Family led and culturally responsive	Have we persevered despite resistance?	Are decisions family led ?	Are plans culturally responsive ?
	Strengths and evidence based	Are we clear about role and power?	Are professionals working together?	Are services and plans being reviewed as agreed?

Source: Connolly (2007), reproduced with permission.

Within this weave of perspectives and phases, key messages were drawn from the research and turned into succinct practice triggers – reminders for practice that captured the essence of the research and good practice findings. Each phase, intersecting with each perspective, has its own set of practice triggers, which guide work and create a synthesis of knowledge and practice. The 'engagement and assessment' phase provides an example of the synthesis (see Figure 2.2). Research supports the importance of engagement and relationship-building between the worker and the family (Marshall et al. 2003; McKeown 2000). Meta-analyses of which practices positively influence outcomes indicate the importance of the good working alliance (Horvath & Symonds 1991; Trotter 2004), so practice triggers specifically reinforce this importance of engaging

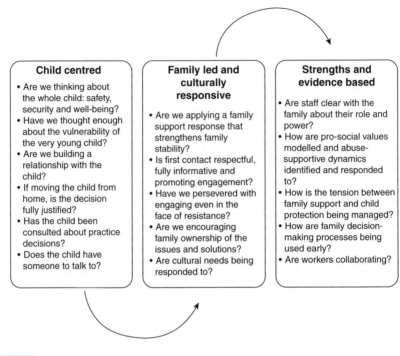

Child centred

- Are we thinking about the whole child: safety, security and well-being?
- Have we thought enough about the vulnerability of the very young child?
- Are we building a relationship with the child?
- If moving the child from home, is the decision fully justified?
- Has the child been consulted about practice decisions?
- Does the child have someone to talk to?

Family led and culturally responsive

- Are we applying a family support response that strengthens family stability?
- Is first contact respectful, fully informative and promoting engagement?
- Have we persevered with engaging even in the face of resistance?
- Are we encouraging family ownership of the issues and solutions?
- Are cultural needs being responded to?

Strengths and evidence based

- Are staff clear with the family about their role and power?
- How are pro-social values modelled and abuse-supportive dynamics identified and responded to?
- How is the tension between family support and child protection being managed?
- How are family decision-making processes being used early?
- Are workers collaborating?

FIGURE 2.2: *The engagement and assessment practice triggers*

Source: Connolly (2007), reproduced with permission.

well with children and their families. Trotter's (2004) summary of his own research and that of others indicates that practice also works in the context of role clarity, collaborative problem-solving, pro-social modelling and reinforcement, and a sound worker–client relationship. These findings resonate with many of the theories we will explore later in the book, particularly those relating to behavioural change (Chapter 5) and solution-finding (Chapter 6). When workers are clear about their role and have open and honest discussions with family members, they have been found to be more effective (Chapter 7). In supporting collaborative problem-solving, effective workers are able to encourage and support a process of client agency over plans and decisions relating to their children. By weaving together theory and research, we can see how this fundamentally supports strengths-based and resilience-focused approaches (Chapter 6). It also supports the notion that people do rebound from serious trouble and adversity, and can grow through dialogue and collaboration (Saleebey 1992).

Within the context of resilience discourses, good outcomes for children are achieved through positive parenting, a stable family life, strong family and kin networks, community involvement and supportive social networks.

In the second phase of the work – seeking solutions – the knowledge base is similarly used to inform practice triggers that provide a bridge between research and practice. For example, several studies have found that including the extended family in solutions for children can support the safe retention of the child within their kinship network (Pennell & Burford 2000; Titcomb & LeCroy 2005). Researchers have also reported increased rates of relative care for children at risk (Edwards et al. 2007; Koch et al. 2006; Morris 2007) and greater placement stability when children remain with their family group (Gunderson, Cahn & Wirth 2003; Pennell & Burford 2000). Wheeler and Johnson (2003) also found that children in kin care experienced shorter periods in care. Such findings find their way into practice triggers and encourage practitioners to utilise extended family as a rich resource to support safe care for children (see Figure 2.3). At the same time, the framework's child-centred strand provides reflective opportunities to ensure that the particular needs of children are not being undermined by a more dominant family support orientation. There is a tension in practice when responding to the needs of children and the needs or desires of parents. In many ways, this tension rests at the heart of child protection as practitioners work towards providing safety for children while at the same time respecting that families have a key role to play in the care and protection of their children. Alliances and loyalties within families create dynamics that can affect safety issues for children. For example, writers have suggested that it may be more difficult for relatives to enforce protective restrictions during parental contact than it is for foster caregivers to do so (Rubin et al. 2008). Aldgate and McIntosh (2006) also caution against a 'cosy view' of kinship care that might assume families are always somehow 'risk-free zones'. The framework acknowledges these tensions, and encourages practitioners to maintain a strong focus on the needs and interests of the child while at the same time supporting families to care for their children well.

In the final phase of the work (see Figure 2.4), the framework is focused on the security needs of children and their sense of belonging. Children need to feel safe and secure in order to grow and do well in life. Lonne and colleagues (2009) draw our attention to the negative aspects of alternative care for children, and many writers have stressed the importance of stability of care and attachment for the growing child (Cassidy & Shaver 1999; Doolan, Nixon & Lawrence 2004; Thoburn 2007; Watson 2005). The need for us to think

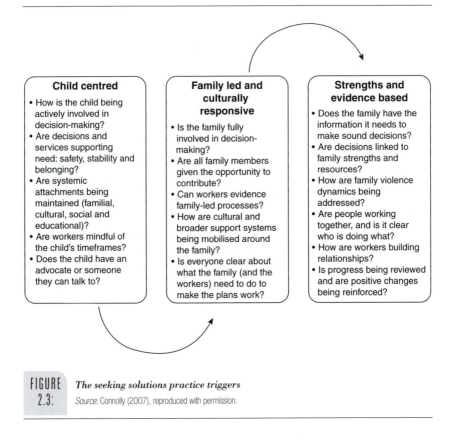

FIGURE 2.3:

The seeking solutions practice triggers

Source: Connolly (2007), reproduced with permission.

carefully about theories of attachment within the context of child protection work has also been noted in the literature (Atwool 2005; Bacon & Richardson 2001; Mennen & O'Keefe 2005). These insights inform the practice triggers in the securing safety and belonging phase of the work.

Both the task-centred model and this more specialist practice framework are examples of the way in which knowledge bridges can be developed to inform practice. We have used the terms 'model' and 'framework' interchangeably. They both provide simplified descriptions of social work processes support- ing theoretical and empirical understanding, and they have much in common conceptually. Both bring together theory, research and ethical components of practice in an accessible format designed to strengthen practice interven- tions, and both enable the eclectic use of other theories and models that are helpful in particular client circumstance. Both represent practical social work responses. Yet, although they have many conceptual similarities, they also have

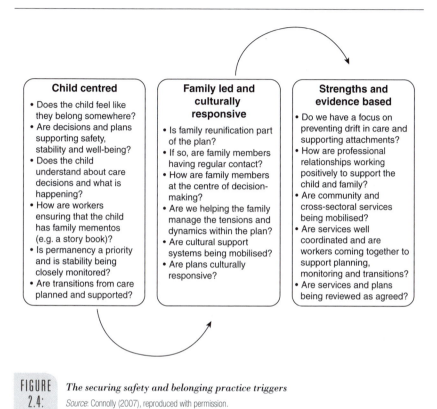

FIGURE 2.4:

The securing safety and belonging practice triggers
Source: Connolly (2007), reproduced with permission.

differences. The task-centred model is a step-by-step illustration of the way in which a practitioner might undertake an intervention with a client, whereas the practice framework provides a higher-level skeleton that supports a set of ideas about what good practice looks like – an exemplar of best practice that can be used to challenge and interrogate practice in key areas. As knowledge develops, new models and frameworks will inevitably develop to strengthen practice and to bring new ideas into practice systems. It is then up to the reflective practitioner to use knowledge and adjust understandings of theory according to the needs of the people with whom they work (Holland 2004).

The frameworks considered in this chapter – and indeed the theories and perspectives we will cover later in this book – rely on practitioners undertaking a good assessment of needs, strengths and concerns. Some approaches describe the focus of this assessment – for example, the problem exploration phase of the task-centred model has an in-built assessment process that provides a foundation for the task-centred intervention. Other approaches leave room for workers to use either general or field-related assessments, discussions of which have also filled volumes. These social work assessments, although not theories or perspectives in themselves, do provide a knowledge–practice bridge, and a means through which intervention decisions can be made. We will therefore explore a number of assessment approaches that can be used as a precursor to the theoretical interventions that follow.

Processes of assessment

Put simply, assessments involve the gathering of information to create a coherent picture that informs interventions with the client (Strom-Gottfried 2002a). They can be formal, using tools or assessment instruments that have been developed for specific areas of practice, or they can be fluid and holistic in alternative ways that respond to cultural needs and interests (Ruwhiu 2013; Mafile'o 2013). We will look at both formal and less formal assessment processes, beginning with the more formal social work assessments that are often referred to as multidimensional or psychosocial assessments.

Multidimensional and psychosocial assessments

Multidimensional or psychosocial assessments are undertaken across a range of practice settings: health and mental health, child protection, disability and criminal justice assessments, to name a few. In all these areas, assessments help us to understand the background to the presenting issues, the influence this has had, and the supports that may be available to assist. According to Strom-Gottfried (2002a), a deficit focus emphasising dysfunction and pathology has persisted in social work assessments despite a strong professional commitment to strengths-based practice ideals (see Chapter 5). Strom-Gottfried argues that this focus under-estimates, and ultimately fails to harness, the potential for client strengths in finding solutions. A preoccupation with pathology can also create professional perceptions of permanent human damage and the impossibility of enriching lives despite limitations and challenges. This preoccupation with deficits can also have a negative influence on the client's sense of self (Strom-Gottfried 2002a: 191):

> Troubled by self-doubts, feelings of inadequacy, and even feelings of worth-lessness, [a] lack of self-confidence and self-respect [can] underlie ... behav-ioural patterns, including fears of failure, depression, social withdrawal, alcoholism, and hypersensitivity to criticism – to name just a few.

While there are clear dangers in assessment processes being dominated by notions of dysfunction and deficit, needs and strengths-based ideas have filtered into many assessment approaches in recent years (e.g. see Rapp 1998 in the context of mental health work and Turnell & Edwards 1999 in the context of child protection).

Drawing upon ecological systems theory (see Chapter 3), Germain's (1991) identification of factors that influence behaviour and human potential provides us with a high-level framework that can be used in developing psychosocial assessments (see Figure 2.5). The framework demonstrates the complex interplay of factors in human development and across human relationships. Within it, individual well-being can be influenced by a range of factors. Objective features include physical characteristics – for example, cognitive and intellectual functioning – and biological factors, including developmental needs and wants (Strom-Gottfried 2002b). For example, the developmental needs and wants of an adolescent are likely to differ from those of an elderly person.

The framework reinforces the importance of understanding the stresses associated with life transitions. Becoming pregnant is likely to present different challenges depending on the age and circumstances of the woman involved. Some transitions and role changes may be experienced as normal or traumatic, thus creating stressors that may be beyond individual and/or family coping

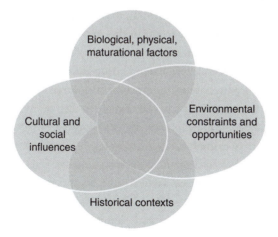

FIGURE 2.5: *Interrelated factors influencing behaviour and human potential*

capabilities. A person's physical appearance – for example, a stooped posture, lack of spontaneity or poor personal presentation – could indicate feelings of depression. There may be physical manifestations of anxiety, tension or an inability to keep still. Hand tremors, restlessness or irritability may indicate physical problems or illness, and it is important not to assume that problems necessarily relate to psychosocial factors. Personal factors that affect health and safety are important to know about, including dangers to self or others. As the biological, physical and maturational factors are assessed, it is also important for domains of strengths and resilience to be explored. Assessing for strengths includes attention to talents, skills and knowledge.

Within the context of social and cultural spheres, ethnocultural factors influence the ways in which people seek help, how they view solutions and their responses to professional services. Internalised cultures can have an important influence on how people perceive the world and their place within it:

> Culture and related social processes influence the development of individuals' self-definition and, consequently, their thinking, feeling, and behaviour ... People from different social groups construct their own cultural self-definitions in a way consistent with and viable in their own cultural context. (Lee & Greene 1999: 29)

These subjective features include the relationships, values, beliefs and meanings that contribute to or detract from well-being (Bowes & Hayes 1999). Patterns of experience within the family or social network, such as drinking patterns, must be understood. According to Strom-Gottfried (2002b), female drinkers are more likely to come from families in which alcohol and drugs were used, and it is clear that maternal drug and alcohol abuse can have serious implications for unborn children. Parental drug and alcohol abuse also has the potential to influence the care and protection of children negatively. Assessing for strengths in the social and cultural domain is also of critical importance. Discovering what people hope for in their lives, working with cultural strengths and valuing diversity caution us against the use of simplistic stereotypes and assumptions about the way a particular person thinks or feels.

The significance of historical factors must be understood if interventions are to hit the mark and be successful. Cultural dislocation can result in social alienation. The erosion of personal and cultural identity as a consequence of migration or colonisation can affect a person's sense of themselves and their worthiness within an alien or dominant culture. Research indicates that refugee and asylum seekers have histories of torture and trauma, which can have lasting consequences (Briskman & Fiske 2009: 143):

> Cultural expectations and interpretations of health and ill-health, experi-
> ences of trauma, and issues of mental health intersect to generate a complex
> set of interconnected factors that require skilled professional responses.

Traumatic histories of violence, sexual abuse or criminality can also present on-going issues, and it is important to understand the intergenerational
influence of these dynamics. Previous negative experiences of social agencies
may result in people becoming withdrawn or distrustful of professional services. This reaction to professional help may result in them failing to apply
for entitled benefits or cause them to avoid important health services, thus
allowing simple illnesses to worsen due to a lack of treatment. Assessing for
strengths in the historical domain provides opportunities to counter-balance
tragedy and past abuses with stories of resilience, dignity and hope (see
Chapter 6).

Environmental constraints and opportunities can enhance or compromise
individual and family functioning. Adequate income, a reasonable place to live,
and access to basic health care and educational opportunities all create conditions within which people have a chance of functioning well. Living in remote
communities where there are limited job opportunities can put additional pressure on families, and create stress and conflict in family relationships. This may
be compounded by social isolation and conservative attitudes to the unem-
ployed. Environmental factors influencing health and safety include freedom
from threat and the importance of feeling safe and secure within one's neighbourhood. Environmental assessments would include, for example, the care
and safety needs of an elderly person to ensure that the home resources meet
the person's functional needs.

While these factors could be seen as creating a lineal effect with respect to
human development, they also influence one another. Biological factors intersect with cultural attitudes if, for example, sexuality is perceived negatively
within a particular cultural milieu. The historical context can influence the person's cultural system and their environmental opportunities when processes
of colonisation or prejudice have threatened the fabric of the person's cultural
community. Equally, experiencing disability can influence factors within the
cultural and social sphere, where prejudice may be located, and in the environmental sphere, where economic conditions constrain the person's ability to live
a good life.

There are a number of reasons why an ecological analysis can be useful
in social work assessments. The conceptual framework of Germain (1991)
includes the network of extended relationships that can be found in families – for

example, kinship networks (grandparents, aunts, uncles), relationships of psychological significance (alternative caregivers, neighbours, friends) and broader support networks (teachers, church contacts, support professionals). An ecological analysis reveals sets of relationships that interact, overlap and engage in reciprocal exchanges. Knowledge about these interrelationships is important for social work, and should inform the choice of intervention. Practitioners in a range of different practice settings need to know the ways in which these relationships interact, how they influence and motivate the individuals involved, and how they affect family systems as a whole.

Specialist assessments

Although Germain's conceptual framework provides a good basis for a generic assessment, specific fields of practice have developed frameworks that respond to the particular needs and concerns of the agency mandate. For example, the Framework for the Assessment of Children in Need and Their Families (Department of Health (UK) 2000; HM Government 2010: 146) was first introduced into child protection practice in the United Kingdom, and has subsequently been adopted in many countries. The framework is presented in an assessment triangle that explores three domains: the child's developmental needs; parenting capacity; and family and environmental factors (see Figure 2.6). It was intended that the framework would extend the worker's focus beyond safety alone and incorporate the child's broader needs.

Within the context of the child's developmental needs, the assessment explores areas of health, education and their emotional and behavioural development. Identity needs and the strengths and challenges of the child's family and social relationships are considered, along with their social presentation and capacity for self-care.

Assessing parenting capacity is very important in child protection work, as parental neglect is a key issue in many child protection inquiries. The assessment framework explores the basic care provided by the caregiver and assesses their capacity to be protective. The caregiver's understanding of the child's needs is important, as is their ability to provide emotional warmth and stimulation needed for the growing child. As we noted earlier, children grow well when they have a stable home base and a sense of belonging. In this context, they can safely explore their surroundings and rely on the adults in their lives to look after them. Children's care and protection assessments consider all these areas

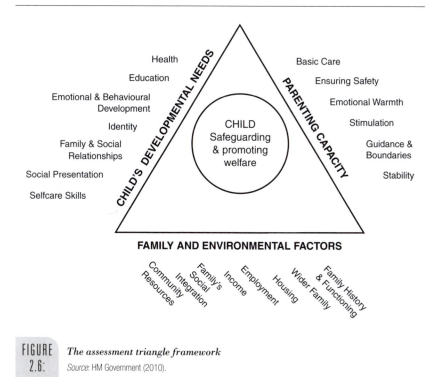

Health

Education

Emotional & Behavioural
Development

Identity

Family & Social
Relationships

Social Presentation

Selfcare Skills

CHILD'S DEVELOPMENTAL NEEDS

CHILD
Safeguarding
& promoting
welfare

PARENTING CAPACITY

Basic Care

Ensuring Safety

Emotional Warmth

Stimulation

Guidance &
Boundaries

Stability

FAMILY AND ENVIRONMENTAL FACTORS

Community Resources

Family's Social Integration

Income

Employment

Housing

Wider Family

Family History & Functioning

FIGURE
2.6:

The assessment triangle framework

Source: HM Government (2010).

of parental functioning, including their ability to provide appropriate guidance and boundaries.

An important aspect of any social work assessment is an exploration of the broader family and environmental factors, including the impact of poverty, the adequacy of housing and the strength of the family's social networks, such as their connectedness to community networks of support. The family's history and family functioning provides important insights when working within the child care and protection area, and attention to the interconnectedness of factors is common when undertaking a psychosocial assessment.

Sometimes absent in mainstream assessment models is the importance of spirituality. According to Lee and colleagues (2009: 173), 'Spirituality entails cognitive, philosophical, experiential, emotional, and behavioural aspects', including religious and non-religious world-views. The Integrative Body–Mind–Spirit Social Work developed by these authors is an example of social work that brings together Eastern philosophies and techniques that create more holistic social work practice.

Holistic assessment processes and cultural dimensions

Modern thinking around cultural wellness and health continues this theme of interconnectedness and is generally described as 'holistic' (Durie 1998). Writers have also developed ways of understanding the cultural dimensions of health, development and well-being (Durie 1998; Mafile'o 2013; Ruwhiu 2013). Durie's important *whare tapa wha* model of Māori health (representing a four-sided house) reinforces the interrelatedness of factors that contribute to Māori health and resilience. The model demonstrates the interaction of four areas of well-being: *taha wairua* (the spiritual dimension), *taha hinengaro* (emotional or mental dimension), *taha tinana* (the physical dimension) and *taha whānau* (the extended family dimension). According to Durie, *taha tinana* (physical well-being) relates to the importance of good physical health and reinforces the need for optimal conditions for growth and development. *Taha hinengaro* (mental well-being) reinforces the inseparability of the mind and body, a key aspect being the person's capacity to communicate, think and feel. The *taha whānau* (family and extended family) dimension places the individual within the context of the family and recognises the individual as part of the wider social system. Central to this is the individual's capacity to belong to and feel part of this wider system in a process of reciprocity and sharing. *Taha wairua* (spiritual dimension) connects the individual to their spiritual side, reinforcing the importance of faith and health being related to 'unseen and unspoken energies' (Durie 1998: 69). Central to the Māori health perspective captured in this model is the notion that these four areas of well-being are 'basic ingredients' of good health, and that balance between them is important.

The Fonofale Framework is another example of a culturally responsive model that is widely accepted and used within Pasifika services (Mafile'o 2013). It captures the importance of family, culture and spirituality for Pacific peoples and, like the *whare tapa wha* model, is based on a metaphor of a house – in this case, a Samoan *fale* (see Figure 2.7). The extended family provides the foundation of the *fale*. The roof of the house represents culture, sheltering life, and the poles of the house provide the framework of spiritual, mental and physical well-being. A circle surrounds the *fale*, representing broader influencing factors upon well-being – context, time and environment.

The significance of extended family networks resonates across Pasifika cultures, providing an important foundation for lifelong health and well-being:

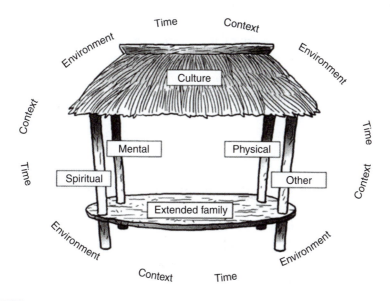

FIGURE
2.7:

The Fonofale Framework

Source: Reproduced with permission from Oxford University Press.

> The history and genealogy of family finds people together and connects them
> to their lands, islands, the sea, and places of identity and nourishment …
> problem-solving and social development within Pasifika social work occurs
> largely within the mechanism of extended family. (Mafile'o 2013: 146)

Culture, represented by the roof of the *fale, is* all-encompassing, thus critically influencing the physical, mental and spiritual elements of well-being. In the same way as the roof of the *fale* protects the house, so too culture provides protection, 'a refuge and source of meaning for Pasifika people during the course of major life events' (Mafile'o 2013: 146).

The importance of spiritual well-being features prominently in cultural models of health and well-being. Over the years, this area has been somewhat neglected by Western conceptualisations, although it has emerged more strongly in contemporary writings (e.g. see Harms 2010). The spiritual dimension within cross-cultural practice operates inclusively in both assessments and interventions and, according to Mafile'o (2013: 147), 'spiritual matters are a key to realising changes in the natural, physical and psychological domains'. Aspects of mental and physical well-being are intricately connected with culture, and with the broader influences of context, time and environment. In this sense, while there may be common issues and experiences across cultural domains, it is nevertheless critical to appreciate context – for example, differences in experience with respect to new immigrant and more settled populations, and the unique differences of particular cultures. The circle of context, time and environment cautions against a one-lens perspective when striving to understand peoples.

There is no single Indigenous culture across Australia, and while Aboriginal and Torres Strait Islander peoples may share common values – for example, the valuing of children, respect for Elders and the significance of culture – important differences exist in terms of instilling cultural values and developing stories of traditional lore. Bromfield and colleagues (2007) explored the appropriateness of using standard assessment processes with Australian Indigenous communities. In a study that involved professionals from government and non-government Indigenous services, carers of Aboriginal and Torres Strait Islander children and the young people themselves, mainstream assessment processes were found wanting in their cross-cultural application:

> Current assessment procedures are based on Anglo-European, middle class values and parenting standards and are inappropriate when used to assess potential Aboriginal and Torres Strait Islander carers, or potential non-Indigenous carers of Indigenous children. The strict assessment criteria may also exclude some Indigenous adults with past criminal history that has no current bearing on their capacity to provide appropriate care for a child. Further, the current assessment procedures use a communication style that is alienating to potential Indigenous carers. (Bromfield et al. 2007: 8)

In response, Bromfield and colleagues note that some states and territories of Australia have been successful in adapting practices and assessment tools to make them more effective in work with Indigenous peoples. In particular, taking a flexible approach to assessments, using more appropriate communication styles and harnessing community knowledge within processes of assessment were seen as more responsive to the particular needs of Aboriginal and Torres Strait Islander peoples.

Models that explore dimensions of culture provide important knowledge that can be incorporated into assessment processes and intervention practices. In this way, practices can be developed that respect Indigenous ways of knowing, build on Indigenous values and provide flexible responses to local traditions.

Conclusion

In this chapter, we have looked at ways in which models and frameworks have been developed to provide bridges between theory, research and practice. Social work writers and theorists will continue to package knowledge in accessible frameworks such as these, and will continue to push the boundaries to strengthen the knowledge base of practice. This is particularly evident as we have explored innovative assessment models that are more responsive to cultural need. The critiques that gave rise to these alternative models are also critically relevant to the discussion of social work theory. In the following chapters, we will return to these important critiques as we explore a range of theories and perspectives that have been important to social work.

Useful resources

Bennett, B., Green, S., Gilbert, S. & Bessarb, D. (eds) 2013. *Our Voices: Aboriginal and Torres Strait Islander Social Work*. Melbourne: Palgrave.

Mafile'o, T. 2013. Pasifika social work. In *Social Work: Contexts and Practice*, 3rd edn, ed. M. Connolly & L. Harms. Melbourne: Oxford University Press, pp. 138–150.

Ruwhiu, L.A. (2013). Indigenous issues in Aotearoa New Zealand. *In Social Work: Contexts and Practice*, 3rd edn, eds M. Connolly & L. Harms. Melbourne: Oxford University Press, pp. 124–37.

3 Systems theories

Social workers will often say that they use systems theories in their practice. People are inextricably linked to their environments, and theories that call on systems of experience and interaction tend to make logical and practical sense to workers in daily practice. Systems theories help us to think about these interactions between people and their social and physical environments, and they also help us to understand how change can occur through the use of ecosystem interventions. In Chapter 1, we talked about how social work theory helps us to explain human experience and how people and their environments change. For the profession, this has often meant engaging in a search for a single, unifying theoretical approach. This was particularly pursued during the first half of the twentieth century, when social work was criticised for being more of a 'cause' than a profession, particularly given that it had no scientific theoretical base (Austin 1983; Flexner 1915; Leighninger 1987). This seems an unusual critique these days, as no profession would be able to argue that it adheres to a particular causal explanation of the world and its role as a profession within it. Back then, however, the pressure was on to justify professions according to their scientific bases. From the second half of the twentieth century, systems theory looked as if it might just be the foundation needed to save the social work profession by providing this elusive unifying approach. In recent decades, we have reduced our expectations that systems theory will save the profession, as we have gained an appreciation of the value of multiple perspectives in response to complex needs. Nevertheless, systems theory has continued to be important to social work thinking and practice, as it provides a foundation for much of social work's understanding of human adaptation and coping in the face of adversity.

In this chapter, we will explore the development of systems theory and how some key thinkers in the systems theory approach have informed social work practice. As Healy (2005) notes, there have been three key waves of systems theories, moving from a focus on general system theory to ecosystemic and, more recently, complex systems theories, as systemic thinking has evolved in response to contemporary needs. An examination of some of the key systemic thinkers and their understandings of systems theories will serve to illustrate how these theories have evolved, and how they have shaped practice in different and significant ways. We will start with Mary Richmond and her *social diagnosis* approach.

Mary Richmond and *Social Diagnosis*

As discussed in Chapter 1, in her book, *Social Diagnosis* (1917), Mary Richmond set out one of the first analyses of social work practice, which is now recognised as a systems approach. Richmond worked with people who were affected by the devastating food and housing shortages in the United States during the early 1900s. She identified the interdependency of people and context, which later characterised more developed systemic ideas. Written at a time when psychoanalytic theory oriented practice towards people's inner worlds, she provided a way of thinking about people's coping, motivation and agency in the context of their wider networks of support or stress.

Richmond challenged the notion that there was one cause of the difficulties families were experiencing:

> The common inclination is to seek for one cause. Social workers, however, need to bear in mind that where cause must be sought in human motives, as is apt to be the case in their work, they must expect to find not that it is a single, simple cause, but that it is complex and multiple. (Richmond 1917: 92)

In many ways, she was identifying the systems within which poverty was occurring for families, and identifying the sources of information that could be gleaned to help form an assessment and an intervention. She concluded:

> Social diagnosis, then, may be described as the attempt to make as exact a definition as possible of the situation and personality of a human being in some social need – of [their] situation and personality, that is, in relation to the other human beings upon whom [they] in any way [depend] or who [depend] upon [them], and in relation also to the social institutions of [their] community. (Richmond 1917: 357)

The types of institution seen to be relevant included family, neighbourhood, civic and private charitable and public relief institutions, as described in Figure 3.1. Family forces include the capacity of each member to provide affection, and to generate endeavour and social development. Personal forces include kindred and friendship networks. Neighbourhood forces include

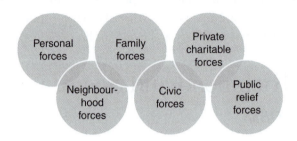

FIGURE
3.1:
Richmond's areas of person: environment assessment

those in the immediate external network – for example, landlords or doctors. These are primarily people but also include agencies and services. Civic forces include school teachers, truant officers, policy-makers, magistrates, mail deliverers, parks, neighbourhood baths and the like. Private charitable forces would include the church to which the person belongs, people and agencies of support – for example, nurses, relief societies, employment agencies and children's homes. Finally, the public relief forces included alms houses, public hospitals and dispensaries.

For Richmond, these interlocking institutional systems created interdependencies and a conceptual framework that could be used to support people in their troubles and to find solutions within the broader context.

While Richmond identified many of the aspects of an individual's social environment that were relevant to their particular concerns, her approach did not provide a way of theorising these interactions. There were gaps in understanding the connections and influence of these interactions on well-being – either personal or environmental. General system theory increased the depth of thinking in these areas and, with it, solutions for social work practitioners.

Bertalanffy and general system theory

As we noted earlier, throughout the early 1900s social work was building primarily on a psychodynamic theoretical base. Social work's professional focus on the person and their environment as the source of stress or support was nevertheless strong, and it was clear that this systemic analysis could not be sustained through the psychodynamic reliance on inner world theory (see Chapter 4).

In the 1920s, an Austrian biologist, Ludwig von Bertalanffy (1968), published his *General System Theory* and developed new insights into understanding 'the growth and change he saw in living organisms' (Norlin et al. 2003: 30). Bertalanffy was transforming thinking in the sciences by looking at the whole, and at the order of the parts, rather than the more conventional scientific approach of trying to understand the whole through an analysis of each part. One of his core assumptions was that an underlying order exists in both human experience and the wider ecology. As Norlin and colleagues (2003: 31–2) note, 'General systems theory focused on wholeness and causality in interactive rather than in linear terms. Here at last was a way of viewing human behaviour that focused on the person and his or her total situation.' Although this was a theory of interactions in the biological world, it was seen to be generalisable to our social worlds, to people's interactions with one another and with their environments. As Bertalanffy (1968: vii) himself noted:

> Systems theory is a broad view which far transcends technological problems and demands, a reorientation that has become necessary in science in general and in the gamut of disciplines from physics and biology to the behavioural and social sciences and to philosophy.

General system theory provides a way of understanding interactions and adaptation through elaborating the core concepts of emergence, open and closed systems, boundaries, entropy and steady state. These concepts are now outlined briefly.

Emergence

The concept of emergence, or of emergent entities, refers to the fact that the 'whole is more than the sum of parts' (Bertalanffy 1968: 55); that is, a new entity continually emerges from many parts coming together – a family, for example, emerges from a system of individuals. A social network such as Facebook is something over and above its millions of individual members.

Open and closed systems

General system theory identifies certain systems in the environment as being open or closed. Derived from physics, systems that are seen as closed are those that are seen to be 'isolated from their environment' (Bertalanffy 1968: 39).

Bertalanffy argues, however, that 'every living organism is essentially an open system. It maintains itself in a continuous inflow and outflow, a building up and breaking down of components' (1968: 39). Later in his book, he describes this as 'systems maintaining themselves in a continuous exchange of matter with environment' (1968: 156). As such, open systems are constantly interacting with the environments around them, responding to the influence of the inputs of others and in turn outputting to others. Each individual is an open biological system, constantly adapting to the environment around them. As individuals, we are thus part of many other open systems in our daily lives – for example, relationships, families, workplaces and communities. For example, thinking about these systems as being open or closed has been very useful in considering the risk and protective factors within families or communities. Are they, too, closed to positive inputs from other resources around them? Are they too open and too diffuse to function well?

Boundaries

When we think about a system, we are encouraged to think about the bound-ary around it – that is, what is within the system and what is beyond it. In gen-eral system theory, 'every social system will possess a boundary and will exert energy to maintain its boundary' (Norlin et al. 2003: 61). This translates into thinking about the rules and roles within a system and what kinds of boundary are maintained between family members and others. Think of your own fam-ily system and the degree to which extended family members are considered core to your family system or as operating under different rules and roles of relating.

Notions of transactions and reciprocity across these boundaries become critical as systems open or close themselves off to resources within or beyond them. Again, reflecting on our own family systems helps to illustrate how we rely on family for certain resources or interactions that we don't expect from other friendship networks. How reciprocal do these interactions need to be to keep everyone in harmony? How taken for granted are some of these interac-tions? How open are family systems to the input and involvement of others?

Much of this thinking has transferred into thinking about social networks. For example, many people who are addressing drug and alcohol issues face dif-ficulties staying clean when they return to their social networks (their closed systems), where old patterns remain and they find it difficult to establish new ways of behaving in relation to drugs and alcohol. For some, it is easier to sustain these old, albeit problematic, ways of being rather than face the realisation that their networks undermine their potential to live their lives differently. In drug and alcohol counselling, often an emphasis is placed on finding new networks or systems of support that can enable change to occur.

Entropy

One of the qualities of closed systems that can also usefully be applied in practice is entropy. Entropy 'refers to the fact that closed systems inevitably run down, become disorganized and are then unable to transform energy, matter and information, or to produce further work' (Germain 1991: 465). This is in contrast to open systems, which can continue to survive and change, given their ability to take in new inputs and adapt to a new steady state. The relevance of these concepts for individuals and families can be seen at numerous levels: functioning as closed systems, for example, is not sustainable for individual or family well-being.

Steady state

The notion of steady state is also central to systems theory, although controversial within it. Steady state refers to the overall identity of a system that remains unchanged, even though there are inputs and outputs to the system. A related concept is that of *homeostasis*, 'a state of equilibrium produced by a balance of functions and related properties of a system' (Norlin et al. 2003: 35). According to Norlin and colleagues, 'the homeostasis process operates through a feedback system with the goal of returning the system to a fixed state' (2003: 35). For people, this means constant adaptation to circumstances – at a micro level, for example, maintaining adequate sleep and exercise for wellness. Or it may mean looking at social interactions and what helps someone to maintain balance. Later theorists called this the 'self-righting tendency' (e.g. Vaillant 1993).

One of the frequently asserted criticisms of this concept of homeostasis relates to the maintenance of the status quo. For example, systems may be oppressive and the maintenance of steady state does not provide a context for challenge. This may imply that change is not possible and that people may strive to maintain the status quo – albeit an oppressive status quo. Interpreted in this way, homeostasis from a radical perspective is likely to be very unappealing (see Chapter 7).

Hudson (2000) challenges this concept of homeostasis, or equilibrium, claiming that the concept is not properly interpreted in relation to how feedback loops operate. Positive feedback loops lead to change and growth of a phenomenon, whereas negative feedback loops lead to stability (Hudson 2000: 218). This critique has been similarly challenged by Germain (1991), who explored the ways in which systems are undergoing constant adaptation and therefore can undergo radical change, depending upon the influences upon them. Systems theories have been critiqued for being too focused on orderly, linear change and for over-simplifying notions of cause and effect. Recent developments in complex systems theories (chaos and complexity theories) have enabled the development of more sophisticated theories of change within systems. This more recent wave of development in systems thinking, which responds to the complexity of the contemporary environment, means that it continues to be relevant to social work practice, an area to which we return later in the chapter.

These concepts have been enduringly influential in practice, and in particular enthusiastically embraced in the area of family therapy. In this regard, general systems theory has enabled the family to be seen as its own system, with its own boundaries, roles, adaptive mechanisms and steady states. For example, Minuchin and Fishman (1981: 16) note that:

> Families are highly complex multi-individual systems, but they are themselves subsystems of larger units – the extended family, the block, the society as a whole … In addition, families have differentiated subsystems. Each individual is a subsystem, as are dyads, like husband and wife. Larger subgroupings are formed by generation (the sibling subsystem), gender (grandfather, father and son), or task (the parental subsystem).

Family therapy focuses on understanding these interactions, and challenging maladaptive aspects of the system when a problem occurs. Family therapy can also focus on systems of meaning with families. Patterson and Garwick (1994), for example, have written about the levels of meaning in family stress theory and highlighted the ways in which families build understanding about situational meanings (specific to what is going on), family identity and family worldview. These levels (or systems) of meaning interact with each other, and come to influence family coping styles and changes in them over time.

Although most strongly adapted as a theory supporting family therapy approaches, general system theory has broader relevance to social work practice. It provides a way of thinking about the social work role in interaction with clients' lives – as we enter people's lives, we become part of their systems and co-create new systems of involvement, influence and understanding with them.

As individuals and as a profession, we are part of a professional system that critically interacts with people's lives. System theories keep us aware of how our roles, rules, boundaries and transactions critically influence ourselves, our profession and everyone we work with. General system theory has therefore provided a critical base for social work thinking for more than half a century, and no doubt will continue to do so as the field is transformed by new waves of development in systems thinking.

Bronfenbrenner and ecological theory

In 1979, Uri Bronfenbrenner, an American psychologist, wrote the landmark book *The Ecology of Human Development*. In it, he outlined the ways in which human development takes place within four particular layers of context: the micro, meso, exo and macro systems. He also placed these layers or systems within a chronosystem, or time context. He saw each of these layers as a series of reciprocal, mutually influential ways to understand individual experience and development. The interconnectedness of these layers or systems of influence is illustrated in Figure 3.2.

A microsystem is defined as 'a pattern of activities, roles and interpersonal relations experienced by the developing person in a given setting with particular physical and material characteristics' (Bronfenbrenner 1979: 22). This layer refers to direct one-on-one or interpersonal connections within the system. He emphasises the importance of the face-to-face relationships we have across a wide range of settings, with each microsystem providing different resources, supports and demands. Some people may have very few microsystems, thus becoming dependent on a small number of close friends or family members. Different microsystem configurations have different strengths and limitations. This has become ever more complex with the emergence of social networking technologies. What these technologies highlight is that microsystems do not always need to rely on face-to-face interactions, yet many social work practice theories are focused at this level of interaction.

Mesosystems refer to the layer of relationships *between* microsystems, 'the interrelations among two or more settings in which the developing person actively participates' (Bronfenbrenner 1979: 25). This layer refers to what goes on between our various networks of relationships: our social connectedness or isolation, and the extent to which our groups of friends or family interconnect and form a web of connection or risk in and of themselves. For example, in

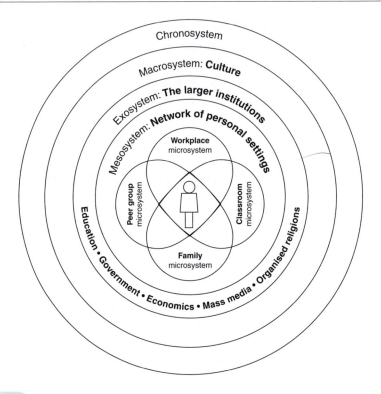

FIGURE
3.2:   *Mapping Bronfenbrenner's layers of the social environment*

small rural communities people may feel that everyone knows them. While a person may have relationships with many people, these people in turn have relationships with others. This degree of interconnectedness has both strengths and limitations.

The exosystem 'refers to one or more settings that do not involve the developing person as an active participant, but in which events occur that affect, or are affected by, what happens in the setting containing the developing person' (Bronfenbrenner 1979: 25). The exosystem refers to the settings that belong within our broader social systems; these, for example, make policies and legislation that directly affect our lived experience. While we do not have face-to-face interactions with these settings, we are nevertheless affected by this wider social context. These settings may interface directly with other members of our family (such as school or work), which then indirectly affect our own individual experiences. They represent wider health, legal, educational or religious institutions or settings, where decisions are made that may influence us quite profoundly. Again, this system is understood differently by different systems theories, so in Table 3.1 an attempt is made to illustrate the similarities and differences between different conceptualisations.

The fourth layer, identified by Bronfenbrenner (1979: 26) as the macrosystem, involves 'consistencies, in the form and content of lower order systems (micro-, meso- and exo-) that exist, or could exist, at the level of the subculture or the culture as a whole, along with any belief systems or ideology underlying such consistencies'. This is typically thought of as the cultural system within which we live. As discussed in Chapter 1, this system shapes our expectations, responses and behaviours. In return, as individuals and groups, we shape and change cultures. This layer is often difficult to articulate until we step outside it and find ourselves in a different cultural context. In Chapter 7, we will look at mountain-moving theories, which locate both the influence on individuals and the change agenda for individuals at this level of the system.

The final layer identified by Bronfenbrenner is the chronosystem, the time dimension. In this layer, he considers a range of time influences: historical time, as well as biographical, chronological, cyclical and future time dimensions. Bronfenbrenner's concepts are often portrayed as a circular interaction of these layers. Figure 3.2 shows this interconnectedness between various layers of the systems he identified as critical in understanding human and social ecology.

The nested conceptualisation of these various layers of influence signifies that change in any part of the system can lead to change for a person or for their environment. Cultural change can radically transform an individual's experience – for example, addressing cultural attitudes to mental illness could prevent an individual becoming stigmatised and isolated in their depression. In turn, individual experience can change cultural attitudes, with consumer perspectives shifting the broader society's attitudes towards mental illness, for example. Intervening in any or many parts of the system – whatever the system might be – can bring about change.

Reflection: Thinking about change at a cultural level

At various times, advertisements on television and publicly distributed posters highlight the everyday experiences of depression and other mental health problems. The strategy informs and supports people with mental health problems, and creates the potential to influence wider public attitudes.

TABLE 3.1: *Comparing the language of systemic approaches*

ECOLOGICAL (BRONFENBRENNER 1979)	ECOLOGICAL (US AUTHORS OFTEN USE THIS THREE-LEVEL APPROACH INSTEAD)	PERSONAL, CULTURAL, STRUCTURAL OR ANTI-OPPRESSIVE (THOMPSON 2003; MULLALY 2002)	MULTIDIMENSIONAL (HARMS 2010)	DOMAIN-SPECIFIC THEORIES LEAD TO INTERVENTIONS OR PRACTICE APPROACHES
Microsystems: Settings in which activities and relationships occur	**Microsystems:** Settings in which activities and relationships occur	**Personal**	An individual's 'inner-world' dimensions	For example, psychodynamic, cognitive, behavioural and narrative approaches
			'Outer-world' dimensions: **Relational:** Our direct linkages with people	For example, psychodynamic, cognitive, behavioural, feminist, narrative, couples and family systems approaches
Meso: The relationships between the various microsystems	**Mezzo**		'Outer-world' dimensions: **Social** (networks): Our networks of relationships	For example, systems, anti-discriminatory, anti-oppressive, feminist, critical theory and social network approaches
Exo: The settings that belong within our broader social systems that influence our well-being		**Structural**	'Outer-world' dimensions: **Structural:** The organisations and institutions that determine resources, policies and legislation, such as health and educational organisations	For example, systems, anti-discriminatory, anti-oppressive, feminist, critical theory and social network approaches
Macro: The 'social blueprint' (Bronfenbrenner 1979) – taken-for-granted ways of doing things expressed via the media, institutions, etc.	**Macro:** Taken-for-granted ways of doing things expressed via the media, institutions, etc.	**Cultural:** Taken-for-granted ways of doing things expressed via the media, institutions, etc.	'Outer-world' dimensions: **Cultural:** Taken-for-granted ways of doing things expressed via the media, institutions, etc.	For example, systems, anti-discriminatory, anti-oppressive, feminist and critical theory approaches

Within social work, Bronfenbrenner's ecological theory has had a profound influence. We talked about the work of Carel Germain in Chapter 2 as she developed the central tenets of ecological theory for social work application in her classic text, *Human Behavior in the Social Environment*. In this text, she introduced the use of an ecological perspective in social work for thinking about assessment and intervention across the life-course.

This was connecting even more deeply the person–environment or person-in-environment (PIE) configuration. As Green and McDermott (2010: 3) note, 'Person-in-environment begins from a position that recognizes the interdependence of phenomena in affecting, changing and sustaining human life.' Explanations for how and why change and adaptation occurs rest at the heart of systems thinking. Germain (1991) took this a step further by talking about the 'person:environment' unit of analysis, a term she used metaphorically (an issue we will revisit later in this chapter). The emphasis in her terminology was on the inseparability of the two: a person is embedded in and influenced by an environment, and similarly an environment is embedded in and influenced by people. As Germain (1991: 17) notes, the use of the colon was critical in this relationship: 'Its use seeks to repair the fractured connection caused by the earlier use of a hyphen.' By making the words inseparable, their constant transactional, interdependent nature is emphasised.

Social work practice occurs at this very point of interaction: the interface between people and their environments. To work with people without consideration of their environments, and similarly to work with environmental change without considering the individuals within the environments, would be to lose the distinguishing strength (and the complexity) of social work as it is practised in real situations. Thinking in this way gives social work its focus on both the micro and macro aspects of intervention. It justifies a focus on interpersonal counselling with someone who has experienced a sexual assault, for example, and on the wider macro issues relating to education and advocacy. It justifies a focus on interventions that more broadly address causation, which may be at a different point of interaction than with a client, such as political or cultural interventions.

In later writings, Germain and Bloom (1999) responded to many of the critiques of ecological approaches, in particular the view that the approach failed to provide a theory of change. They argued that power, homeostasis, self-righting tendencies, and conflict and change *could* all be accommodated within the theorising of person:environment exchanges.

Systems theory influences: Personal/cultural/structural theories

Despite Germain and Bloom's (1999) response, the extent to which core concerns of social work, human rights and social justice can be accommodated within system or ecological perspectives has remained a major criticism of these approaches (Wakefield 1996a, 1996b). Theorists more concerned with these aspects of practice have adapted systems theories to better accommodate this broader social justice focus. For example, Thompson (2006) and Mullaly (2002) have incorporated these concepts into what has become known as the personal cultural structural (PCS) model. In many ways, PCS is informed by systems thinking in that it sees these dimensions as constantly interacting within reciprocal translation: where 'P' denotes the personal, 'C' denotes the cultural and 'S' denotes the structural dimensions of focus. Within these transactions, and within an anti-oppressive approach (see Chapter 7), the PCS model emphasises an understanding of the role of power and relationships, of resources and of identities, that is played out across these dimensions. The oppressive nature of many transactions is highlighted, and the emphasis is on the influence of higher-level systems (such as the economic, political and legal systems) rather than on the more traditional familial systems.

Complex systems theories

Since the 1990s, systems theories have continued to evolve as technology has enabled deeper insights to emerge. Complex systems theories and neuroscience have arguably had the most influence on understanding further the implications of the person:environment configuration. What was general system theory has transformed into complex systems theory, as understandings of chaos and complexity have increased. Thus systems theories continue to be attractive to social workers as social problems and environments have increasingly become complex systems.

In looking at their application to psychology and other life sciences, Robertson (1995: 12–13) notes three major theoretical contributions to systems theory from new insights into chaos and complexity:

> Change isn't necessarily linear; that is, small causes can have larger effects.
> Determinism and predictability are not synonymous – deterministic equations

can lead to unpredictable results – chaos – when there is feedback within a system. In systems that are 'far-from-equilibrium' (i.e. chaotic), change does not have to be related to external causes. Such systems can self-organize at a higher level of organization.

Chaos theory has highlighted the importance of non-linearity. As distinct from linear relationships, where cause and effect have a 'proportional relation', non-linearity emphasises 'the non-proportional relation between cause and effect, and is exemplified by the adage of the "straw which broke the camel's back", or the idea of a critical mass or threshold' (Hudson 2000: 220). Practitioners can relate much more easily to this understanding, which illustrates how, when and why people and/or environments change. Someone dealing with multiple, serious stressors, for example, can be overwhelmed by a seemingly simple, even minor, stressful event that occurs at the same time; conversely, sometimes people living in profoundly disorganised and self-harming ways can seem suddenly to engage in positive change and recovery.

Hudson (2000) proposes that feedback, too, is a core concept that is retained in complex systems theory. What chaos theory has emphasised, however, is 'sensitivity to initial conditions' – sometimes referred to as the 'butterfly effect'. This effect recognises that even a small change in the atmosphere caused by the movement of a butterfly's wings can set off a chain of events of increasing significance – essentially, small events can have major consequences. As Hudson notes, 'A single act of kindness or particularly well-timed intervention on the part of a social worker can have major repercussions' (2000: 221). It can also mean the opposite: that major events may have relatively small consequences.

Similarly retained from general system theory is the concept of equifinality. Equifinality ensures that a steady state can be maintained in open systems, referring to the fact that 'the same final state, the same "goal", may be reached from different initial conditions and in different pathways' (Bertalanffy 1968: 132). A metaphor for this concept is a handful of pieces of paper being flung into the air. All of them end up on the floor – that is, in the same end state – but they have arrived there from different directions. Translating this into a practice setting, many people recover from alcohol addictions, but make their way through recovery in vastly different ways. A system – in this case, a drug and alcohol system – has to be able to accommodate a range of interventions and approaches in order to support people through to the final step of self-management or harm minimisation.

Another core concept in complex systems theory is the notion of attractors, and particularly 'strange attractors'. Chamberlain (1995) defines them in this way: 'Think of strange attractors as an idealized state toward which an unpredictable or dynamical system is attracted. Essentially, a strange attractor is the process that unfolds through the complex interactions between elements in a system.' This concept of strange attractors has gained traction in family therapy: 'Despite the appearance of chaos in relationships, there are certain boundaries that limit behaviors' (Chamberlain 1995: 268–9). A seemingly unpredictable and chaotic situation can have its own ways of limiting itself.

Complex systems theory is now used in a wide variety of disciplines, and is particularly useful in understanding notions of resilience. Resilient people, communities and environments are all of interest within complex systems theory. In studying and responding to ecological disasters, for example, resilience is an important process and outcome to understand. Complex systems concepts provide a map for understanding the ways in which community or environmental systems retain, build or lose resilience (Cork 2010).

The other key influence on systems theory – or at least the robustness of the person:environment configuration – is neuroscientific research. Neurobiological understandings have shown the very real influence of environments on people and vice versa. Green and McDermott (2010) propose that neuroscience provides the core explanation for how the person and environment are constantly interacting. They rightly challenge the notion that the expression 'person:environment' (Germain 1991) is only a metaphor. Neuroscientific insights into our emotional lives and research into our physical health all reinforce the notion that our well-being (or lack thereof) is a very real interaction of ourselves and our environments. For example, neuroscience has highlighted the role of mirror neurons, whereby the emotional pathways in the brain are triggered depending upon the response of others (Schore 2002; Goleman 2005, 2006). Although you might not feel angry when a client is angry with you, neuroimaging has shown that the parts of the brain associated with anger will nevertheless be triggered. Similarly, other research has shown that recovery from medical procedures is greatly enhanced when patients are located physically near windows, where they can engage with the external natural world (Sternberg 2010). This connection between our inner worlds and our social environments is critically important as we seek to understand and make use of the person:environment reciprocal exchanges.

Further, some research is proposing a strong link between human experience and the impact on environments, such as Tumarkin's (2005) analysis of physical places that she defines as 'traumascapes'. These are places where extreme human suffering and distress have continued to linger and be experienced well after the events – for example, places where massacres have occurred. This makes sense if the theoretical approach really does take into account both the person and their inseparability from environments. Similarly, broader ecological theories, such as ecofeminism and ecosocial approaches, have taken these concepts further to embed the reciprocity not just between people and their social environments but also in all environments, including the physical (Payne 2005: 154).

Reflection: Experiencing the physicality of environments

In visiting a couple of places where there has been great suffering, such as a recently closed prison in Melbourne, I have felt a chill run down my spine. Even if I know very little about what has gone on there, there is a palpable sense of sadness or malevolence. It is a very uncomfortable feeling as it has little to do with current experiences.

Social worker

Another arena where complex systems theories can resonate is in relation to Indigenous practice theories. Aboriginal writers and practitioners have always emphasised that well-being and social work practice must be grounded in understanding holistic interactions of people, their communities and the land (Green & Baldry 2008; Bennett, Green & Bessarab 2012). Although anti-oppressive or critical theories ('mountain-moving' in our text – see Chapter 7) might seem the closest theories that address colonisation and marginalisation, in many ways systems thinking is a key strength of many Aboriginal models of and approaches to well-being:

> Although there are differences between Indigenous peoples in Australia and elsewhere, there exists a core of values, which is often expressed in terms of harmony with the land, an omnipresent spirituality, a holistic approach to the world, the centrality of extended family, and the valuing of elders. (Briskman 2007: 69)

All these connections show that systems theory can continue to inform social work practice in a multitude of different ways.

A multidimensional approach

As some social workers have become increasingly sceptical about systems theory – something we will explore later when we consider its limitations – attention has moved from systems approaches to more multidimensional perspectives (Hutchison 2003; Harms 2010). In this approach, many of the dimensions or layers identified in an ecological theory are maintained as a central focus. A 'dimension refers to a feature that can be focused on separately but that cannot be understood without also considering other features' (Hutchison 1999: 17) – that is, the many systems of influence of which a person is a part are acknowledged. Some of the assumptions about relationships and influence are not as strongly maintained, however – the causality assumed in systems theory is not as rigidly adhered to. More consistent with chaos theory, change is seen to be far more complex and unpredictable than GST has conceptualised it as being. The language used to describe Bronfenbrenner's (1979) layers has also become less systemically oriented. Microsystems are referred to as our relational dimensions; the mesosystem as the social dimension; the exosystem as the structural dimension; and the macrosystem as the cultural dimension. As systems thinking has evolved, dimensions of the inner world have been reassessed as significantly influential. This has resulted in much greater attention being paid to biological and physical, psychological and spiritual inner-world dimensions alongside the outer-world dimensions of relationships, social networks, and structural and cultural dimensions. In all our work, we need to consider these dimensions in the context of time and place.

Thinking systemically

One of the confusions in talking about systemic approaches is the interchangeability of the language that is used to describe the various influential layers or systems. This variation is due to different theorists' preferences for language and the prioritising of focus within their approaches. Table 3.1 presented a comparison of the various sets of language that are used throughout numerous ecological and multidimensional approaches to show the points of overlap and diversity. This table highlights how different levels of experience can become the focus of attention, using different theoretical lenses and sometimes quite different terminology.

Applying systems theories in practice

An indication of the enduring influence of systems theories is their extensive use in practice in a wide range of social work settings. Figure 3.3 illustrates how the systemic theoretical explanation translates into a practice approach, then

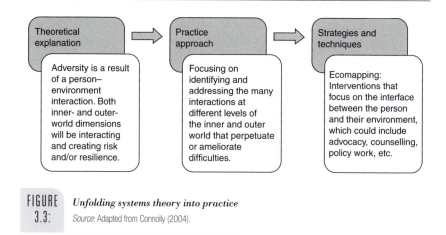

FIGURE 3.3: *Unfolding systems theory into practice*
Source: Adapted from Connolly (2004).

in terms of the practice strategies and techniques that can be used in practice. Whatever the setting – whether it be a large city hospital or a remote community – thinking about people and their interactions within and across their environments informs social work assessments and interventions. Systems theory informs all levels of social work practice, and is relevant to micro-level interventions, such as counselling and casework, through to the macro-level interventions of social policy and advocacy. Changing the impact of systems – be they relational, social, cultural or political – is the aim of the systemic assessment and intervention.

Within the systemic framework, adversity is a result of a person:environment lack of fit, where inner- and outer-world dimensions create risk or resilience. This causal explanation thus unfolds into a practice approach that focuses on mapping out the interface between people and their environments, and the ways in which difficulties are perpetuated or ameliorated. Causation is understood in the interaction of various systems, and the practice approach aims to influence these interactions positively. Strategies and techniques consistent with the theoretical explanation and the practice approach are then used within an intervention framework.

Ecomapping, or social network mapping, is one of the key tools to emerge from systems theory approaches. It enables an assessment of the stressors that may be influencing a person's or family's well-being, and what resources can be drawn upon to help. Bronfenbrenner's (1979) ecological map (see Figure 3.2) is often used as a way of thinking about the influences on a person or a family.

Other ways of mapping the person-in-environment include developing a diagram that encompasses all the critical social linkages in a person's world, then analysing these linkages according to the extent to which they provide concrete or emotional support, criticism or closeness, as well as some of the structural aspects of these networks, such as the frequency and duration of contact (Kemp, Whittaker & Tracy 1997: 111). However, this level of analysis can overlook some of the more structural and cultural dimensions of a person's situation.

An ecomap is another tool that helps to draw out the various linkages in a person's world. Figure 3.4 shows how a person's social network may appear, and highlights the micro- and meso-system interactions. Again, though, it does not

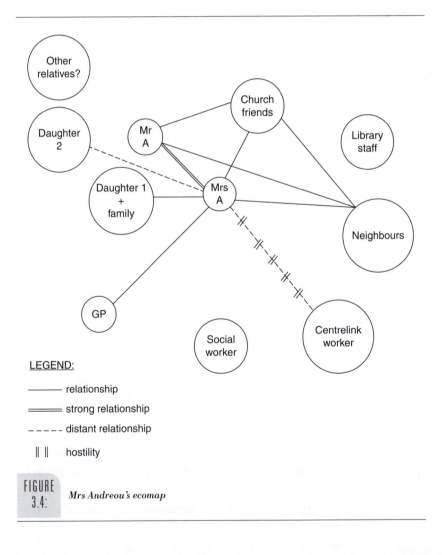

LEGEND:

———— relationship

═══ strong relationship

– – – – – distant relationship

‖ ‖   hostility

FIGURE 3.4: *Mrs Andreou's ecomap*

Case example: Mrs Andreou

Mrs Andreou (aged 68) has been experiencing significant health difficulties. She was diagnosed with chronic fatigue syndrome about five years ago, and in recent months has been experiencing complications with her symptoms. She is visiting the general practitioner regularly. Her husband has become increasingly frustrated about her illness, feeling as if they have no life together. Her eldest daughter and son-in-law drop in each week to see how they are going, but they are balancing their family's needs as their three children are in the last few years of finishing school or starting new jobs. Mrs Andreou's youngest daughter lives overseas and has been home only once in the last three years. She has gone to live in Greece, her parents' birthplace.

Mrs Andreou no longer works part time as a librarian – a job she loved. She no longer walks down the street to go shopping, and only goes out to church on Sundays. At church, they want her to be more involved in volunteer activities, but her depression overwhelms her. Her neighbours occasionally drop in for a coffee and a chat.

She has recently been advised by Centrelink that her Disability Support Pension will be discontinued following changes to the legislation. She is distraught about their financial situation, and worried that she is putting pressure on her husband to stay in his job as a cleaner at the local primary school. She has been referred by her doctor to the Community Health Centre to see a social worker about her situation.

Mrs Andreou's ecomap might look something like the one in Figure 3.4.

show the exo-, macro- and chronosystem factors that Bronfenbrenner (1979) highlighted, and that are still emphasised in the multidimensional approach via the structural and cultural dimensions. The case scenario of Mrs Andreou (see box and Figure 3.4) shows how these links all need to be integrated into an understanding of a person's situation, not just some aspects of her social network.

Some key questions to consider:

- What would you want to know about the interactions in Mrs Andreou's situation?
- Where and why do you think change could best need to occur for her?
- Applying a multidimensional approach, what do you think could be maintaining her problems, and what could change some of the processes that are occurring?

Crisis intervention

Another direct way in which systems theories are applied is through crisis intervention, a key approach that social workers use in practice, based on systems theory approaches. The way a crisis is understood as a systemic experience is shown in Hepworth, Rooney and Larsen's (2002: 382) definition of the word 'crisis': 'an upset in a steady state [state of equilibrium] that poses an obstacle, usually important to the fulfilment of important life goals or to vital need satisfaction'. A hospital social worker's reflection demonstrates how this might be experienced in a practice setting:

Reflection: Understanding a family's crisis experiences

Some families coming to a hospital are anxious, uncertain and often highly distressed. Sometimes they have never been in an intensive care environment in any of their lives, and they are completely overwhelmed by the sounds, smells and sights of the whole unit. It is my job to calmly and clearly support them through this initial shocking phase of the experience. Providing lots of information, or linking them with others for answers to their questions, is a really key part of the role, as is talking about how other families have coped with such unusual and distressing experiences.

Hospital social worker

When a crisis occurs, a person's, family's or community's usual systems of experience and coping are disrupted and overwhelmed. The familiar ways of adapting no longer work, and as a result it is not possible to regain a sense of balance immediately. People in the midst of a crisis are deeply affected in emotional and practical ways, and need to find new ways of returning to some sense of balance. Resuming normal functioning is typically possible, as crisis states are usually temporary states and people tend to have 'self-righting tendencies' (Vaillant 1993), as discussed earlier in this chapter. Crisis-intervention approaches focus on helping people to restore emotional and practical balance – through encouraging the resumption of coping (often by highlighting strengths) and/or introducing new coping skills and resources.

Given that people's usual systems of coping are not functioning well, one of the core tenets of crisis intervention is that they are more open to new ways of coping and adapting (Caplan 1990). Social workers and others can introduce new ways of thinking, acting or being resourced to cope with the new situation. Some key tasks involved in crisis intervention work are:

- initially building high trust and engagement through warmth and rapport
- building a realistic sense of safety through reassurance and information exchange
- initially being highly influential and/or directive if needed
- undertaking a rapid psychosocial assessment

Case example: Crisis intervention

Daniel is an 11-year-old boy who has been placed on a Children's Court order, and is under the supervision of the Secretary of the Department of Human Services. His mother still has guardianship of him. The key issues are that he did not attend school on a regular basis and was often seen in shopping malls during the school day. He was also sometimes left at home alone while his mother went out.

You are the allocated worker supervising the order and started working with Daniel and his family about two months ago. You have just graduated, and this is one of your first cases. You have had a number of home visits to the family in the past six weeks and are making another visit at 3.30 p.m. today.

His mother, Margie, is 36 years old and a sole parent. She has five children (including Daniel) aged 2, 4, 6, 8 and 11. The father of the three younger children died of cancer. The family moved from a rural to an urban community around six months ago, and has been in its current rental accommodation for at least two months. The family appears to have moved around a great deal, and Daniel has had many changes of school and sporting clubs (he is an excellent cricketer and enjoys sport generally).

Margie is a very likeable woman who seems keen to engage with you. You have recently had some concerns that she may be gambling, and that the family is under financial stress. When you visit the family, you note that the house is chaotic, with clothes and goods everywhere, both inside and outside – and children everywhere, both inside and outside.

While Daniel's room is furnished only with a mattress on the floor, his possessions are very ordered, with all his clothes in neat, folded piles around the edge of the room. He speaks about sport a great deal and clearly loves it.

You arrive at 3.30 p.m. for your next home visit, to find Margie and the five children sitting on the front lawn with their cases around them, having been evicted from the house. They are waiting for you as they do not have any money, food or shelter and do not know what to do.

How would you approach this situation?

- drawing upon people's strengths, particularly their psychological and social strengths
- validating and containing feelings that may often be very contradictory
- providing information and resources to help people build a new language and understanding of their experiences.

As the crisis settles, people are able to resume a sense of 'steady state' and control, because they are no longer feeling so emotionally overwhelmed by what it is they are dealing with.

In the case example, the experienced social worker has highlighted a common scenario with which a social worker may be confronted in their practice.

A term that you may also hear used in practice is *psychological first aid* (e.g. see Australian Child and Adolescent Trauma, Loss and Grief Network 2011). In many respects, this term refers to similar interventions. However, the term fails to highlight one of the essential aspects of crisis intervention approaches: namely, that (crisis intervention is about *psychosocial*, not just psychological, responses. In other words, crisis intervention sees people as part of their daily systems, and takes into account that crisis disrupts both these inner and outer systems of influence.)

Criticisms and strengths

Throughout this discussion, you will have noticed that criticisms have been raised about the use of systems and ecological theories within social work. The most significant concerns tend to be theoretical, relating to limitations in terms of meeting the expectations of 'grand' theory: they have little explanatory power; change does not occur in the way we think it will; there are changing complexities in social systems; there is a lack of attention to the inner-world dimensions; and they are derived from disciplines too removed from the social sciences to be readily applicable to human and social contexts. Systems theories have also been criticised for trying to accommodate every aspect of a person's environment and interaction. Paradoxically, it is too prescriptive to be a 'grand' or 'umbrella' theory, and it is difficult to overlay other theoretical frameworks with systems theory as its assumptions and core tenets differ. Despite not having strong explanatory power, systems theories – and in particular ecological theories – can provide an important systemic lens for social work practice. They provide a map for the territory but not necessarily a guide as to *how* to negotiate the territory in terms of priorities in assessment and intervention. For this purpose, it is argued that more domain-specific theories are required to make therapeutic sense (Payne 2005; Wakefield 1996a, 1996b). Although it is recognised that there are interactions between dimensions, cause and effect are not as predictable as they are often made out to be.

Complex systems theories have helped to emphasise the nature of change as non-linear, unpredictable and complex, yet there is some lag in the way change is theorised in social work practice. One of the other untested concepts of systems theories is the nature of reciprocal understandings: 'the extent to which both are mutually influential and in what ways' (Stone et al. 2008: 5). As Stone and colleagues point out, how do we actually measure and analyse reciprocity, and how do we link 'individual and small group functioning to macro forces beyond more proximal environmental settings'?

With technological advances, modern societies are vastly more complex and interconnected than they were in Bronfenbrenner's day – almost 40 years ago. This raises all sorts of questions about the use of the language of a system: what is a 'system' in today's social context? With internet and social networking technologies, the notion of a system as a local and identifiable entity is certainly problematic. Perhaps more importantly, what are the significant interactive forces – the attractors – in these systems? When change may be caused, to use chaos theory's popular metaphor, by a butterfly flapping its wings somewhere else in the world, how do we really understand what has and will cause change? The infinite possibilities for causation and impact can serve to distance the theory from the practical realities of day-to-day social work.

Although the ecological model places the person:environment configuration first and foremost as its primary unit of analysis, the reciprocity in this exchange is sometimes overlooked. If the outer worlds of environments shape the inner worlds of individuals, according to systems theories, the inner also shapes the outer. Yet there does not seem to be enough theory within the ecological approach to account for individual differences and complexities of response in relation to human agency, motivation or intelligence, for example. For this reason, some writers have argued that ecological approaches are not therapeutically useful in that they provide limited, if any, explanation of the inner-world experience, suggesting that a system or layer of experience alone can explain variation in outcomes (e.g. see Wakefield 1996a, 1996b; Walsh 2006).

It has also been noted (e.g. see Healy 2005) that general system theory approaches have emerged from biology, and more recent systems theories that address complexity and chaos are largely derived from mathematics and physics. This imposition of science on social processes has resulted in a reductionist approach to human experience. Other mathematical concepts that drive systems theories, including chaos theories, do not actually translate well to social work practice (Hudson 2000). Hence, in very broad terms, the concepts have a degree of utility within the profession rather than the mathematical concepts themselves being useful.

Despite these significant criticisms, systems theories have played a central role for social workers as a means of understanding the big-picture context of practice. At their minimum, systems theories provide a language for thinking about the interactions between people and their environments that have served the profession well over many decades. They provide a map that helps identify interacting risk and protective factors, including the impact of the worker system as part of that interaction. Sometimes they even provide limited explanations and understandings of causation.

As Payne (2005) notes, social workers have tended to step back from this big-picture theorising to more specialist and localised theories for practice. (The real strength in the systems theory approach is the way it encourages simultaneously thinking and intervening at micro- through to macro-system levels. It shifts the focus of practice beyond an individual who can potentially be problematised and marginalised to an appreciation of their experience in context. Similarly, systemic thinking prevents issues being seen as emerging only in the wider social or cultural arena and having little to do with the micro experiences of individuals and/or families. ⌉

Conclusion

In this chapter, we have tried to capture the enduring influence of systemic thinking on social work. In many ways, it represents a core theoretical approach that has informed social work practice for generations. Despite its limitations, it holds continued relevance for social workers – indeed, its key constructs and broad conceptual framework can often be found supporting eclectic approaches in practice. While the limitations of the systemic approaches are that they can become descriptive rather than prescriptive for interventions, their wide appeal rests in the depth and breadth of factor analysis that are influential at any given time – and the ways in which environments and systems themselves change as a result of these individual interactions. We have highlighted some of the ways in which systems thinking is enduringly helpful, primarily in exploring risk and protective factors from micro through to macro levels of influence.

We will now turn to the first of our metaphorical distinctions, the *onion-peeling theories*, where we have grouped together perspectives that focus on the inner worlds of individuals and highlight the role of insight as a key mechanism for change. As you will see, they have their own set of characteristics that drive intervention pathways, but you will also notice that systems concepts are also very much at the core of psychodynamic thinking – looking at change within our inner systems of functioning and in the interrelatedness with others, many patterns of which emerge from our early childhood experiences in our family systems.

Useful resources

Bertalanffy Center for the Study of Systems Science, http://www.bertalanffy.org.

Bronfenbrenner Center for Translational Research, Cornell University, http://www.bctr.cornell.edu.

Hudson, C. 2000. At the edge of chaos: A new paradigm for social work? *Journal of Social Work Education*, 36(2): 215–30.

4 Onion-peeling theories

In Chapter 3, we explored systems theories and looked at how they have provided an over-arching focus for social work practice. In many ways, onion-peeling theories have some of the same characteristics as systems theories. Within psychodynamic and person-centred approaches, for example, the primary systems of focus are our inner selves and our inner-world organisation, and family or relational systems. These theories propose that the system of the self (both conscious and unconscious) emerges through systems of relationship with others. Unlike the broader ecological approaches, however, they focus on very specific relational systems. They share some of the language of systems theories in relation to boundaries, roles and dynamics, but their use is informed by different theoretical understandings. They are insight-focused.

We have used the metaphor of onion-peeling to describe the characteristics of insight-focused theories because they seek to peel back layers of experience to reach understanding. Like an onion, human experience reflects a layering: layer upon layer, it builds up around us and influences our lives, sometimes in complex and repetitive ways. Accumulated throughout our lives, these layers have the potential to protect us positively and help us to make our way in the world. At other times, they can present barriers to the realisation of important needs and wants. Onion-peeling theories focus on peeling back these layers so that we can see how they influence who we are today. By increasing our awareness of these influences and understanding their origins, it becomes possible to engage in conscious change and develop greater emotional maturity. Awareness and insight lead to change and optimal functioning.

There is another, more ironic, way in which the onion-peeling metaphor works: peeling an onion typically creates lots of tears. One of the Hollywood-style popularised images of this way of working is that a lot of distress and crying are involved in the process of integrating the past with our present selves, developing cathartic insight and resolving our early inner conflicts. This leaves some practitioners cold, yet it is a compelling attraction for others.

Our onion-peeling metaphor is relevant to several key theoretical approaches. In this chapter, we explore two that have been particularly influential in the development of social work thinking: psychodynamic and person-centred approaches. As we look at these theories, we introduce you to some of their key concepts and show how they have been, and continue to be, used by social workers in practice. Psychodynamic and person-centred approaches are used predominantly in the context of individual counselling – the micro practice we talked about in Chapter 2. You will notice this in the language – therapists and counsellors, as well as social workers, use theories of this type, and we draw upon the ideas of different theorists to support and explain theory development over time. Social workers have in fact been significant influences in many of these schools of thought. The onion-peeling theories do not resonate with every social worker's helping style, but their insights do find their way into practice as they provide in-depth analysis of the processes of relationships, including that between the social worker and the client. They provide us with an important foundation for understanding the therapeutic relationship, and have informed many other theoretical approaches because of this. They also have relevance beyond the context of individual counselling – for example, providing useful insights into practices and cultures within teams and organisations.

As with the ecosystem collection of theories, both psychodynamic and person-centred approaches have extensive histories and traditions. Key writers have built a foundation upon which many contemporary theorists have either challenged or used developed key ideas. In this chapter, we draw together core ideas from the psychodynamic and person-centred theories that we think best capture the essence of the onion-peeling tradition.

Psychodynamic concepts

Psychodynamic theories have a core belief that there is an inner world that profoundly influences who we are, how we feel and what we do. This inner psychological world is dynamic in the sense that it constantly interacts with all aspects of the external world in which we live. This inner world includes our dreams, our fantasies, beliefs and unconscious experiences. These can be seen as 'building block' theories, in that one step builds upon another: 'All of the psychodynamic theories emphasize the importance of stages of psychosocial (or psychosexual) development and unconscious mental processes on human behaviour' (Walsh 2006: 28).

Karen Healy (2005: 51) describes the ways in which social workers have been engaged in a 'retreat from psychodynamic theory' as society moved through the 1960s and 1970s to focus more on social concerns. Interestingly, we might be in the midst of a contemporary transformation in using neuro-biological theories to understand human experience. In many ways, this new knowledge confirms, or provides evidence for, what psychodynamic theories have been proposing for more than a century. In this discussion, we focus on four key areas where psychodynamic theory has continued to make a major contribution: the place of the past in the present; inner drives and motivations; the organisation of the inner self; and aspects of relationship dynamics.

The place of the past in the present

Psychodynamic theories focus on the past in forming a person's inner world. But how do we conceptualise the past and its role in present functioning? This inherent problem has been the basis for long-standing tensions between differ-ent schools of thought.

Two key problems emerge in relation to the role of the past in here-and-now living. One is how deterministic we see these past experiences as being. One risk of focusing on the past as the core influence in the formation of who we are today is that we can become reductionist and deterministic. For example, if we see early childhood abuse as causing irreparable damage, how do we account for the many people who experience horrific abuse yet go on to lead fulfilling, happy lives? The second problem is that the past in the present is memory. Memories are not fixed, in that they are constantly influenced by the present context of a person. They are reauthored as new experiences are encountered. If we think about a memory we may have, it has probably been reauthored many times, depending on changing circumstances. Therefore the past is neither fixed nor objective.

Contemporary thinking recognises that, in the context of past experience, we are most likely talking about a person's *subjective past* and, to a lesser extent, their objective past. We are invited to think about 'two apparently contradictory views: on the one hand, that psychic reality is created subjectively and intersub-jectively in the here and now; on the other hand, that psychic reality ... was cre-ated in the there-and-then past' (Chodorow 1999: 45). This dilemma highlights a parallel process within these theories – a challenge that also relates to when you stop peeling back the layers to reach an optimum level of understanding. Like the parallel in psychodynamic practice, when should we stop taking into account past issues that inform today's practice? In theoretical terms, this question becomes when and how we incorporate all the different strands of theory that have informed these approaches. In practice, it relates to how we incorporate the past in understanding, together with the client, what is going on for them today.

Our inner drives and motivations

If our inner lives are in constant dynamic interaction with the external world, our conscious and unconscious lives are driven or motivated by various concerns, priorities and anxieties. Theories about our unconscious and conscious drives have shifted significantly over the century and a half of psychodynamic thinking that has taken place. From seeing our drives as primarily psychosexual in the early days of Freudian thinking, we are now in an era where safety and security are seen as primary drives. Perhaps we see the social concerns of the day reflected in our understanding of the infant's early development and inner world,: from sexually repressed Vienna through to our risk-obsessed society.

Our psychosexual and psychosocial drives

Freud (1975) placed psychosexual drives at the core of his theories, arguing that each phase of early development of the self was driven by sexual preoccupation: from oral to anal and through to the genital phases of development, Freud and his colleagues articulated theories about the conflicts and potential neuroses arising from each of these transitions. Further reading can help you understand the details of the Oedipal and Electra complexes, for example, and of his elaboration of the pleasure principle and the death instinct (e.g. see Freud 1975, a collection of Freudian writings edited by Strachey).

Many came to question Freud's theory of psychosexual drive as the primary motive in human development and behaviour. In response, Erikson (1959) proposed eight crises that need to be negotiated throughout a person's life, with each of these phases focusing on particular aspects of psychosocial bond with others – for example, developing a sense of basic trust in infancy, or ego-integrity in old age.

Our social bonds and the importance of attachment theory

Until recently, a discussion of attachment theory would never have appeared in a chapter on psychodynamic approaches. John Bowlby's (1984) pioneering work in relation to attachment theory and the bonds between infants and primary caregivers was initially regarded as being outside the realm of psycho-dynamic thinking. Indeed, as Peter Fonagy (2001: 1) notes, 'There is bad blood between psychoanalysis and attachment theory.' Attachment was viewed as a social theory, relating to the external world and objectivity, rather than the internal world and subjectivity. The primary drive identified by Bowlby was nevertheless the human drive for social bonds that enabled (or not) the development of an inner self – a primary concern of psychodynamic theory. This attachment-enabled inner self initially was organised through mirroring and responding to primary caregiver interactions, later becoming our internalised 'inner working models' of emotional regulation.

While people have many different relationships with others, attachment relationships are seen as having particular characteristics and functions. Bowlby (1984: 177–234) outlined three core characteristics of attachment bonds as being proximity seeking, the secure base effect and the separation protest. Allen (2003), from the Menninger Clinic in the United States, outlines four key functions of these. The first is a protective and safety function. The infant's survival is utterly dependent on the availability of a primary caregiver. The child must be able to elicit this unfailing protection from a more powerful figure in the environment. The second is the function of assisting with physiological regulation – that is, keeping a balanced state of well-being in relation to physical needs. The third is the function of assisting with emotional regulation – that is, managing or containing intense emotional responses. The fourth is the important process of teaching the child to mentalise, as we will explore later when we look at the theory of mind.

Attachment style has been studied extensively, from infancy through to adulthood and in many cross-cultural contexts. Originally, three major attachment styles were proposed: secure; insecure and avoidant; and insecure and ambivalent (Ainsworth 1985). Attachment theory was later expanded to include a fourth type of attachment behaviour, which was termed insecure and disorganised (Howe 1995). The parenting styles associated with each of the attachment styles have been outlined by Harms (2010: 200–4) as follows:

- *secure attachments:* the parent is available, helpful, responsive, sensitive and attuned
- *insecure, or anxious, attachments:* the parenting style is marked by uncertainty, inconsistency, misinterpretation of signs, frequent separations and rejections
- *insecure, disorganised attachments:* the parenting involves excessive early deprivation or absences.

(These early attachment styles between primary caregivers (primarily but not exclusively mothers) and infants were seen to have a profound influence on later adult functioning. Attachment style is linked with the capacity of the infant to develop their own affect regulation and their sense of relationship with those around them. A securely attached infant is able to explore their world, seek physical and emotional safety when needed, and gradually develop an internal working model that their wider world is safe and that they can emotionally and relationally negotiate their world. Much of the psychosocial trauma caused by the removal of Aboriginal children from their families can be explained through understanding attachment bonds and needs. These concepts are critically important in all child and family welfare interventions.)

Our safety

Other theorists have identified safety as the core drive experienced by infants. Moving from Freud's emphasis on psychosexual drives, the work of Sandler (1985) has had a profound influence on refocusing psychodynamic thinking about what motivates infant behaviour. As Fonagy (2001: 79) notes, when there is an emphasis on maintaining safety, 'The unique emphasis on instinctual gratification is replaced by the pursuit of a prototypical sense of safety as a unifying underlying goal.' These concepts also link strongly with Bowlby's (1984) focus on the importance of a secure base.

Neuroscientific developments

Over the past two decades, neuroscientific research has gone a long way towards providing support and evidence to demonstrate the impact of these influences on the developing infant. Neuroimaging has shown, for example, that early deprivation and trauma significantly affect children's emotional development. The research shows that, within attachment relationships, many neural pathways associated with affect regulation and empathy do not develop as they do for infants who are not exposed to such deprivations (Schore 2002; Koole 2009). Similarly, neuro-endocrine consequences have been identified following trauma in infancy:

> The neuro-endocrine system refers to the system of interaction between the brain, nervous system and hormones; with one of its primary roles the regulation of moods, emotions and stress response. Any disruption to the neuro-endocrine system affects a range of basic psychological and physiological functions. (Coates 2010: 393)

This research has provided evidence of the ways in which these significant patterns of relating and of experiences shape the developing brain of the infant (Shonkoff & Phillips 2000). It confirms in many ways what psychodynamic and attachment theorists have been arguing for decades. Given the strength and weight of scientific discourses, these findings are now being heeded as writers recognise more fully the influence of early negative experience. The fact that the research provides the physical evidence supporting psychosocial processes also provides support for renewed attention to psychosocial interventions.

Organisation of the inner self

If you observe an infant and compare them to a young child ready for school, it is clear that a lot happens within a short number of years to enable the child to function independently in the world around them. Think of a baby and how they experience and express their distress and their survival needs (for example, hunger, thirst, sleep, affection, temperature and toileting regulation). As an infant develops, their inner self (along with their physical self) becomes organised so they can become a functioning person capable of relating to other people.

Psychodynamic theories have proposed different ways of understanding this organisation of the self over time. Freudian theory proposed that there were three aspects of our inner world, using the metaphors of the id, the ego and the superego for our inner-world structures. The id was seen to signify 'the uncoordinated instinctual trends', or the range of impulses we experience, whereas the ego was the organising, realistic part of the self. The super-ego had a 'critical and moralising function', operating like parental or social constraints on our behaviour (Freud 1975: 21).

Ego psychologists proposed different ways of organising the self through more conscious activity, 'toward a greater emphasis on client strengths and adaptability. This was in part a reaction against Freud's heavy emphasis on drives, and highlighted the ego's role in promoting healthy social functioning' (Walsh 2006: 30). Some of the key aspects of self-organisation currently being emphasised include the task of affect regulation, the use of defence mechanisms and the development of a theory of mind.

Affect regulation

Observing infants, one of the most striking aspects is how rapidly their emotions shift, even in the course of a few minutes. These emotions are not under their control, but rely more on the external sources of soothing and containment, such as an adult responding to their crying by picking them up and holding them or feeding them. The settling or soothing of their emotions is highly dependent on these interactions with others. During our early years, we learn to manage our emotions to a far greater extent – after the temper tantrums of toddlerhood, for example, we learn other ways of managing high frustration. This is why we tend to see toddlers, rather than adolescents, having tantrums in the supermarket. The management of our emotions enables us to interact with others and usually control our emotional responses as we relate to others. This is the process of *affect regulation*: being able consciously to control our emotional responses and replace them with more cognitively and socially aware responses.

To do this, certain things need to happen. We learn anxiety management, both consciously and unconsciously. We learn to suppress our frustrations and desires, and in many instances contain our anger or our pleasure. We learn that, even when people are angry around us, we can remain calm. For an infant, this differentiation is not possible. Relationships provide a mirror for the infant – they see out there as 'in here'. They take in, or introject, the world they see outside themselves, and begin to create a sense of being.

Psychodynamic theory proposes that an infant is initially unable to distinguish their own emotional life from that of their primary caregiver – that is, the primary caregiver's emotional life is perceived and accommodated as the child's own. Theorists suggested that infants initially see things as primarily good or bad. Integrating complexity into relationships is too sophisticated a cognitive task at this point in the child's development. This initial splitting into good or bad helps us to make sense of the world, within which primary caregivers are typically seen as good.

Defence mechanisms

Our defence mechanisms are usually not under our conscious control. We become aware of them through reflection and insight. Psychodynamic theories propose that defence mechanisms are one way of protecting ourselves against anxiety. They provide a way of defending from our consciousness the fact that we are anxious or distressed, and thus enable us to function. Defence mechanisms can be both functional and dysfunctional, depending upon the extent to which they create subsequent problems in our daily life. For example, denying the reality of the loss of a particular relationship and acting as if there is no sadness or hurt may protect a person from feeling the intensity of that sadness and hurt.

While theories of defence mechanisms are typically attributed to Freud, it was his daughter Anna who elaborated on nine defence mechanisms, and others have expanded this work further. We provide a brief overview of these defences in the box below, detailed primarily by Goldstein (1995) but with additional mature defence mechanisms identified by others. Vaillant (2002), for example, identified sublimation, humour, altruism and suppression as mature, adaptive coping strategies.

Common defence mechanisms

1 **Repression:** keeping unwanted thoughts and feelings out of awareness.
2 **Reaction formation:** replacing an impulse in consciousness with its opposite.
3 **Projection:** attributing unacknowledged feelings to others.
4 **Isolation of affect:** repressing feelings associated with a particular context or ideas associated with certain emotions.
5 **Undoing:** nullifying an unacceptable or guilt-provoking act.
6 **Regression:** returning to an earlier developmental phase and level of functioning.
7 **Introjection** (or internalisation): turning feelings towards the self rather than directly expressing powerful emotions.
8 **Turning against the self:** rather than turning unacceptable feelings onto others, turning them towards the self.
9 **Reversal:** altering feelings or attitudes into their opposite.
10 **Sublimation:** converting a socially objectionable aim into a socially acceptable one.
11 **Intellectualisation:** thinking about the experience or emotion rather than experiencing it directly.
12 **Rationalisation:** using convincing reasons to justify certain ideas.
13 **Displacement:** shifting feelings or conflicts about one person or situation onto another.
14 **Denial:** non-acceptance of important aspects of reality.
15 **Somatisation:** converting anxiety into physical symptoms.
16 **Idealisation:** over-valuing another person, place, family member or activity beyond what is realistic.
17 **Compensation:** making up for perceived deficits or inadequacies.
18 **Asceticism:** giving up pleasures to avoid conflict created by gratification.
19 **Altruism:** getting pleasure from giving to others what is wanted for yourself.
20 **Splitting:** separating two contradictory feeling states (usually good and bad).
21 **Projective identification:** projecting unacceptable feelings onto another and then fearing and/or seeking control of that person.
22 **Omnipotent control and devaluation:** unrealistic idealisation of self and exaggerated devaluing of others.
23 **Humour:** permitting the expression of feelings through making something painful seem ridiculous or without discomfort.

Sources: Goldstein (1995: 72–85); Vaillant (2002: 63)

Theory of mind

As infants develop and negotiate their relationships, they come to see themselves as a separate entity from those around them, with their own mind or ability to mentalise. This capacity to mentalise is part of what is termed the theory of mind: the essential capacity infants must develop in order to recognise that other people are separate and different from themselves. This is a critical capacity, as it enables children to realise the separateness of self and the reality of an 'other'. Developing a theory of mind also relates to developing human capacity to be empathic towards others and sensitive to their needs, rather than just seeing them as an extension of the child (Baird & Sokol, 2004).

Aspects of relationship dynamics

Psychodynamic theories pay a good deal of attention to the influence of early relationship dynamics on later adult experience, particularly within the context of adult relationships. In focusing on how a person develops in the context of primary relationships, the nature of relationships themselves becomes a primary focus of the theory. Psychodynamic theories provide a way of understanding motivations, expectations, experiences and patterns of relating. Three critical concepts for social workers are transference, counter-transference and intersubjectivity.

Transference

Transference refers to our emotional reactions to others, which originate in patterns established early in life. It is a part of everyday relationships: 'In transference, we use experiences and feelings from the past to give partial meaning to the present as well as to shape the present, as we act and interpret present experience in light of this internal past' (Chodorow 1999: 14–15). These reactions can be tangled up with past reactions or experiences, causing us to relate to someone 'as if' they are the person from the past. This might be quite outside our conscious awareness. Expectations, fantasies and frustrations may be projected onto the person to whom we are responding in the present, or they may be experienced internally. As Nancy Chodorow (1999: 21) states, 'Unconscious fantasies expressed in transference processes of projective and introjective identification are the way we give meaning to our lives and experiences in general.' Michelle's case example later in the chapter highlights the intensity of these reactions and shows how one man's view of his partner can be influenced considerably by his relationships with his parents in ways that are outside his awareness.

Reflection: Experiencing transference

In practice, I am still surprised by how quickly and intensely some clients will respond to me when we talk together – it is not who I am or what I am saying to them that necessarily elicits the response. It is that I am reminding them of something or someone from earlier in their life.

Social worker

Transference is the means by which the work of psychoanalysis occurs. A positive transference relationship is seen to be the container within which change can take place – that is, through a trusting, positive relationship, the client can experience the anxieties of present and past relationships, and work through understanding them to be better able to relate to others around them. Transference emerges in so many different ways.

Psychodynamic theory would propose that a client was connecting with other experiences and 'projecting' into this situation feelings, thoughts and memories from this past experience. For example, if their father or mother was overly authoritarian in their parenting, they may see another adult (such as their employer) as overly authoritarian, and take on a more passive role in relating to them, or not 'rock the boat' because they feared negative consequences. This is a simplistic explanation, but it highlights that in all our relationships with other people – including in our professional worlds – we carry these ideas and expectations about relationships, based on these earlier, primary relationships.

Counter-transference

Counter-transference is the reaction of the social worker or therapist to the client. Freud coined the term as a way of highlighting that 'a therapist is compromised in his or her dealings with the patient because of the therapist's own feelings. These feelings come from the therapist's own psyche, from her or his own interpersonal patterns and habitual resistances' (Gibney 2003: 135). In Michelle's example later in the chapter, note the reaction she initially had to her client when confronted with his anxieties – it nearly prevented her from working with him. Supervision is the space where these reactions are explored – particularly when they become problematic in the working relationship.

Counter-transference reactions emerge from the worker's unconscious, as well as from their past world and their reaction to the client's past experience.

As mentioned in Chapter 2, neurobiological research has provided an evidence base for these processes in which one person elicits a response from the other. Research tracking mirror neurons has shown that when one person expresses anger towards another, the area of the brain where intense emotion can be seen through imaging is similarly aroused in the listener, even if they do not become angry themselves. Understanding this research and its implications for practice is an important developing knowledge base that can help practitioners and their supervisors to appreciate these normal relational dynamics and how to respond to them in the context of practice.

Intersubjectivity

Initially, psychodynamic theories and therapies emphasised the idea that the therapist was like a blank screen, onto which the client projected their fantasies, expectations and reactions. The therapist was a neutral, objective listener, forming interpretations of the nature of the client's projections over time. They were literally out of sight, sitting behind the client who was lying on the couch, and symbolically maintaining an objective position – as if outside the relationship. This supposed objectivity and neutrality came to be questioned. Carl Jung and others challenged this dynamic, recognising the interactivity of the therapeutic encounter – neither party was neutral or objective. Later in this chapter, we explore person-centred approaches that highlight the necessary conditions for change in the therapeutic relationship: warmth, congruence and unconditional positive regard. We will see that these are not neutral conditions.

This shift of emphasis within the therapeutic relationship has led to an understanding of the intersubjectivity that exists within it – that is, it is 'co-constructed between two active participants with the subjectivities of both patient and analyst contributing to generate the shape and substance of the dialogue that emerges'. Importantly, this places the worker 'as a participant in a shared activity (analyst as inside)' (Fonagy 2001: 123–4). These shifts now mean that positive supportive relationships, rather than neutral or objective ones, are emphasised as the space in which ego strength can be developed.

Interesting insights from research are starting to clarify which treatment factors in relationships are important for therapeutic success (Miller et al., 2014). Lambert and Barley (2001) conducted a meta-analysis of psychotherapy studies in which – despite being somewhat cautious about the accuracy of such a crude percentage breakdown – they demonstrated that extra-therapeutic factors (factors outside the therapy process) actually accounted for 40 per cent of therapeutic success, compared with 15 per cent from expectancy and 15 per cent from specific therapeutic techniques. Nearly one-third, or 30 per cent, of the outcome could be explained by 'common factors' such as 'therapist credibility, skill, empathic understanding, and affirmation of the patient, along with the ability to engage the patient, to focus on the patient's problems, and to direct the patient's attention to the affective experience, all of which were highly related to successful treatment' (Lambert & Barley 2001: 358). These qualities are very similar to the facilitative conditions within the onion-peeling approaches that require us to pay increased attention to the therapeutic relationship. As Lambert and Barley (2001: 359) note, 'Therapists need to remember that the development and maintenance of the therapeutic relationship is a primary curative component of therapy and that the relationship provides the context in which specific techniques exert their influence.'

Psychodynamic theory and practice

Using our theory-to-practice framework, we will now look at the way in which psychodynamic theory unfolds into a practice approach and a repertoire of psychodynamic techniques. As you may recall, the theoretical explanation clarifies why difficulties have occurred, which then informs the practice approach and essential characteristics of the method. Importantly, the strategies and techniques that emerge are consistent with both the theoretical explanation and the practice approach (see Figure 4.1).

Within this unfolding of the theory-into-practice framework, we see that unresolved conflicts cause responses that inhibit optimal functioning. The practice approach uses insight as the primary means of working through conscious and unconscious processes that prevent the person from functioning well. Various techniques that support this approach are then used to increase awareness, and in doing so facilitate change. Some of the goals of intervention in psychodynamic approaches (Harms 2007: 203) are to:

- free individuals and family members from unconscious restrictions, and therefore establish less neurotic patterns of relationship and communication
- work towards eliminating unhelpful patterns of relating
- delineate roles clearly, through establishing the fantasy compared with the reality of expectations

- find a balance between autonomy and mutuality
- develop affect tolerance and impulse control
- restore or develop an integrated self-identity.

These goals are about expanding a person's inner capacities and resources to function optimally in daily life.

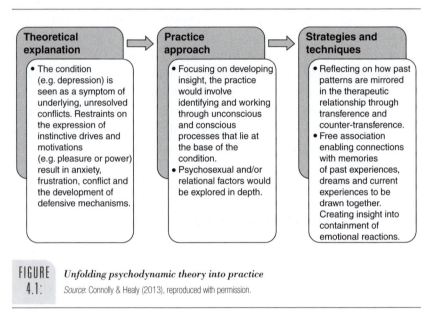

Theoretical explanation

- The condition (e.g. depression) is seen as a symptom of underlying, unresolved conflicts. Restraints on the expression of instinctive drives and motivations (e.g. pleasure or power) result in anxiety, frustration, conflict and the development of defensive mechanisms.

Practice approach

- Focusing on developing insight, the practice would involve identifying and working through unconscious and conscious processes that lie at the base of the condition.
- Psychosexual and/or relational factors would be explored in depth.

Strategies and techniques

- Reflecting on how past patterns are mirrored in the therapeutic relationship through transference and counter-transference.
- Free association enabling connections with memories of past experiences, dreams and current experiences to be drawn together. Creating insight into containment of emotional reactions.

FIGURE 4.1: *Unfolding psychodynamic theory into practice*
Source: Connolly & Healy (2013), reproduced with permission.

Although the approach initially was used in private psychotherapeutic services, and has continued to be utilised in this way, many aspects of psychodynamic theory have been embraced across a range of settings and fields of practice. They have organisational application as well. Psychodynamic approaches provide a useful way for thinking about the management of anxiety in organisations such as the police force or defence forces, or in hospitals, highlighting how both individuals and groups function in highly stressful situations. Isabel Menzies Lyth (1988), for example, studied the ways in which nurses used psychological defences in the face of the anxiety and stress associated with their role in hospitals.

Some of the specific psychodynamic skills or techniques used by social workers and others include establishing a trusting relationship; promoting a corrective emotional experience; providing a safe space to talk; offering containment; undertaking interpretive exploration; and managing defence mechanisms (Gibney 2003; Harms 2007; Nelson-Jones 2006; Walsh 2006).

Establishing a trusting relationship

The quality of the therapeutic relationship is absolutely fundamental for positive outcomes within the psychodynamic approach. A key skill or technique for psychodynamic practice is the ability to establish trusting relationships, enabling the relationship and the process of relating and discussing to build an understanding of a person's patterns of relating and of their neuroses. Trust is established in many ways. In practical ways, it is established through reliability and consistency. For example, as social workers, it is important to ensure that we are available when we say we will be, that we are punctual and/or that we return telephone calls (Trevithick 2012). Maintaining confidentiality appropriately or being transparent about what information will be shared with others will also build trust. At other levels, trust is built through an accurate empathy and emotional containment, which we explore below.

Promoting a corrective emotional experience

The development and maintenance of the therapeutic relationship over time is seen to be one of the most critical skills within psychodynamic approaches. As we have discussed, this enables the experience of positive transference to emerge, and for insight-oriented work to be undertaken within a supportive yet challenging environment (Harms 2007: 198–9). Ideally, the therapeutic relationship provides the opportunity for the client to re-experience or experience a 'good' adult relationship (mirroring a protective parenting relationship). This experiencing of a good relationship enables clients to experience and internalise the good aspects of themselves while learning about and acknowledging the bad. Change and healing occur through the relationship with the social worker.

In the common factors approach (Lambert & Barley 2001; Miller, Hubble & Duncan 1996) described earlier, the relationship is assessed by the client at the end of each session to assess how they are experiencing the process. This enables the client to talk about what is working or not working for them within the supported environment of therapy, also modelling the possibility of relationship review and enhancement.

Providing a safe space to talk

Psychodynamic approaches are 'talking cure' approaches: they operate on the understanding that giving voice to inner experience, making connections with origins and links between the past and present, and conscious and unconscious thought brings about a new sense of coherence and understanding of self. Through cathartic expression and sense-making, a person can be released from the emotions, thoughts and behaviour that have been holding them back or keeping them in problematic ways of being. Insight is the driver of change.

Free association is encouraged – the client says whatever comes into their mind. The content of the discussion might include everyday events, past experiences, dreams and fantasies, and other dimensions of relationships to enable a better understanding of a person's beliefs and reactions. Links are then made with what was said, why it was said and what it means. The rationale for this approach is that free association enables awareness to emerge – from what is experienced by way of feelings, and through naming and verbalising them, a coherent narrative can form and awareness can be achieved. Some ways of doing this can be to ask, 'Who does that remind you of?' or 'What are you thinking right now?' The emotion or difficulty can be reduced in terms of its intensity or 'hold' on the client – again, insight is the driver of change. In Chapter 5, we will explore cognitive behavioural approaches and you will read some similar questions. But while cognitive behaviour therapy focuses on beliefs and cognition, here the focus is relational or process elements of the therapeutic process.

Offering containment

Often we can feel a lot of anxiety in talking about past and present events and difficulties, leading to a need to feel safe and secure in our inner worlds. Containment refers to 'an exquisite empathy and thoughtfulness with which the [worker] responds to the client throughout the session' (Gibney 2003: 46). Containment is an important skill that is used frequently in practice and with ourselves as practitioners. Gibney (2003: 46) proposes six key interventions that lead to containment:

- *An accurate assessment and the sense of safety.*
- *Setting details of time (duration and frequency) and space (boundaries) as containing features.* Unlike other approaches, a psychodynamic approach is typically employed in a structured setting, with clear boundaries around your meeting times and space. The certainties of this contract are seen to provide some safety and boundary, and therefore provide an opportunity for the client to experience safety and boundary also in their inner world.

- *Containment of the client within the therapy session.* Gibney (2003: 51) describes this as relating to the fact that the client feels absolutely understood, accurately and genuinely. He and others argue that this leads to the client being able to get in touch with their feelings, irrespective of their nature. Thus there is a containment and affirmation of inner-world experiences.
- *Containment of the client in relation to external threats.* Through the giving of advice and direction in decision-making, the worker in many ways models adult decision-making processes and does not hesitate to advise on particular situations, particularly those of risk. In this sense, the role of 'good' parent is often enacted. This is a controversial aspect of intervention, with many workers believing that directive practice is not effective practice. Others would see that there is a time when dependence on advice is needed, given client vulnerability (Trevithick 2012).
- *The therapeutic alliance and a probable map of the territory.* If a client knows what the boundaries and expectations of both the counselling and the counsellor are, this eradicates the anxiety about how, when and why, for example, therapy will end.
- *Contextualisation as containment.*

Undertaking interpretive exploration

Within psychodynamic approaches, non-directive, 'uncovering' techniques typically are used to listen and elicit the history, thoughts, ideas, feelings and perceptions of a person about their circumstances, now and in the past. Using summaries, making observations or invitations and using 'why' questions are all part of an interpretive process. Interpretations are usually made in the context of well-established, trusting relationships, where they can be discussed fully in insight-oriented work. Timing is often critically important to the synthesis of worker interpretation and client insight.

Managing defence mechanisms

Anxiety experiences are understood to lead to a distortion of reality, a loss of control and inner conflict. As we have explored in this chapter, psychodynamic theory proposes that in the face of anxiety, we unconsciously use defence mechanisms, which enable us to channel impulses 'into acceptable behaviors' (Walsh 2006: 31). Learning about these patterns is a core focus of psychodynamic work.

Michelle, a social worker who applies psychodynamic concepts in her practice, has provided the following case example, which illustrates many of the psychodynamic concepts and strategies explored in this chapter. You are encouraged to think about the psychodynamic concepts and skills she is using as you read through the practice scenario. Some details have been altered to ensure confidentiality, both in this example and throughout the following chapters.

Case example: Psychodynamic approaches

Gary is a 27-year-old man who has requested counselling because of relationship issues. Gary states that he has been dating his girlfriend, Sara, for ten months and that for the most part they have enjoyed a good relationship. He describes Sara as his 'dream girl'. They met via an internet dating site, and he says they share many common interests. Gary says he struggles at the thought of Sara having been with other men, and that he ruminates about this constantly. He also says he feels jealous when she talks to males and often questions her interactions with others. Recently he called her a 'slut' when she accepted a car ride home from a male colleague because it had been raining.

Gary appeared nervous when he first attended counselling and displayed anxiety in response to some of my exploratory questions about his past history. He informed me that he did not believe he needed to provide details of his family history, as he did not believe his past would have any influence over his current issues. He also avoided talking about aspects of his relationship with Sara by deflecting on to other topics.

I noticed that I was having countertransference reactions to Gary. I felt that he was trying to take complete control of the counselling process and that he was making it difficult for me to complete an assessment because he was unwilling to provide me with the information I needed. I wondered whether I should refer him to someone else who might be able to engage him more effectively. Luckily, I was able to process this reaction and consider the impact it could have on the therapeutic relationship. I had ignored the fact that this person was indeed asking for help and wanted to change. I considered that the very thing about which Gary was seeking help was relationships, and in fact my own experience of being in a relationship with him was valuable information. I guessed that his need for control stemmed from an experience of not feeling in control, and I wondered whether others felt a desire to reject him. I also reminded myself that Gary's defences were not a personal attack on me but Gary's way of protecting himself from hurt, and this helped me to get back in touch with my compassion for him. I decided I needed to spend time building trust with Gary and did some behavioural work to assist him with his anxious thoughts and his poor impulse control when it came to insulting his girlfriend. This provided him with some strategies he could implement immediately.

Eventually, Gary appeared to feel more comfortable, and I decided to revisit his personal history. He disclosed that he was an only child. He said his father was controlling and overly critical of him, and he described his mother as depressed, passive and emotionally distant. I felt that Gary's experience in his current relationship was most likely related to his attachment experience with his primary caregivers, and asked for more details about his childhood experiences. For the first time, I noticed tears well in Gary's eyes as he spoke about his mother's lack of responsiveness when he tried to please her and his father's on-going ridicule and unrealistic expectations of him.

I was able to help Gary identify internal working models that he developed; these led him to believe he was unlovable and someone who was not good enough. Gary and I explored how this was affecting his current relationship. He identified that he feared Sara rejecting him, and he was unable to trust that she truly wanted to be with him. This led him to search for evidence that she had feelings for other men, and Gary was able to see how he was sabotaging the relationship and setting himself up to be rejected. Gary felt that if he could prove she had feelings for someone else, he could end the relationship before she had the chance to hurt him. This insight was important in changing Gary's behaviour in his relationship, and helped Gary to relinquish a good deal of his anxiety. I assisted him to understand how this relationship was different from that with his parents, and Gary was able to share his insights with Sara, thus deepening their relationship. Exploration of his relationship with his parents also allowed Gary to process some of the anger and hurt that he felt towards them.

Psychodynamic approaches have been important to the development of social work over time, and with the development of new research and knowledge there is a sense that these approaches have reinvented themselves to remain relevant in the context of contemporary practice. The person-centred approach, another theoretical strand within the onion-peeling tradition, has shown itself to be equally enduring as it has evolved to meet the contemporary challenges of practice.

Person-centred approaches

In many ways, person-centred approaches can be seen as 'psychodynamic' approaches in that they are concerned with 'the changing dynamics of what comes to awareness, the changes in the processes of the mind, and the dynamics of human relations' (Owen 1999: 166). In other ways, however, they have become the foundations of much more radical approaches to working with people, putting people and their right to self-determination at the centre of practice.

Person-centred approaches emerged primarily from the work of Carl Rogers (1965). As a therapist, Rogers (1965: 22–4) was aware of the attitudes of objectivity and implicit superiority that often played out in therapeutic relationships, particularly in the dominant psychoanalytic approaches of the time. He saw the potential of the therapeutic relationship – that is, the co-created relationship – as a space in which change could occur. This was in contrast to the idea that the therapist was a 'blank screen' upon whom projections were made, a notion that is inherent in more conservatively practised psychoanalytic approaches. Rogers and other person-centred therapists and researchers provided the building blocks for thinking about intersubjectivity and the co-creation of meaning and experience that occurs within the therapeutic relationship. Rogers (1965: 65) states, for example, that 'it has become increasingly evident that the probability of therapeutic movement in a particular case depends primarily not upon the counsellor's personality, nor upon [their] techniques, nor even upon [their] attitudes, but upon the way all these are experienced by the client in the relationship'.

Earlier in this chapter, we noted Lambert and Barley's (2001) meta-analysis, which found that 30 per cent of change was a factor of the therapeutic relationship. Rogers' statement pre-dates their findings by some 40 years, but nevertheless supports some of the ideas of the early theorists. Rogers was clear that the philosophical orientation of the therapist or counsellor is critical to what occurs within that relationship, and that it is necessary to interrogate our professional motivations: 'Is our philosophy one in which respect for the individual is uppermost? Do we respect [their] capacity and right to self-direction or do we basically believe that [their] life would be best guided by us?' (Rogers 1965: 20)

These questions were critical at the time of developing the person-centred, non-directive approach to working with people, and helped to identify the core or necessary conditions of this new way of working. The questions remain critical as we support the development of empowerment models and approaches that support rights-based ideals (see Chapter 7). Notions of dignity and respect lie at the heart of person-centred approaches. Richard Sennett (2003: 23) explores three themes in relation to respect: focusing on 'the demeaning effects of adult dependence, the difference between self-respect and recognition from others, the difficulty of showing mutual respect across the boundaries of inequality'. Many social work clients have experienced disrespect in so many ways, and person-centred or client-centred approaches are one way of redressing these demeaning experiences.

The key focus of a client-centred or person-centred approach is on the 'internal frame of reference of the client, to perceive the world as the client sees it, to perceive the client [themselves] as [they are seen by themselves], to lay aside all perceptions from the external frame of reference while doing so, and to communicate something of this empathic understanding to the client' (Rogers 1965: 29). Thus, in contrast to the more traditional psychodynamic approaches, which prioritised the listening and the subsequent interpretations of the worker, the key focus of person-centred approaches was on the client's sharing of their inner-world experiences, in a safe, supportive and empathic relationship. Although the phrase 'starting where the client is' came much later, it was unquestionably foreshadowed by Rogers' non-directive, empathically oriented approach.

Reflection: Carl Rogers in practice

I remember seeing an old video recording of Carl Rogers when I did my training. It struck me that he personified the essence of person-centred practice. He was gentle, caring and steadfast in his trustworthiness. Everything about him spoke of humanistic values.

Social worker

Through the three facilitative conditions of the relationship – congruence with the client, the warmth expressed in that relationship and unconditional positive regard – the client is able to explore their inner world and the ways in which their experience of self is disorganised or distressing, and take responsibility for knowing this self and living life with greater satisfaction (Rogers 1965: 136). Importantly, Rogers identified these three conditions as the fundamental facilitative conditions of any relationship 'in which the development of the person is a goal' (Rogers 1980: 115).

By congruence, realness or genuineness, Rogers meant 'a close matching, or congruence, between what is being experienced at the gut level, what is present in awareness, and what is expressed to the client'. By unconditional positive regard, he meant the attitude of 'acceptance, or caring or prizing'. Empathic understanding was the third facilitative aspect: the social worker 'senses accurately the feelings and personal meanings that the client is experiencing and communicates this understanding to the client' (Rogers 1980: 116). Many of these qualities are now recognised as central to culturally safe practice (Ramsden & O'Brien 2000), where recognition of the client's reality, their conditions for safety and their full identity expression form the basis of practice.

Person-centred theory and practice

Using our theory-to-practice framework, we now illustrate the ways in which key theoretical constructs of humanistic or person-centred theory unfold into practice (see Figure 4.2).

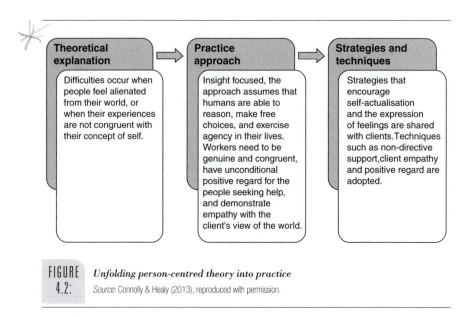

Theoretical explanation	Practice approach	Strategies and techniques
Difficulties occur when people feel alienated from their world, or when their experiences are not congruent with their concept of self.	Insight focused, the approach assumes that humans are able to reason, make free choices, and exercise agency in their lives. Workers need to be genuine and congruent, have unconditional positive regard for the people seeking help, and demonstrate empathy with the client's view of the world.	Strategies that encourage self-actualisation and the expression of feelings are shared with clients. Techniques such as non-directive support, client empathy and positive regard are adopted.

FIGURE 4.2: *Unfolding person-centred theory into practice*
Source: Connolly & Healy (2013), reproduced with permission.

Within this framework, it is the alienation from the world that creates distress and the loss of personal meaning (theoretical explanation). That is, a person experiences incongruence when their world is different from how they want or need it to be. Like the psychodynamic approach, the practice approach is insight-focused, but here notions of worker congruence and positive regard within the therapeutic relationship become centrally important. Consistent with a humanistic approach, techniques are then client-centred, empathic and non-directive, assisting the client to develop an honest, affirming sense of self. As we noted earlier, person-centred approaches share characteristics with psychodynamic perspectives in that they both seek to build awareness and insight. They are also not dissimilar in terms of their intended outcomes and their use of the relationship primarily to achieve these outcomes. There are differences, however, in the focus within the therapeutic encounter.

With unconditional positive regard, congruence and warmth as the key facilitative conditions for positive therapeutic outcomes, these conditions are operationalised by a repertoire of techniques or skills for us to use in our practice.

Unconditional positive regard

As Rogers (1980: 152) notes, 'It is impossible to accurately sense the perceptual world of another person unless you value that person and his or her world – unless you, in some sense, care.' It is about unconditional positive regard in the present moment with another person, regardless of what may have occurred in their past or may occur in their future. It is not about condoning unacceptable behaviour by any means, but accepting that person as a valued human being. Thinking about unconditional regard in the context of caring – that the person matters to us – may help to locate this within a contemporary practice setting.

Being empathic

There is an extensive literature in relation to empathy, and whether it is an attitude, a quality or a skill (Egan 2007). There are things we can do to increase the empathic qualities of our listening and responding. One of the extraordinary qualities of Rogers' work was his ability to reflect on, paraphrase, summarise and clarify what his client was saying and what they meant. He would highlight inconsistencies that he was hearing – perhaps within a narrative a client was relating or within the match between verbal and non-verbal behaviour. Or he would highlight incongruities between what a client wanted and what they were doing or saying. This ensured that he and his client developed a mutual understanding of their story, leaving very little room for misunderstanding or misinterpretation, and focusing on the goal of being an aware, attuned human being. Interestingly, Rogers noted that counter-transference was not as much of an issue in person-centred approaches. If the client, rather than the therapist, is driving the agenda and insights, then the therapist is less likely to influence the process of therapy in the same way through their reactions and their personal history of relationships.

The skill of highlighting reflected in this level of listening and understanding is now referred to as advanced empathic highlighting: sharing with the client the incongruities or underlying messages often expressed by clients.

For example, while they may talk about feeling sad about something that has occurred, their non-verbal communication or tone of voice may convey anger and resentment. These discrepancies might be noted and/or reflected to the client in the context of supportive discussion.

Being genuine

Sharing the reality of the dilemmas for the client is one way of expressing the genuineness of concern. This means adopting an unconditional positive regard for the client's attempts to resolve their situation and acknowledging that they have genuinely tried to find the optimal solution but not been able to, and that they want to be the best person they can.

Both the person-centred and the psychodynamic perspectives have been part of social work's theoretical landscape for many decades. Indeed, they probably represent our longest-standing theories for practice. Yet, while they have both been influential in shaping the ways in which we think and undertake social work, they have also been subjected to criticism.

Strengths and challenges

The criticisms of both psychodynamic and person-centred approaches are quite similar. They relate particularly to the lack of evidence for their effectiveness; their Western, individualistic and inner-world focus; their lack of political emphasis; and their suitability across social work practice settings.

The lack of evidence for their effectiveness

Relative to other approaches – particularly cognitive behavioural therapy (see Chapter 5) – there is far less empirical evidence to support psychodynamic and person-centred approaches (Roth & Fonagy 1996). The evidence that is available is typically from small qualitative studies or case studies rather than randomised, controlled trials, and from high levels of client satisfaction. That said, as we noted earlier in the chapter, trauma studies have shown the impact on neural pathways of early trauma and the inability to develop empathy and insight with and about others. Therefore, while many of the very specific concepts of psychodynamic theory may be difficult to prove, general concepts of psychodynamic theory (that we have a rich inner life, that our early emotional development profoundly influences our later self-organisation and so on) are consistent with this more recent research. Neuroscientific studies of empathy and the interpersonal zones of relating highlight the importance of deep listening (Goleman 2006). It is therefore not surprising that, in the United Kingdom, person-centred practice approaches are incorporated into trauma work (Murphy et al. 2013) in many specialist trauma services. This is despite the fact that the National Institute for Health and Care Excellence (NICE) guidelines recommend that trauma-focused cognitive behavioural therapy is the preferred intervention.

Subjective reports of satisfaction are also typically high in psychodynamic and person-centred therapy. Therefore, for many people the interventions of deep listening and interpretation, of experiencing positive relationships and of sense-making have healing outcomes. Many of the terms have transferred from these very specific theories into everyday life – in particular, 'denial', 'containment' and 'psychosomatic' are terms we often hear in media reports or in organisational life. These concepts make sense to people, and help to explain everyday interactions.

A Western, individualistic and inner-world focus

Many of the popularised images of psychodynamic therapy are of self-indulgent, neurotic people of middle-class means, soaking up the attention of another human being. The term 'worried well' has been used to define this group of people, who may in fact experience few everyday external problems, yet whose lives are filled with anxiety and existential angst. This criticism highlights the evolution of the theories within a Western and individualistic cultural context, and these origins are indisputable.

Whether they are relevant to cross-cultural and Indigenous practice is an important question. Many authors have been highly critical of the fundamental ideas about individuality, developmental trajectories, family and cultural identity that have been at the heart of psychodynamic approaches in particular (Berzoff, Flanagan & Hertz 2008). Taking a person-centred approach in which you are not the expert requires that you genuinely follow the client's lead, wherever that may take you.

A lack of political emphasis

Related to these cultural criticisms, many social workers challenge these theories as lacking in political emphasis. With a focus on the inner world only, to what extent does this enable us to see people within their social, political and/

or economic contexts? To what extent do the practices marginalise people as individuals rather than becoming part of more collective forms of oppression? For example, most of the clients Freud saw as part of his clinic in nineteenth- and twentieth-century Vienna were women caught in a pre-feminist world. Could their frustrations, concerns and anxieties have been understood better as emerging from social and relational oppression under patriarchy than as arising from their own inner worlds and blocked desires? Feminist theorists would undoubtedly think so. Psychodynamic and person-centred approaches do not lead to radical social change, nor is it necessarily part of their agenda, although some argue that the insights people have gained about their frustra- tions and anxieties have led to the emergence of social and political movements (Trevithick 1998). Others do argue explicitly that psychodynamic approaches can and must incorporate political action by the practitioner – for example, Boulanger (2012) argues that there is a moral obligation for practitioners to not only individually and therapeutically witness people's stories but also to engage in political acts of witnessing, such as actively participating in court processes. This demonstrates an integration of the social work interpretive lenses within these onion-peeling theories (see Chapter 1).This would then provide the theories with social work's critical edge, which might be lacking in application across other disciplines.

Interestingly, Thorne (1997) notes that critics of person-centred approaches have suggested that they are out of step with modern imperatives, which value efficiency and the importance of seeking quick solutions. In response, he argues that it is the development of our competitive society that makes person-centred practice ever more important – a powerful antidote to the 'culture of contempt' (1997: 179). In this sense, he sees the on-going influence of person-centred practices as a 'quiet revolution'.

Suitability across social work practice settings

Some social workers and other practitioners have argued that these approaches do not relate well to many of the crisis-oriented and often chaotic environ- ments of practice: 'in short the concept of the "helping relationship" as the vehicle for change is problematic in contexts where the social work role is not only about helping, as is the case in statutory social work' (Healy 2005: 57). Yet, even in these complex areas of practice, a social worker can hold to being person-centred, bringing with them the three facilitative conditions of empathy, genuineness and unconditional positive regard. Some have also argued that the approaches are counter-productive at times when people may feel very unsafe psychologically, because they focus on insight-oriented work rather than on providing direct support for people.

Insight and self-understanding nevertheless remain important areas of concern for social workers, both as a critically reflexive tool and as an important aspect of work with clients in helping them to develop new understandings of their past and their potential. Both psychodynamic and person-centred approaches have had an important influence in social work supervision, providing a frame of reference for talking about work with clients and for understanding the dynamics of the supervisory relationship and other organisational interactions and patterns. They provide useful ways of thinking about processes that are occurring within relationships, whether professional or personal.

Conclusion

Although many social workers have not used onion-peeling approaches in a purely theoretical sense, many of their key concepts retain their relevance in contemporary practice. In thinking about the complex dynamics within any relationship, the life of groups and what occurs within them – or indeed the dynamics within organisations – both person-centred and psychodynamic theories provide useful frameworks that help to conceptualise the issues and suggest ways of intervening. In focusing on the inner worlds of clients and those of ourselves as workers, onion-peeling theories bring rich insights into the relational lens that we bring to our practice. The challenge is not to neglect the importance of multiple interpretive lenses – in particular, the social justice lens – that will ultimately characterise the social work response.

Useful resources

Fonagy, P. 2001. *Attachment Theory and Psychoanalysis*. New York: Other Press.

Tavistock and Portman Clinics, http://www.tavistockandportman.nhs.uk.

5 Faulty-engine theories

In Chapter 4, our onion-peeling theories focused primarily on insight as the key mechanism for change. It was frustration with this insight focus that created the impetus for the development of more action-oriented theories, in particular behaviourism and cognitive-behavioural responses. These relatively new theories, which we have grouped together using the 'faulty engine' metaphor, brought with them ideas and techniques that would shift practice attention to the present and more concrete evidence of change. In many ways, our 'faulty-engine' metaphorical distinction is a bit unfair when describing behavioural and cognitive behavioural theories, although they have received critical appraisal for their perceived mechanistic, almost uncaring characteristics (Trevithick 2012), something to which we return later in the chapter. They do tend to be more structured and directive than other theories, and they do focus on actively changing thoughts and behaviour in the here and now. But there is no reason why they can't be as engaging, respectful and empowering as any other theory when interpreted through a social work lens. We will start by looking at behavioural approaches.

Behavioural approaches

As already noted, approaches based on the modification of behaviour largely emerged in response to a general sense of frustration with psychoanalytic approaches that delved into the past, focused on insight and were grounded in a hope that greater awareness would actually change things for the better. During the 1970s, psychodynamic approaches increasingly came under fire from a strengthening radical social work movement, which saw the micro focus on individual pathology as deeply discriminatory and as failing to address issues of social justice and empowerment (Howe 2009). From another camp entirely, social workers with an inclination for science were questioning the effectiveness of psychoanalytic approaches that seemed to go on forever in what they perceived as some kind of confused morass. Social work was an applied science:

Like all good applied sciences, social work should be rational. Its techniques, when applied, should bring about the desired change. If social work is about helping people to cope better and change their behaviour, it seemed logical to suggest that social workers should have a good look at behaviour modification and its techniques for inspiration. And this is what happened. (Howe 2009: 49)

As the name suggests, behavioural approaches focus on human behaviour – not on what people think or feel, not on what might be causing problems, but on what people actually *do*. Much human behaviour is learned through life experience, and learning processes are formative in terms of the development of individual and group behaviour. Coping behaviour is acquired through learning and, as such, can create helpful or unhelpful behavioural responses. In simple terms, this goes towards explaining causality – faulty learning environments can result in problems when they give rise to so-called dysfunctional behaviour.

Based on the early work of Pavlov (memorable for his canine experiments, which demonstrated an animal capacity for learning and conditioning responses), and Watson, who has been identified as 'father' and 'charismatic leader of a larger social movement' (Kazantzis, Reinecke & Freeman 2010: 1), behaviourism's classical conditioning principles provided the basis for behavioural approaches to come.

Conditioning principles

Two early studies tested classical conditioning, which became the foundation stone for behavioural therapy: Pavlov's experiment with dogs and Watson's experiment with Little Albert, an 11-month-old child who, following a period of conditioning, would develop a fear of rats (Howe 2009; Teater 2010).

Pavlov observed that dogs salivated when food was offered to them, and that they also salivated upon seeing their handler, even though they could not yet see or smell the food coming. He was taken by this, and decided to construct an experiment to test the dogs' responses. The experiment began by introducing a noise immediately before the food was brought to the dog. Quickly, he found that the dog began to salivate upon hearing the noise alone, a conditioned response that the animal had learned during the experiment. This technique of introducing a stimulus to engender a learned response has become known as *classical* or *respondent conditioning*.

Watson, who was particularly interested in the development of phobias, proceeded to test these ideas in his research with children. In an experiment that would not receive ethical approval these days, Watson observed Little Albert playing with tame rats, demonstrating no natural fear. Little Albert was nevertheless startled by loud noises, so Watson sounded a loud noise as the rat was introduced. By the end of a week of subjecting the child to this treatment, Little Albert only needed to see the rat alone, without the noise, to become alarmed and distressed. Watson concluded that Little Albert was *conditioned* to fear the rat, which had held no fears for him before. This forms the basis of the notion that behaviour can be learned and, importantly, therefore also unlearned.

Another key idea that forms a foundation for behavioural approaches relates to *operant* or *instrumental conditioning*. In essence, this relates to what happens when positive and negative consequences are introduced into the equation. Early researchers (for example, Thorndike and Skinner) also undertook animal experiments, which encouraged them to conclude that behaviour could be changed through positive and negative reinforcers (Teater 2010). Positive reinforcers result in increasing desired behaviour while negative reinforcers cause the behaviour to reduce. Disappointingly for Watson and his colleague, Mary Jones, Little Albert's mother, would not let her boy take part in any further experiments, and we can only wonder how the whole thing affected poor Albert's development (Howe 2009). Experiments with children nevertheless continued. Jones undertook further experiments using the positive reinforcement conditioning technique with a child who had a fear of white rabbits and other white objects. Gradually, by exposing the child to positive reinforcers along with the white rabbit, the child's fear reduced until he lost his fear altogether. These early insights laid the groundwork for important therapeutic advances in the deconditioning of phobic responses, procedures that have become known as *systematic desensitization* (Wolpe 1990).

Drawing upon these key principles, we now use the unfolding of the theory-to-practice framework to conceptualise the way in which theory translates into a practice approach, and then into strategies and techniques for practice (see Figure 5.1).

Theoretical assumptions relating to causality position behaviour at the forefront. Behaviour is acquired through learning, and faulty learning environments can result in the creation of unhelpful behavioural responses. Because behaviour can be learned, it can also be unlearned. The practice approach, then, is to create a learning environment in which unhelpful behaviour can be reduced or extinguished, leading to the conditioning of positive behaviour. Practice techniques are specific and measurable. Understanding the behaviour is critical – in order to create positive reinforcers for change, you need to know

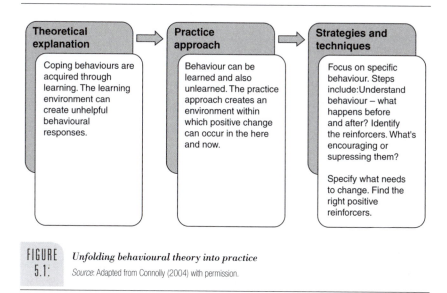

FIGURE 5.1: *Unfolding behavioural theory into practice*

Source: Adapted from Connolly (2004) with permission.

what is currently reinforcing the undesirable behaviour. Usually, when people seek help, they have tried all kinds of things to solve their problems. Sometimes, however, the actions they take can serve to reinforce the very behaviour they hope to ameliorate (Watzlawick, Weakland & Fisch 1974). Experienced practitioners find the right reinforcers, a skill that Howe (2009: 57) identifies as 'part of the art of behaviour modification'.

Modelling desired behaviour is also part of the work of the behavioural practitioner. According to Trevithick (2005), modelling occurs in two ways: inadvertently and deliberately. Most of us learn through watching others. We learn from our parents, our peers, teachers, media and the like. Many experiments have confirmed that we pick up skills through modelling (Hudson & MacDonald 1986). We are more likely to learn from people we respect, where

Case example: Assertiveness

Mary, a middle-aged woman who lived alone, was finding it difficult to say no to her neighbour, who kept coming over to borrow things. She didn't want to hurt her feelings, but it was just another example of Mary being unable to say what she really wanted to. The worker brought another person in and role-played a few different responses that Mary practised on the spot. They continued to work on responses over the next few weeks until she tried out her new assertiveness with her neighbour, to good effect.

we share an identity with the person and where the behaviour is reinforced. This type of learning is a consequence of inadvertent modelling. It is not a consequence of a planned intervention – it just happens. Deliberate modelling doesn't just happen, though: it is a specific intervention to reduce negative and increase positive behaviour. Trevithick (2005) notes that modelling can be particularly effective for reducing anxiety and helping to tackle daunting situations.

Behavioural approaches in contemporary social work practice

Behaviourist theories and practices have had a significant influence on social work. Elements of behavioural approaches have found their way into a variety of perspectives: strengths-based practice and solution-focused work, to name but two. Social workers will apply behavioural techniques in a variety of contexts. Behavioural approaches as specialist practice approaches in themselves are not widely practised, however, and Bronson and Thyer (2001) note that the status of behavioural practice remains unclear: 'While many social work interventions borrow heavily from the behavioural approach, few social workers are thoroughly trained in the theory [and] . . . misconceptions continue to limit acceptance of behavioural methods.'

Behavioural approaches are used in a range of areas – for example, with autistic youth, with people suffering chronic mental illness and in the areas of drug and alcohol work (Thyer & Myers 2011). Bronson and Thyer (2001) nevertheless note Gambrill's (1995) concern that social workers have shifted their interest to cognitive-behavioural approaches, but are overlooking the behavioural while privileging the cognitive. Therefore, we now turn to the cognitive theorists to see how thinking has been brought to the forefront of the theoretical picture.

Cognitive-behavioural approaches

Just as behavioural approaches emerged in response to dissatisfaction with psychoanalytic approaches, interest in cognitive theory and practice emerged through a growing critique of behaviourism's limited focus on behaviour. Psychologists recognised the importance of what people thought and felt, as well as what they did. The new focus on cognitive-behavioural therapy (CBT) spawned a raft of cognitively focused psychotherapies that used behavioural techniques, but now added a greater emphasis on thoughts and feelings. Early theorists talked about the 'mind as an information-processing computer', and such metaphors dominated both theory and practice (Berlin 2002).

As ideas developed, there was an appreciation that the mind-as-computer conceptualisation did not adequately represent the complex thinking processes involved in human experience, and greater attention was paid to notions of constructivism – the idea that the mind constructs reality. This found a measure of fit with similar ideas emerging from the social sciences and the humanities (see Chapter 1); as Berlin (2002: 25) notes, this 'recognizes the relationship between constructivism and theories of social constructionism, which posit that personal and social meanings are the result of social processes of defining meanings and organizing social structures such as norms, boundaries, roles, and power-relationships'. This interpretation of cognitive-behavioural thinking is likely to resonate with social work thinking, given the influence of social constructivism on social work theorising in recent years (see Chapter 6).

Cognitive-behavioural assumptions

Put simply, three fundamental assumptions rest at the heart of the cognitive-behavioural approach: thinking mediates emotions and behaviours; distorted or 'faulty' thinking leads to psychological distress and dysfunction; and by changing faulty thinking and behaviour, you can reduce distress and dysfunction (Teater 2010). Distorted or irrational beliefs tend to be self-defeating ideas, with which we have been indoctrinated – either intentionally or unintentionally – throughout our lives. A number of ideas have been proposed relating to the nature of irrational beliefs. Granvold (2011), for example, draws the following examples of faulty information processing from the work of Beck et al. (1979):

- *Absolutist/dichotomous thinking:* things are right or wrong, good or bad – 'I am a total failure.'
- *Overgeneralisations:* things are always this way – 'My boss is on my back all the time.'
- *Selective abstraction:* one example colouring a whole perspective – 'My essay was hopeless' when the essay had a good mark but there was also some critical feedback.
- *Arbitrary inference:* reaching a conclusion without anything to support it – 'He wouldn't like me, I know it' and 'I'll never find someone who will love me.'

- *Magnification and minimisation:* distorting extremes so that small things become big things and big things become small things – 'Anyone could have done it' when actually it was a very skilled or brave thing to do; or the situation is catastrophised – 'He'll resign because of this' when actually the issue is a relatively small one in the grand scheme of things.
- *Personalisation:* things have gone wrong because of me – 'If I'd only been there it wouldn't have happened.'

These self-defeating thinking processes can be problematic to a greater or lesser degree. They do not apply to everyone, nor do they need to be used as a list of things to cover when working with people. They are provided only to expand our thinking about the range of ways in which people may perceive their world and how they can create unhelpful emotional responses.

That our behaviour is driven by what we think, not necessarily by what happens to us, is captured in the often-used quote by Epictetus Enchiridion, a classical Greek philosopher: 'Men are disturbed not by things, but by the view which they take of them.' The idea that it is our interpretations of external events that cause distress, not the external events themselves, was central to the ABC of CBT: an activating event (A) creates beliefs (B) that result in an emotional consequence (C). As the theory goes, it is not A that causes C, but B. This raises the potential for our interpretation of A to be inconsistent with the reality of A. The case example illuminates the interpretive possibilities inherent in human interactions.

The activating event in our example is Lucy and her lecturer passing each other in the quad (A). Lucy's belief, which in cognitive-behavioural terms might be assessed as an irrational belief (B), is that the lecturer purposefully ignores her because she has failed her recent exam. It may well be, of course, that Lucy's lecturer was thinking of other things, not even seeing Lucy or giving her a second thought. She may have been distracted by something across the quad. She may not have even marked Lucy's paper yet. And even

Case example: ABC

After the completion of her exams, Lucy, a social work student, walks across campus and sees her lecturer walking towards her (A). The lecturer walks straight past, looking away from her. Lucy is immediately struck by what she sees as the lecturer avoiding her (B). She thinks this is because she has done badly in her exam. Now she will fail the course and never achieve her goal of becoming a qualified social worker. She knew that she was never going to be good enough to get through. She feels depressed and sad (C).

if she had and found it to be wanting, it does not necessarily follow that this marks the end of Lucy's career hopes. But Lucy is already feeling low about her failure and the consequences of this for her life chances (C). It is Lucy's *interpretation* of the interaction that causes the sadness, not necessarily what actually happened.

Albert Ellis, a key writer in the cognitive-behavioural field, developed the ABC model, and extended it to include D = disputation and E = evaluation (Trevithick 2012). These additions provide for the helping response: D – the exploration of the irrational beliefs that create the emotional disturbance and the replacement of these with rational beliefs, and E – the re-evaluation of the activating event in the light of these insights. The ABC model lends itself well to the conceptualisation of theory into practice (see Figure 5.2).

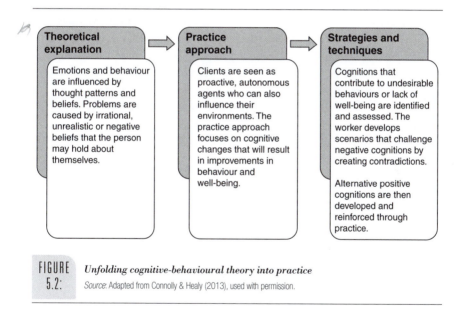

FIGURE 5.2: *Unfolding cognitive-behavioural theory into practice*
Source: Adapted from Connolly & Healy (2013), used with permission.

That emotions and behaviour are influenced by thought patterns makes sense and creates an accessible theoretical basis for causality – when the thought patterns are irrational or negative, they are likely to create problems and under-mine a person's sense of their own well-being. The practice approach, then, is to challenge the irrational thoughts. Understanding the influence of negative thinking is critical here: 'Distorted thinking and irrational logic are based on negative *cognitive schemas* [original emphasis] . (. anxious people tend to overestimate the chances of bad things happening and, if the bad thing did happen, exaggerate its impact and effect) (Howe 2009: 62).

This approach appreciates the power of negative thinking and the way in which it becomes an automatic response that may be quite outside the person's awareness. Importantly, the practice response recognises that people are autonomous beings who can proactively influence their environment. Although the cognitive-behavioural worker may be more directive in suggesting strategies for change, there is nevertheless a strong emphasis on collaboration, openness and transparency in practice. The approach is based on learning, so the more the person knows and understands about what makes the ABC process work, the better. Techniques create opportunities to challenge irrational thinking. This includes a detailed analysis of what needs to change. Socratic questioning is used skilfully to explore the person's reality. Granvold (2011: 186) describes this method of questioning:

> The Socratic method (1) stimulates the client's development of self-awareness and self-observation; (2) facilitates the shift from vague, ill-defined concerns to focused definitions of the problem; (3) opens up topic areas rather than leaving them minimally explored; (4) gives the therapist access to the client's characteristic patterns of perceiving, reasoning, information processing, and problem solving; (5) exposes the client's belief system; (6) exposes the client's coping mechanisms and tolerance of stress; and (7) is effective in the therapist's modelling of reasoning, the challenging of irrational beliefs, and problem solving.

Cognitive-behavioural approaches in contemporary social work practice

Cognitive-behavioural approaches have the strongest evidence base supporting their effectiveness. The vast amount of research undertaken in a range of practice domains (see Granvold 2011 for a summary) points to an impressive success rate:

> The results of systematic reviews and experiments show that in the juvenile justice and probation, in cases of depression, in relapse prevention, in schizophrenia, in the field of child behavioural problems, in helping families cope with an autistic child, and so forth, cognitive-behavioural approaches never come second to anything. (Sheldon & Macdonald 2009: 64)

In the following New Zealand case example from Jim, a psychologist at the Auckland-based Te Piriti Special Treatment Unit of the Community Probation and Psychological Services, we see CBT principles used in reintegrating child sexual offenders into the community. We invite you to think about how CBT is integrated into direct practice approaches.

Case example: Cognitive-behavioural principles

Treatment programs for child sex offenders based on CBT principles have received worldwide acclaim as the treatment of choice for these offenders, achieving very low recidivism rates around the 5 per cent mark over a five-year period (Nathan, Wilson & Hillman 2003). These results are attained despite the fact that child sex offenders are still not readily accepted into the community upon their release from prison.

These treatment programs typically address a number of risk factors believed to be related to reoffending, including insight into offending patterns, intimacy and relationship deficits, mood-management problems and sexual deviance. CBT principles are used to identify problematic beliefs, thoughts, feeling and behaviour in all of these areas. However, perhaps the clearest illustration of the use of CBT to help child sex offenders refrain from reoffending can be found in the relapse-prevention model.

The relapse-prevention model was adopted from the drug addiction treatment literature and adapted for use with sex offenders (Pithers et al. 1983). Relapse prevention was instantly popular among those who treated child sex offenders because of its compatibility with CBT. The relapse-prevention model assumes that child sex offenders will experience lapses from time to time. Some will be able to correct and contain their abusive thoughts and urges, while others may give in to them and experience a relapse. The model guides the offender to identify a typical sequence of events or set of circumstances that will precede them from offending, usually known as an offence chain or cycle. The offender is then taught techniques to prevent or manage any high-risk situations they encounter. Offenders would first be taught how to recognise high-risk situations, then how to avoid them and, if that is not possible, how to

control them. Should these strategies fail, escape from the situation may be the only remaining option.

The essence of these techniques is to provide offenders with a level of cognitive control over behaviour that previously had been impulsive or driven by a need for short-term gratification. More recently, the relapse-prevention techniques were augmented by the introduction of the good lives model (Ward 2002), which aims to provide the offender with options that will steer them away from offending and towards more socially appropriate and rewarding goals, such as successful employment.

While these techniques are usually effective for most offenders, there are those who have been identified as being at particularly high risk of reoffending, and who may lack the necessary self-discipline to apply the relapse-prevention techniques in the long term. In a recent case of a high-risk prisoner being considered for release after completing the treatment program at the Te Piriti Unit in Auckland, New Zealand, the Parole Board was prepared to approve the release only if the offender could show proof of a 'robust release plan'. Evidence that he was well versed in relapse-prevention techniques was considered to be useful but insufficient.

With the cooperation of the offender, a number of volunteers were then recruited to form a circle of support and accountability around him. Their task would be to have daily contact with him, inquire about his well-being and support him to find accommodation and employment. Because they were fully informed about the offender's offending pattern, they were able also to challenge him should they become aware of him being in high-risk situations. The circle of volunteers met frequently to discuss any issues among themselves and with the offender. They also remained in contact with the treatment unit and probation officers, thus ensuring a seamless continuity of the expected behaviour that would enable the offender to remain offence free.

In that case, the Parole Board approved release. Apart from a range of positive supportive activities, the circle of volunteers had to challenge the offender on a few occasions, such as when he was seen in the children's section of the local library and on another occasion when he admitted to taking out videos intended for teenagers. He was able to provide reasons for both situations, but Socratic questioning was used to assist him in discovering why his behaviour was inappropriate. At the time of writing, the offender had been free for more than a year and had not been recalled for any breach of his conditions, providing further support for CBT-related interventions to ensure the successful release of even high-risk child sex offenders.

Cognitive-behavioural approaches are not consistently used by social workers, despite this history of success and the fact that they lend themselves to social work adaptation. Berlin (2002: 31) illustrates the way in which the social work lens can be used in adapting practice theories to support the multifarious needs of people:

> My work to revise more orthodox versions of cognitive therapy constitutes an attempt to … increase the breadth of targets and the range of interventions to encompass social interventions for difficult social situations. These efforts are occurring at a time in which the life chances of many people are being systematically undercut as a result of shifts in popular sentiment and political leadership that emphasize the high costs of welfare benefits and adhere to the old belief that the good life is available to anyone who is willing to work for it. Especially in these times, it seems critical to have a cognitive perspective that acknowledges that willingness … is only a part of the social mobility/personal adaption story.

One of the criticisms of cognitive-behavioural approaches has been its individualistic focus. Attention to life circumstances and the ways in which these influence life chances have been paid less attention than working on cognitive distortions and how they can be changed. Berlin's integrative perspective draws on a broader set of understandings that incorporate notions of empowerment, critical theory and practice. She considers it possible to shift from a focus on the individual to one that moves into the real world of the client, where external factor – such as politics, bureaucracy and cultural beliefs – are intertwined with individual concerns. She identifies a number of ways to stay grounded in the concerns of the client while working within a cognitive-behavioural paradigm.

Avoiding a narrow focus on the extremes

Focusing on the specifics of a person's thinking and behaviour can provide a shield behind which we can hide and avoid very real problems that may be confronting the client. Conditions of poverty can seem overwhelming, and it is easy to take the route of psychodynamic processes of change. To do so, however, neglects our disciplinary commitment to reducing disadvantage and working towards a more equal society. Searching for possibilities, identifying what can be done, then taking steps to mobilise action is part of an integrated response. Communities are resourceful, and so are people within communities. That is not to say that workers develop romantic notions that idealise communities: this can leave already vulnerable people at further risk. But being open to the opportunities to mobilise community action, along with supporting clients to think differently about their problems, can help us to avoid a narrow focus on purely individual change.

Rushing in to save

Saving people from themselves and adopting the role of rescuer is always a risk when working with people whose lives seem chaotic and whose circumstances seem disastrous. A commitment to responsiveness can create a need to do something, particularly when we think we know exactly what that should be. Added to this, professional expectations – developing expertise, expensive training – and all the trappings of the 'expert' can lead us to believe that change lies in our hands. Yet the social work disciplinary lens of change reminds us that change is achieved through collaboration and through people being experts in their own lives. As we noted in Chapter 1, this positions the social worker's role as one of professional supporter and facilitator of change. As Berlin's (2002) example illustrates, within a clinical setting there is still room for a person–environment response where a balance of hope and reality come together to support change.

Rising to the challenges

Social work often operates in the space where people experience multifaceted problems, involving losses, crises, personal problems and systemic disadvantage, and where they may have long histories of involvement with social services. In what may seem overwhelming odds, it is important to help people 'gain a foothold' and begin a process of 'constructing meanings of personal worth and possibility' (Berlin 2002: 285). While there will be a larger socio-political context, social workers practice at the meso level, where extended family and friends become a collective resource for change. Social work is a hopeful profession that rises to the challenge of complex and difficult problem-saturated environments. Building on strengths is a critical part of this, and so too is developing collaborative relationships.

Collaboration

Collaboration is associated with our earlier discussion relating to notions of the 'client as expert'. Collaborating with clients is not 'doing to', but rather 'working with'. When people don't respond to the challenges they face, and even seem to sabotage possibilities for change, collaboration can feel too hard and seem a waste of time. On those occasions, it is important to listen again to what the person has to say, and look for practical and straightforward helping strategies that are relevant to them.

Collaborating with other professionals to strengthen the client's supportive network will also pay dividends. Collaboration between mental health services and child protection, for example, is likely to result in a better service for the family.

Case example: Change through collaboration

Valerie, a 30-year-old African American woman, applied for services at a local mental health centre where she was assigned to work with an intern. She was dishevelled, poor, living in a shelter and occasionally delusional. The intern was surprised that she asked for therapeutic help, but was compelled by her insight into her experiences of professional help: people didn't listen to her or help her, they just wanted to label her and give her drugs. Valerie and the intern worked together. Her child had been removed from her care, and she wanted to regain custody. The intern found her a lawyer and went with her to court. When the court required that she take her medication as a visitation condition, the intern found a psychiatrist who would listen to her, and he advocated on her behalf when protective services dismissed her on the assumption that all her beliefs were delusional. The intern thus helped her find subsidised housing and enrol in job training. He worked with her for four years. In that time, she became stable, managed her medications, lived independently and started an apprenticeship. Her son was being taken care of by his father, and she visited regularly. She decided against applying for custody.

Berlin (2002: 284–5), abridged

Finding meaning in the concrete dimensions of life

Having enough to get by on is a fundamental component of a dignified existence. It means something when a parent cannot respond in important ways to their child's basic needs, even if their own actions have resulted in them having no money for food only a day after getting their wage or benefit. Having their own place to which they can return also means something. Helping clients address basic needs is a practical response that may include planning, modelling and support to work out ways of getting what they need, and feeling the difference that it makes to their daily lives. What some people may take for granted – a home in which to live – can represent a significant achievement for someone who has never had one. Renting something of their own, working to make sure they have the coping skills to keep it, and finding a niche in the neighbourhood are likely to provide them with an important sense of their place in the world. Positive changes in the external environment can create positive mind changes, thus increasing feelings of worthiness, confidence and achievement.

Collaborating with people and organisations to generate resources

Advocating for clients involves negotiating with services and organisations and applying well-developed skills of persuasion, reasoning, persistence, collaboration and sometimes confrontation. It is interesting to know that some workers have a real knack for getting what clients need, whereas others struggle. This is often because workers go unprepared, without a plan of attack, or because they leap into confrontation when persuasion is a better skill to use in the circumstances. Alternatively, they might think that because they have been unsuccessful with the person on the front desk, that's all they can do. The person on the front desk is just the first person in a chain of increasingly powerful people along a decision-making line. Being reasonable and calm, and hopefully successful in negotiating for resources, is a powerful modelling experience. In general, people in bureaucratic situations also want to do their best for people, and they also experience the personal rewards of helping people. It is important to identify leverage points and avoid creating situations where officials feel that they have been taken for a ride. This just harms the next person's chance of success.

This cognitive-integrative perspective illustrates the way in which a cognitive approach can be knitted together with a social work interpretive lens. It builds on the basis of strong relationships, is strengths based in its collaborative responses, and is mindful of the social work commitment to fairness and justice. It also sees thoughts and emotions as 'conveyers of culture' (Berlin 2002: 133). Cultural meaning is constructed from the person–environment reciprocal exchanges that signal the ways in which we might think, feel and act.

Cognitive ways of working have also been seen as particularly optimistic methods when working with families (Elliott 2000). Knowledge about cognitive frameworks create options for family workers to develop a greater focus on thoughts, and not just the feelings expressed by family members. Beliefs in family systems can be very powerful, and reframing is an important skill that aims to change both thoughts and behaviours. Watzlawick, Weakland and Fisch (1974: 95) describe reframing as a way to 'change the conceptual and/or emotional setting or viewpoint in relation to which a situation is experienced and to place it in another frame which fits the "facts" of the same concrete situation equally well or even better, and thereby changes its entire meaning'.

In the same way that our interpretation of an activating event can shape our belief about what happened, so a reframing can change the thinking without any change in the supposed reality. In fact, the reality might be unchangeable. What changes is the meaning that is attributed to it. An example might help.

Case example: Reframing

A couple bring their six-year-old child, Billy, to a child and family clinic that they have heard helps with children's behavioural problems. Billy's behaviour has become unmanageable at home. He is swearing and is becoming aggressive with his baby sister. After a few sessions, the worker realises that all is not well in the couple's relationship. The pressure of having two young children, compounded by financial concerns, is creating tension within the relationship. In the course of the sessions, the worker tells them that, in her experience, children are attuned to parental disharmony and behave in ways that can signal that the family needs help. The father says, 'Like a scout going ahead? That's a brave thing to do.' He takes the boy in his arms and holds him. Over the next few sessions, the parents report a change in Billy's behaviour.

Reframing creates the potential for an alternative reality, and can also influence a person's attributions of blame and engender more compassionate understanding. As Trevithick (2012: 243) notes, it can be particularly valuable when people are affected by guilt or are self-blaming: 'Often the messages that service users give to themselves can be deeply critical, harsh and self-punishing. Reframing offers a way to replace these painful, negative *internal conversations* with words that are more understanding, optimistic and caring.' Trevithick provides us with another nice example of positive reframing:

> *Service user:* I am too lazy to get out of bed.
>
> *Practitioner:* Perhaps what you describe as being lazy is a feeling that there is nothing to get up for?
>
> *Service user:* I think I'm a horrible mother. I'm really tired and bad-tempered and shout at my kids all the time ...
>
> *Practitioner:* The fact that you felt able to tell me about how you are with your children shows that you want to have a better relationship with them – that you care about them. It takes courage for a parent to admit that things are going wrong – as you just did. It gives us a chance to build on the fact that you want to do something about these difficulties.
>
> *Service user:* I decided yesterday not to come to see you today because I felt you would criticise me.
>
> *Practitioner:* Then you were very brave to come.
>
> (Trevithick 2012: 243–4)

Although cognitive approaches are not broadly used in mainstream practice, they are nevertheless used in a range of social work practice contexts. Changing the way people think about aspects of their lives, their relationships and themselves is key to a cognitive-behavioural worker's methodology, and examples of using cognitive approaches can be found in the areas of couple work (Kayser 2011), and drug and alcohol work, in response to depression and in some other areas of mainstream practice (Mikhailova & Nol 2011). Perhaps not surprisingly, cognitive-behavioural approaches are used in response to such conditions as phobias and panic disorders, anxiety disorders, anorexia and bulimia, where distorted thinking processes prevent people from functioning well. As we noted in our case example earlier in the chapter, cognitive approaches have also been used significantly in the area of sexual offending, where distorted underlying beliefs create cognitive distortions (Keenan & Ward 2003). In this complex area of practice, cognitive-behavioural approaches have been adapted in ways that are more relationally responsive and mindful of cultural imperative, as this example from a sexual treatment program in a prison illustrates. In the same way, Berlin (2002) explores an integrative perspective that uses social work ideas, adapting practices in the area of sexual offending work in ways that are less directive and are empowering of self-reflection. Being self-change driven is also considered important:

> Using the strength of the therapeutic relationship to model openness and responsivity to others is more likely to reinforce positive modes of inter-action ... by creating a climate of reciprocity and mutual learning, and exploring ways in which the client can both experience and understand the processes of reflexivity and reflection, the potential to build insight and skill acquisition is enhanced ... the work becomes less didactic and more natural-istic and evolving. (Frost & Connolly 2004: 379)

Despite the long-standing position of behavioural models and the demon-strated effectiveness of cognitive approaches, neither has been widely applied in social work practice. Behavioural approaches have been strong in the past, particularly during the 1960s and 1970s, but have waned over time, although practitioners continue to use techniques of behaviour modification in a range of ways. While important in specialist areas, cognitive approaches have not gained the traction in mainstream practice that might have been expected given their demonstrated efficacy. At least in part, this is due to the perceived limita-tions and challenges of each approach, which we explore later in this chapter. Where cognitive-behavioural approaches *have* gained traction more recently has been under the range of approaches of mindfulness practice.

Mindfulness

Mindfulness approaches are increasingly being used by practitioners in a range of settings, with a strong evidence base emerging for their efficacy (Garland 2013; Kabat-Zinn 2013). Lee et al (2009: 40) suggest that

> mindfulness, by enhancing one's awareness of and ability to attend to the moment-to-moment experience, allows a person to recognize movements and changes in the self and external environment, regulate behaviours, and make adjustment based on current needs and interests, instead of being trapped by past experiences, future desires, or isolated, rigid standards.

Mindfulness approaches have emerged from two different traditions – Western traditions of social psychology and Eastern traditions drawn from Buddhism

(Walsh & Shapiro 2006; Lee et al 2009). Both share some common elements, on which we focus here, but they also differ in important ways.

The approach that is consistent with our 'faulty-engine' discussions in this chapter is the Western tradition. In 1978, Langer, Blank and Chanowitz published an article on 'the mindlessness of ostensibly thoughtful action'. They were examining the links between behaviour and full awareness, and highlighted how frequently we fail to pay 'attention to the substantive details of the "inform-ative" environment' (Langer, Blank & Chanowitz 1978: 635). This in turn led to a focus on mindfulness as a key component of well-being – by staying con-sciously attuned and aware of our thoughts, feelings and wider relationships and environment, we can live in deliberate and focused ways (Kashdan & Ciarrochi 2013). The emphasis of mindfulness strategies is on developing cognitive aware-ness, and challenging the beliefs we hold on to in our daily lives.

From the Eastern traditions, mindfulness has been based more on strong philosophical grounds, not so much psychological ones, and connected with a spiritual value base drawn from Buddhism. It is similar to Langer's con-ceptualisation, in that 'Simply put, mindfulness is moment-to-moment non-judgemental awareness. It is cultivated by purposefully paying attention to things we ordinarily never give a moment's thought to' (Kabat-Zinn, 2013: xlix). However, strategies for mindfulness strive to integrate full awareness, both psychologically and physically, in the present moment, through medita-tion, breathing exercises and awareness-building. Bringing together empiri-cally based approaches from both Eastern and Western traditions, Lee and colleagues (2009) promote holistic practices that integrate body, mind and spirit in response to individual and family needs. As noted in Chapter 2, this includes an important emphasis on spirituality.

Strengths and challenges

Behavioural and cognitive-behavioural approaches have been subjected to a fair amount of criticism. They have also developed and evolved in response. As we have seen from Berlin's (2002) integrative treatment, applying a rela-tional, social justice and reflective social work lens in the context of person–environment thinking creates a somewhat different contemporary approach from early applications of the theory. Also, somewhat confusingly, some strengths can be seen as weaknesses and some weaknesses as strengths. That said, it is useful to explore limitations and how these can be moderated so that the approaches can continue to evolve and grow.

The focus on the here and now

As we mentioned earlier in the chapter, approaches that focus on behavioural change emerged in response to frustrations with the insight-focused psychodynamic models that lack time boundaries and evidence of effectiveness. These new approaches, which paid attention to the client's immediate concerns and how they affected their ability to live their lives well, were an important departure from psychoanalytic responses that dug into past events to develop insight into the here and now. This focus on the present is seen as a real strength of the behavioural and cognitive-behavioural approaches. Working with parents to find ways to manage a constantly screaming child is practically helpful. Creating environments within which people can function relatively quickly in the real world can free them from debilitating thinking processes that negatively influence their lives.

The challenge here is that some thinking processes are deeply entrenched and are not necessarily amenable to quick change. This is appreciated in some areas of practice – for example, sexual offending treatment programs are anything but brief. Influencing distorted schemas takes considerable time and effort, and participants in these programs can be in treatment for extensive periods. While we recognise the need for in-depth and intensive treatment services in the context of sexual offending, we do not necessarily use the same rationale for the provision of services in other areas. For example, the emphasis on quick therapeutic solutions has had a critical influence on the funding of other services when it is assumed that brief therapy can address client issues in limited timespans over a limited number of sessions. Short-term services may be successful for some, but others will require longer, more intensive work. Expecting quick changes in these situations is likely to be unrealistic and potentially undermining of the client's confidence when brief interventions do not result in the expected outcomes.

The focus on individual thinking and change

Traditionally, behavioural and cognitive-behavioural approaches have emphasised individual behaviours and their underpinning irrational beliefs as the focus for change. Some writers have nevertheless noted that the beliefs may, in fact, not be irrational at all but a natural and appropriate response to life events – for example, bereavement, victimisation or discrimination (Trevithick 2012). Overlooking these factors can result in pathologising normal human reactions and reinforcing past oppressions. This is where third-generation or third-wave notions of cognitive-behavioural approaches are important (Kazantzis, Reinecke

& Freeman 2010). As theories evolve, inevitably they are influenced by new thinking and developments in knowledge. More recent responses to these theories incorporate a greater emphasis on contextual factors: 'These treatments tend to seek the construction of broad, flexible and effective repertoires over an eliminative approach to narrowly defined problems, and to emphasise the relevance of the issues they examine for clinicians as well as clients' (Hayes 2004: 658). Most social work interventions focus on the influence of contextual factors, and behavioural and cognitive-behavioural approaches need not be an exception to this. Applying a social work interpretive lens that is cognisant of a bigger picture will help to find a balance that responds to the needs of social work clients.

The mechanistic versus relational approach

As we noted earlier, the terminology in behavioural and cognitive-behavioural approaches can seem mechanistic, and consequently uncaring (Trevithick 2012: 313). To some degree, the ABC model and its structured process reinforce a formulaic step-by-step model that may be perceived as having more to do with the method than the person on the other end. The language used may be off-putting: schemas, cognitive distortions, irrational, dysfunctional – all of which are anathema to postmodernist ideals. Yet the qualities of positive social work practice also rest at the heart of cognitive-behavioural approaches – for example, the importance of the worker–client relationship and collaboration.

In the end, it seems to us that it is the way in which these approaches are applied that is of greatest importance. If the worker values a relational response, then this will form the basis for whatever model or theory is used. Key aspects of the cognitive-behavioural approach are easily accessible, and if the worker knows and understands the behavioural and cognitive-behavioural approaches so that the practice comes naturally to the client, it is unlikely that it will be perceived as mechanistic. When and how to use theory will always be a matter of social work judgement, and good supervision helps to make sure responses are appropriate and consistent with the values of social work.

The directive rather than empowering response

It is true that within the behavioural and cognitive-behavioural approaches, workers are more likely to make suggestions and create challenging environments within which thinking processes can be tested and disproved. On the basis of learning theory, they create learning contexts that may have specific and detailed instructions for clients to try out. They are also likely to have structured homework tasks – quite different from the non-directive approaches we discussed in Chapter 4. Whether such dialectical approaches are disempowering is debatable, and again it probably depends on how they are applied. According to Staples (1990: 37), 'Empowerment requires practical knowledge, solid information, real competencies, concrete skills, material resources, genuine opportunities, and tangible results.'

Cognitive-behavioural approaches – particularly in the context of the third-generation models – would also see these components of empowerment as being critical aims of the work. Looking for tangible results developed from a good knowledge of what is causing the difficulties is critical. Then creating learning processes that will enable them to gain greater agency in their lives and maximise opportunities – including the resources needed to realise them – is all part of the cognitive-behavioural approach.

Theory as a Western construct

Like many other practice theories, behavioural and cognitive-behavioural approaches have emerged from a Western paradigm – indeed, a predominantly male Western paradigm. We therefore need to question whether it is archetypically Western, or whether it offers possibilities in terms of working across diverse cultural groups. According to Berlin (2002: 135), 'Cultures transmit the most fundamental definitions of the self and the social world'. Cultural thinking is deeply embedded, to the point where it can blind us to alternative views and perspectives. Beliefs are so familiar to us, and the way we live our lives and what we consider important can feel internally so 'right', that different views can seem very odd to us: 'It is other people who are ethnic, idiosyncratic, culturally peculiar. In a similar way, one's own views are reasonable, while other people are extremist' (Eagleton 2000: 26–7).

In the context of such powerful internal belief systems, we need to consider whether professionals are able to use such theories as these as if practising in a culture-free zone. We are, of course, never practising in a culture-free zone. Culture defines us and provides cultural signposts that help us to navigate pathways through life. How, then, does all this influence the application of theory? It has to do with working with culture and within cultural meanings in ways that are responsive to the needs of the people with whom we work. This requires us to challenge personal assumptions and beliefs as we work with people, whether or not they are culturally different from ourselves. If we remain blind to culture, we run the risk of confusing culture with dysfunction (Falicov 1995). At the same time, although cultural messages define our understanding of the way the world is and our place within it, some cultural messages can nevertheless be oppressive and can reinforce relationships of dominance and subjugation. People can be left vulnerable when workers are blind to these dynamics through misguided notions of cultural respect.

These challenges are relevant regardless of what social work theory or intervention is used, and point to the importance of understanding cultural meanings and how they influence people's perception of the world. In a way, a practice theory that focuses so strongly on the understanding of thought processes and their idiosyncrasies might be helpful when working across diverse cultures, as long as a reflective lens is applied and the worker remains grounded in the real-life concerns of the person with whom they are working.

Science versus art in practice

As we noted earlier, behavioural and cognitive-behavioural approaches have been the most interrogated by research of all the practice theories, and it is perhaps not surprising that they have therefore found themselves in the middle of the evidence-based practice debate on which we touched briefly in Chapter 1. At the heart of this debate is whether practice should be more or less influenced by scientific outcome research or clinical lore (Chaffin & Friedrich 2004). A real strength of the cognitive-behavioural approach is the impressive evidence supporting effectiveness, causing Howe (2009: 73) to describe it as 'a top-rank social work theory'. Alternatively, Plath (2009: 176) explores a counter argument:

> Effective social work practice, however, also involves the application of ethical principles, such as promoting social justice and self-determination. While fundamental to social work practice, these principles are interpreted according to context and values. As such, they cannot be measured and so evaluation of their effectiveness is open to interpretation.

We are inclined to take the view that there are many forms of knowing, and many ways of helping people work through the challenges they face. Behavioural and cognitive-behavioural approaches may or may not resonate with a practitioner's personal style. But if they do, and are practised through a social work interpretive lens, they can be important practice theories within the social work repertoire. Of course, mindfulness – which could be seen as an approach that brings together art and science – might also provide practitioners with an holistic practice option that meets both art and science needs.

Conclusion

Behavioural and cognitive-behavioural approaches have developed in response to new ideas and thinking about the nature of change and ways of helping people to resolve complex issues in their lives. Behavioural approaches can provide confidence that change is possible, and give clients something to hang on to while working on the challenges they face. Cognitive-behavioural approaches provide a framework for understanding unhelpful assumptions and beliefs that work against the realisation of potential. Like everybody else, social workers have beliefs and processes of cultural thinking that can be more or less helpful in the context of professional practice (Connolly 2003). Insights gained from cognitive approaches challenge unhelpful assumptions and encourage reflexive responses that are the hallmark of reflective social work practice. That said, in the end what is most important is that workers use their judgement about whether theories have a goodness of fit with the people with whom they are working. To appreciate whether this is the case, they need to listen carefully to their clients' concerns and take time to get to know them.

Useful resources

Albert Ellis Institute, http://www.rebt.org.

Berlin, S. 2002. *Clinical Social Work Practice: A Cognitive-Integrative Perspective*. New York: Oxford University Press.

Lee, M., Ng, S.-M., Leung, P. & Chan, C. 2009. *Integrative Body–Mind–Spirit Social Work: An Empirically Based Approach to Assessment and Treatment*. New York: Oxford University Press.

6 Story-telling theories

Human beings have always gathered stories. Long before we could keep them in any recorded form, stories have been gathered as oral traditions and passed down through families for many generations. They become powerful narratives that influence human well-being and identity. In the same way as these life narratives create meaning for us, story-telling theories in social work focus on the stories we live by, as individuals, families and communities. This group of theoretical approaches proposes that stories of strength and resilience can influence how we think, feel and act. By listening to our own internalised stories and others that are shared with us, we can begin to understand both their meaning and the influence they have on the ways in which people live their lives. Story-telling theories are critically interested in this, and in the ways stories can be reauthored to enable more positive and rewarding life outcomes.

Story-telling as a therapeutic process has been most fully articulated in narrative therapy. We explore throughout this chapter how narrative work enables people to cope more effectively with adversity and difficulty. Stories also transform communities and societies, and we will look at how giving voice and transforming marginalised, silenced and oppressed stories can do so. But before we explore narrative ways of working, we will first look at a broader influence that has supported narratives of strength and resilience: the strengths perspective in social work practice.

Strengths-based perspectives

As introduced earlier, a movement in social work practice reflecting this emphasis on narratives of resilience and strength is represented in two landmark texts: Dennis Saleebey's *The Strengths Perspective in Social Work* (1997) and Charles Rapp's *The Strengths Model*, specifically responding to issues of mental health practice, which was published the following year. These two books provided an important foundation for the development of strengths-based ideas, and both have significantly influenced social work practice in recent decades.

The strengths-based approach asserts the fundamental belief that people have strengths and are motivated towards well-being and optimal functioning. It asserts that the focus should be on what is 'changeable and attainable, rather than being daunted and disempowered by the size of the problem' (O'Connell 1998: 8). Problems emerge because people have tried to use their resources in ways that they believe will solve their circumstances and have been unable to do so. From a strengths-based perspective, they are able to find new solutions to old problems without having to go into lengthy therapy to explore past problems in order to find these solutions. As Saleebey (1997: 164) notes:

> We must discover how people have managed to survive ... Tapping into the energy and imagination, the will and the promise of clients is to help them recover or command the power to change, using old skills and resources and/ or discovering and developing new ones.

These perspectives are optimistic about people's capacity for change and their ability to find new solutions. In some ways, there are links here with systems theories and with the notion of self-righting tendencies or homeostasis, concepts we explored in Chapter 3. Here they go much further in terms of confronting what Saleebey (1997: 8) calls 'the obsession with problems and pathologies'.

Saleebey's lexicon of strengths

Saleebey identifies key strengths-based concepts as part of a 'lexicon of strengths'. Within this lexicon, the agenda of *empowerment* is central:

> To discover the power within people and communities, we must subvert and abjure pejorative labels; provide opportunities for connections to family, institutional, and communal resources; assail the victim mind-set; foreswear paternalism; trust people's intuitions, accounts, perspectives, and energies; and believe in people's dreams. (Saleebey 1997: 8)

Notions of *membership* and engagement with community are critical, and are seen to provide an antidote to alienation, oppression and marginalisation. Beliefs about *resilience* are important: the notion that people have the ability to overcome serious adversity means that trauma and distress do not necessarily lead to a life of vulnerability or psychopathology. The human capacity to heal itself and to survive as a species points to the strengths-based concept of *healing and wholeness*: 'At some level of consciousness ... we have a native wisdom about what is right for us and what we should do when confronted with organismic or environmental challenges' (Saleebey 1997: 10).

The emphasis on *dialogue and collaboration* reinforces the human need for relationships with others: 'a caring community is a community that confirms otherness; giving each person and group a ground of their own, affirmed through encounters that are egalitarian and dedicated to healing and empowerment' (Saleebey 1997: 10). One of the more controversial concepts within Saleebey's lexicon of strengths relates to what he calls *suspension of disbelief*. In many ways, it resonates with Carl Rogers' (1965, 1980) *unconditional positive regard*, a concept we discussed in the context of person-centred practice (Chapter 4). In essence, it relates to the need to set aside thoughts of pessimism and cynicism, or professional worries about being manipulated or hoodwinked by a cunning client. According to Saleebey, these are self-protective mechanisms that undermine the potential to harness strengths, and ultimately prevent workers from truly engaging with the people with whom they work.

Practising in a strengths-based way requires a fundamental belief that people have strengths and are able to overcome adversity in their lives. In the context of strengths-based practice, trauma and abuse become potential sources of strength as people confront the challenges of the victim mindset. A practitioner who is committed to these ideas assumes that there are no boundaries to potential, and that growth and change are not only possible but also part of an innate restorative capacity that humans possess. Shifting from the position of 'expert', the strengths-based practitioner understands that clients are best served by collaborative professional responses that recognise the ability of clients to find their own solutions and become experts in their own lives. Contrasting with the traditional perception of clients as passive receivers of professional services, the consumer rights movement also presents clients as 'rights-bearing citizens who have the right and the capacities to fully participate in determining their health and welfare needs' (Healy 2005: 70–1). Within the context of collective support, narratives are reconceptualised from victimhood to resilient survivor and expert.

Interviewing for strengths

Narratives of resilience and strength characterise the practice approach – narratives of incompetence and inadequacy can easily undermine the work and serve to reinforce notions of failure. Connections with narrative theory and narrative ways of working are clearly evident here, something to which we return later in the chapter. Strengths-based practice aims to facilitate a context within which the client can discover, or rediscover, their sense of self, purpose and power. The exploration of the client's skills and competencies is important – interviewing for strengths involves an assessment process that is very much in the here and now, and it is recognised that people are self-determining agents who can be supported to work through complex issues in their lives. Intrinsic strengths are identified: their emotional structure, and their ability to express feelings and to develop motivation or use coping skills; perhaps also a sense of humour. Extrinsic strengths are also important – for example, the person's interpersonal network, family and friends, or the potential for these interpersonal networks to be developed within the client's life.

The identification of client-determined goals is also an important component of strengths-based practice. Teasing out what the client wants and arriving at measurable short-term goals provides a foundation for developing strategies to achieve them. The strengths approach assumes that a client will have a greater investment in working towards goal achievement if the goals belong to them. The strengths-based practitioner avoids taking the lead in goal setting as worker-driven goals that are not owned by the client are less likely to be successful. The role of the social worker is to facilitate the development of goals, to advocate and to link the client to a network of institutional and community resources.

Harnessing the strengths of the families towards the realisation of their own aims and goals has also been a strong theme in the strengths-based literature. The family strengths perspective can be located within an ecological framework, and Froma Walsh (1998: 3), from the University of Chicago, has been a strong advocate of incorporating notions of resilience into family practice:

> A resilience lens shifts perspective from viewing distressed families as damaged to seeing them as challenged, affirming their potential for repair and growth. This approach is based on the conviction that both individual and family strength can be forged through collaborative efforts to deal with sudden crisis or prolonged adversity.

Although the strengths perspective has been particularly influential in the Australian and Aotearoa New Zealand family practice literature (Elliott 2000; Munford & Sanders 1999; Connolly 1999), it is the ground-breaking work of Australasian writers White and Epston (1990) that has put story-telling theories on the international map.

Narrative ways of working

Unlike the other approaches explored in earlier chapters, narrative theories and therapy have Australasian origins. Narrative approaches emerged throughout the 1970s and 1980s, articulated by two social workers, Michael White (2007) from Adelaide, and David Epston from Auckland, New Zealand (Beels 2009; Furlong 2008). They and colleague Cheryl White established the Dulwich Centre in Adelaide, which remains an international hub for writings and resources related to narrative therapies. We will focus primarily on their work, and that of their colleagues, Barbara Wingard and David Denborough. In addition, solution-focused therapy is attributed to Steve de Shazer (1994) in the United States, who was part of a larger therapeutic centre. Many others have contributed to these bodies of knowledge, but these particular authors tend to be acknowledged as the founders of the approaches.

Although there may be differences in emphasis, these key thinkers argue that understanding narratives and their influence on a person, a family or a community is of vital importance to the understanding of the self within context. Some authors and practitioners have focused more on the importance of telling or narrating stories as the most important step – giving voice or primacy to particular experiences. Others have seen this as the first step and then highlighted the importance of transforming or reauthoring stories so that they become coherent, positive, strengths-based narratives by which people can live more fulfilling lives. In the first part of the chapter, we look specifically at narrative practices and the ways in which they have engaged the interest of practitioners. There is a developing body of international literature relating to narrative therapy, and Beels (2009) and Furlong (2008) provide two excellent overviews of the history and legacies within narrative therapy from an international perspective. In this chapter, we look at the particular way in which narrative practices have developed in Australasia, primarily through the work of the Dulwich Centre (see http://www.dulwichcentre.com.au).

Key concepts

Story-telling theories have emerged from a number of different theoretical traditions, including systems theories – particularly family therapy (e.g. see Bateson 2002), anthropology, feminism, and postmodern, post-structural (particularly the work of Foucault – see Gordon 1980) and social constructionist theories (Gergen 1985; Crotty 1998). These social theories have all seen narrative as critical in shaping experience. This is an important distinction between narrative approaches and the other perspectives considered in earlier chapters. Rather than drawing on inner-world theories to understand coping and change, story-telling theories have been developed from primarily outer-world theories in order to understand the inner worlds of individuals.

Systems influences

In Chapter 3, we looked at systems approaches. In many respects, story-telling approaches are a specific form within the systemic tradition. Story-telling theories focus on the ways in which stories create or hold meaning for people, and come to form a system of meaning at the individual, family or community level. This system of meaning shapes interactions, expectations and internalised experiences; hence an important part of the narrative approach is to understand and challenge problematic systems of meaning. The systems theory work of Gregory Bateson influenced Michael White's thinking profoundly in relation to narrative therapy. As Furlong (2008: 407) notes:

> White took up key elements in Bateson's conceptual vocabulary ('double description'; 'the difference that makes a difference'; 'negative explanation'). And, in so doing, White was using a systems/cybernetics frame as his root metaphor, albeit one that was far more reflexive than the first-order variation that is most often associated with systems thinking.

It is no surprise, then, that narrative therapy has its origins in family therapy and is particularly relevant to it. In this context, the family can be seen as a system that develops its own levels of meaning, often sustained and expressed through the stories that are told.

Cultural and anthropological influences

Narrative approaches have been embraced by many Indigenous practitioners and communities, both within Australia and internationally. The appeal of narrative approaches is twofold. First, the rich oral traditions of many Indigenous communities are embraced within narrative approaches and held to be central. Storying is a way in which culture and history have been preserved through many hundreds of years. Aboriginal author Barbara Wingard highlights this in *Telling Our Stories in Ways That Make Us Stronger*:

> As Aboriginal people, we have always told stories about our lives, and we know how important it is for people to be connected to their own stories, the stories of their family, their people, their history. These stories are a source of pride. When people become disconnected from them, life can be much harder to live. (Wingard & Lester 2001: v)

Second, narrative approaches have focused in particular on listening for and challenging dominant, oppressive stories, as we explore later in this chapter. Many Indigenous peoples have been silenced in and by dominant Western and monocultural discourses. In Australia, a focus on power and dominant stories has provided insight into the internationalisation of oppression, and has led to the reauthoring of Indigenous stories that have profoundly influenced Aboriginal well-being.

These narratives, along with the many stories that had been documented earlier in *Bringing Them Home*, the report on Australia's Stolen Generations (National Inquiry into the Separation of Aboriginal and Torres Strait Islander Children from Their Families 1997), have shifted public perceptions of the impact of intergenerational trauma resulting from processes of colonisation. They have challenged non-Indigenous Australia to engage with Aboriginal issues and redress Indigenous disadvantage at structural levels within the community. Stories can change communities as much as they can change individuals.

Social constructionist influences

Postmodern and constructionist theories have challenged the notion that there is such a thing as 'reality':

> Through a postmodern lens, knowledge is multiple and only ever partial. Knowledge is understood to be socially and historically specific and insepa-rable from social relations of power. From a postmodern perspective, there are always competing stories of truth. (Brown 2007: 5)

Social constructionism proposes that, as humans, we construct shared mean-ings, and this helps us create coherence and ways of understanding the world around us. We live in the context of constructed dominant stories that have the potential to influence the directions of our lives in important ways. A major area of focus in story-telling approaches is on identifying the domi-nant stories, for individuals, families and their community. Dominant stories are often held up as truths, indisputable and fixed. For example, families will have particular dominant stories about members of a family, and the family as a whole. This may relate to particular ways in which the family sees itself in relation to others – for example, as survivors or victims of circumstance – or it may relate to particular individuals – for example, matriarchs or the baby of the family.

Broader cultural influences provide a critical framework for our meaning-making and functioning. As Crotty (1998: 53) notes, 'Culture has to do with functioning. As a direct consequence of the way in which we humans have evolved, we depend on culture to direct our behaviour and organise our experience.' These meanings, both at individual and cultural levels, come to influence our well-being. Whether individual or cultural, they may be taken as truths, and can be positive in terms of both our identity and well-being. If they are not positive, however, they may lead to distress and difficulty:

> There are useful interpretations, to be sure and these stand over against interpretations that appear to serve no useful purpose. There are liberating forms of interpretation too; they contrast sharply with interpretations that prove oppressive. There are even interpretations that may be judged fulfilling and rewarding – in contradistinction to interpretations that impoverish human existence and stunt human growth. (Crotty 1998: 47–8)

Social constructionists nevertheless reinforce that these 'truths' will only ever represent interpretations of reality, and that they can therefore be reinterpreted in different and positive ways. Story-telling approaches are concerned with understanding these interpretations, or dominant stories, and seeing how they serve to reinforce problems and create contexts in which people struggle to realise their hopes and dreams. A key goal of narrative therapy is to understand these dominant stories and reauthor them towards more liberating, rewarding or fulfilling stories and possibilities. Within story-telling approaches, change is achieved through this reauthoring: 'changing these stories often involves challenging larger social stories within people's problem-saturated stories about themselves and their lives. All individual stories are social stories' (Brown & Augusta-Scott 2007: xvii).

One example of this relates to what was the dominant story of homosexuality in early 1970s. It was seen as deviant behaviour, and indeed a psychiatric condition: homosexuality could be diagnosed using the *Diagnostic and Statistical Manual of Mental Disorders* (DSM). This subjected people to all sorts of psychiatric treatments until its removal from the DSMIII in 1973 (Spitzer 1981). Today in Australasia, and in many other parts of the world, the dominant stories of homosexuality are increasingly of recognition and celebration – although this is not necessarily seen in all areas of the community. These differing dominant stories have had a profound influence on people's sense of well-being and their acceptance by their families and communities, serving also to challenge unacceptable homophobic attitudes.

Post-structural influences

Post-structural theories, such as those of Foucault, have also importantly influenced narrative approaches. In emphasising dominant discourses and the ways in which they shape experience, post-structural theories have helped narrative therapists think particularly about power and knowledge. In this regard, White and Epston (1990: 27) note that, 'When engaging in language, we are not engaging in a neutral activity. There exists a stock of culturally available discourses that are considered appropriate and relevant to the expression or representation of particular aspects of experience.'

These discourses reflect and normalise certain 'truths' and silence others. We, in turn, internalise them as truths, subjected to the power of dominant stories. As Brown (2007: 17) states, 'Narrative therapy is interested in helping people resist certain practices of power, including the internalized problem stories, which often become totalizing in their lives.' Importantly, reauthoring stories and identities 'requires moving beyond simply telling and retelling stories to an active deconstruction of oppressive and unhelpful discourses' (Brown 2007: 3).

Narrative approaches understand these dominant stories that create difficulties for people through a particular *externalising* lens: they seek to externalise the problem – that is, although someone might have a problem story, which includes accounts of its causation and its consequences, the person is not the problem. It is the narrative or story that is the problem. How the narrative or story fits into a person's life and influences it becomes the focus of intervention. Both the client and the social worker talk about the story as external to the person. This externalising process and deconstruction of the problem allow 'for greater distance from the influence of the problem and more likelihood of being able to live according to one's preferences' (Brown 2007: 17). Through externalising the problem, it becomes possible to focus on uncovering unique outcomes or exceptions, and to concentrate on the 'absent but implicit', as we will explore later in this chapter.

Consideration of power relations also led White and Epston (1990) to be concerned about the ways in which the therapeutic relationship could mirror broader power relations within the community. Here the potential exists for professionals to be oppressive of clients through the application of theoretical and therapeutic knowledge and interventions. Thus White and Epston (1990) propose that the client is the expert in their problem, decentring both the problem and the worker. Narrative approaches therefore focus on the ways in which problem stories are co-created (de Shazer 1994: xvi). Decentring the power and influence of the social worker is critical.

From theory to practice

So far, we have explored the wider theoretical influences that have shaped story-telling approaches. This broad pool of social theories or philosophical approaches has formed a coherent but complex foundation for practice. This is particularly so given that these foundational social theories privilege fluidity of knowledge, uncertainty of truths and challenging power relations – translating these principles into an intervention is not without challenge.

Our theory-to-practice framework provides us with a conceptualisation of key ideas within the narrative approach and the ways in which this unfolds into practice (see Figure 6.1).

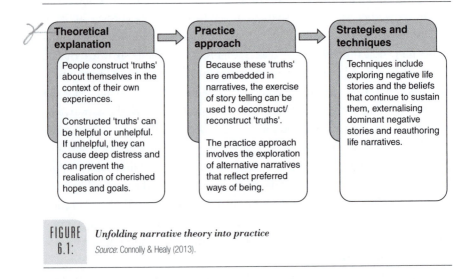

Theoretical explanation	Practice approach	Strategies and techniques
People construct 'truths' about themselves in the context of their own experiences. Constructed 'truths' can be helpful or unhelpful. If unhelpful, they can cause deep distress and can prevent the realisation of cherished hopes and goals.	Because these 'truths' are embedded in narratives, the exercise of story telling can be used to deconstruct/reconstruct 'truths'. The practice approach involves the exploration of alternative narratives that reflect preferred ways of being.	Techniques include exploring negative life stories and the beliefs that continue to sustain them, externalising dominant negative stories and reauthoring life narratives.

FIGURE 6.1: *Unfolding narrative theory into practice*
Source: Connolly & Healy (2013).

In terms of causality, narrative ways of working assume that, when they are unhelpful, constructed truths and dominant stories create disjuncture and deep distress, thus preventing people from realising their hopes for a rewarding and satisfying life. The practice approach and intervention strategy therefore involve seeking to deconstruct these negative stories and reconstruct narratives of strength and preferred ways of being. The narrative approach then provides a repertoire of strategies and techniques that promote the development of alternative narratives, including establishing and sustaining the relationship; telling the story and reauthoring narratives; externalising the problem; and seeking a preferred way of being.

Establishing and sustaining the relationship

Narrative approaches recognise the importance of establishing a client–worker relationship and therapeutic alliance. Unlike onion-peeling approaches, however, the relationship is not the focus of the work – the narrative or problem story is the focus. Therapeutic relationships are co-created relationships, and are typically short-term. As highlighted earlier, core to Michael White's approach is a decentring of the 'therapist' or social worker, focusing instead on collaboration, or a co-creation of meaning. The social worker using narrative approaches becomes engaged in 'journalistic inquiry' rather than being an interpreter or discerner of meaning. You are there to stimulate new ways of thinking through your questions and inquiry into the problem story. The client–worker relationship provides a safe, supportive engagement in which a person's stories can be heard, witnessed and validated. Within this relationship, a strong emphasis is placed on client expertise and empowerment in finding the solutions they need (McQueen & Hobbs 2014). The emphasis in client–worker contact is on translating that expertise and empowerment into everyday life (O'Connell 1998: 85). The client is encouraged to think further about the problem story outside the therapy context. This is consistent with White's concern with the use of power in the therapeutic relationship. We see how this plays out in the various techniques that are encouraged within narrative therapy.

Telling the story

At their heart, story-telling approaches emphasise the importance of story-telling skills on the part of both the listener and the narrator. Denborough (2008: 75–9) uses a 'Tree of Life' methodology with children who have experienced trauma to support story-telling in four parts:

1   Tree of life; introducing the tree metaphor and explaining that the children would be drawing their own 'tree of life'. This would include exploring: the roots of their tree – where they come from, extended family, history,

origins, etc.; the branches of their tree – their hopes and dreams; the leaves of their tree – the people who are important to them; and the fruits of their tree – the gifts that the child has, not necessarily of a material kind, but things such as acts of kindness or care.

2 Forest of life; the trees are put up onto a wall creating 'a forest of beautiful trees' (2008: 81). This encourages children to share and contribute their stories, offering opportunities for re-telling.

3 When storms come; in ways that are not re-traumatising, the children explore and speak about some of the difficulties they have experienced – drawing on strengths and sources of resilience, initiatives for self-protection are explored.

4 Certificates and song; certificates honour the contributions that the children and other special people in their lives have made to their Tree of Life.

Just by bearing witness to a person's stories and helping to co-create stories of strength and healing, change can occur. This often provides a cathartic release of a particular story of guilt, shame or sadness. Research highlights the importance of narrating stories and identifying related emotional reactions (Pennebaker 1995). Many people experiencing difficulties or traumas find that others do not want to or cannot listen to them, given their horrific or distressing nature. There is a sense in which their stories remain unable to be narrated (Laub & Auerhahn 1993; Kleinman, Das & Lock 1997). Developing easily accessible methodologies, such as Denborough's Tree of Life, provides opportunities to engage people in a process of reauthoring, even when their lives have been marked by trauma and tragedy.

In the United States in particular, a strong literature and practice have emerged in relation to listening to illness narratives (Frank 1995; Charon 2006). This emphasis has been driven not only by patients and their negative experiences of illness, but also by the people they encounter in the systems of care – the doctors, nurses and social workers. These narratives have illuminated the human side of illness: the loneliness, distress and suffering many people endure, in often becoming a number or diagnosis in a vast and busy health system. Illness narratives reground people in the human face of these experiences, and typically restore empathy and understanding. Illness narrative work has also been important in influencing the training of health professionals. Story-telling has become important in training health professionals to listen to their own experiences and reactions, and to engage in critical reflexive practice to ensure better patient outcomes and health practitioner self-care (see Chapter 8).

Having someone listen to your story in a concentrated way can itself be a transforming experience. As Moore (2004: 58) notes, 'The repeated telling of a story gradually allows the pieces of life experiences to find their relation to each other.' It also enables these pieces to form a coherent whole, which we can then assess as to whether it reflects who we want to be or whether change is needed. In telling stories of our lives, we often discover that these stories are incongruent with the person we want to be. Story-telling approaches take this one step further, in identifying the problem story, challenging the narrative, asking questions and establishing an understanding of how a problem comes to be understood in particular ways. The source of the narrative, its plot, its assumptions and its actors are all of critical importance, but changing the problem story is at the heart of the work.

Reauthoring the story

Story-telling approaches aim to transform unhelpful stories, or the inhibiting and self-defeating stories, by restoring (or restorying) them with narratives of strength, transformation and empowerment. As we have noted, this reauthoring can be at the individual, group or community level, but often also involves the challenging of dominant social stories. Thus social change can occur as a result of story-telling approaches as much as it may influence individual change. For example, racism and other forms of discrimination can be challenged (Augusta-Scott 2007). Through deconstructing and reauthoring individual or group stories, representation of these at broader social, structural and cultural levels is transformed. A story can be reauthored in a number of different ways, and the techniques we now consider are just some of the more commonly used in narrative therapies.

Externalising the problem

The technique of externalising the problem involves inviting the person to speak around and about the problem, as a separate entity from the person themselves. Questions are asked about the problem, including its influence and effects and how a person feels about these influences and effects. The focus is on relative influence questioning (White & Epston 1990: 42–8). This process of questioning involves two sets of questioning: 'The first set encourages persons to map the influence of the problem in their lives and relationships. The second set encourages persons to map their own influence in the "life" of the problem' (White & Epston 1990: 42).

The purpose of this questioning approach is to assist people 'to become aware of and to describe their relationship with the problem. This takes them out of a fixed and static world' (White & Epston 1990: 42). In externalising the problem, people may highlight instances where the problem story has been experienced differently and less problematically. These become the focus of work, as they are understood to be the alternative or preferred stories.

Listening for unique outcomes: Alternative or preferred ways of being

In telling stories, White (2007) noted that many people were able to tell a dominant story of themselves and their problems and to tell alternative or preferred stories. They were able to reflect on a time when the problem did not control them, or when they acted differently from most other times. You can hear that asking about alternative stories presumes that people have strengths and resources that enable them to overcome difficulties and problems at times. Building on these stories is a key focus of the work. These stories were about exceptions to difficulties, about situations where there were unique outcomes. For example, questions that were used in a group with young women who had survived sexual abuse were:

- Can you think of a time when terror wasn't travelling with you?
- What was different about this time?
- How did you feel?
- What were some of the things you felt when terror wasn't with you?

(McPhie & Chaffey 1999: 51)

Note the externalising of terror in this exchange, and the way in which these questions focus on exploring different experiences in relation to the sexual abuse. These questions enabled these women to be in touch with their strengths and their moments of resistance.

Most problem stories have an exception story – that is, a time when the problem was dealt with or experienced differently. These unique outcomes or exceptions provide an insight into new ways of being, rather than focusing on a lengthy exploration of the nature of the problems themselves. This has some similarities with the 'faulty-engine' theories, but differs from onion-peeling theories in terms of the skills and emphases of the approaches. For example, while someone may see themselves as having been a victim of bullying throughout their childhood, and developed a narrative of themselves as a victim in adulthood, they may be able to identify unique instances when they thought, felt or acted differently. This exception provides useful insights into how the person would like to be or can be. The preferred story of self can emerge, thus enabling the person to build on the strength and often success of the preferred story.

Story-telling approaches affirm that strengths and resources are what need to be amplified, rather than the overwhelming nature of the problem situations themselves. The focus of narrative therapy is on these preferred stories and how they can become the new dominant stories in a person's life. The emphasis is less on insight into current behaviour, thoughts, feelings and events, and more on foresight about the future and a capacity to influence that future.

As Carey, Walther and Russell (2009: 320) highlight, Michael White came to use the notion of scaffolding in his questioning style. By this, he would

> use therapeutic questions to provide stepping stones for people to 'learn' previously unknown things about themselves in the as yet unexplored territories of their preferred stories. Thoughtfully scaffolded questions can support people to step from the 'known and familiar …'

Listening for what is absent but implicit

The 'absent but implicit' concept is one that emerged later in White's work. Influenced by the thinking of French philosophers such as Derrida, he recognised that the 'absent but implicit' was an important focus of listening. As Carey, Walther and Russell (2009: 320) explain, it is a way of listening to the making of meaning and how it is based on 'the distinctions we make between what is presented to us (privileged meaning) and what is "left out" (subjugated meaning)'. Translating this into practice:

> If we accept the proposal that people can only give a particular account of their lives through drawing distinctions with what their experience is not, then we can tune our ears to hear not only what the problem is, but also to hear what is 'absent but implicit' in their descriptions of what the problem is not. (Carey, Walther & Russell 2009: 321)

It involves listening for and valuing what sits behind experience – for example, what is being used as the basis of comparison for functioning well. In many ways, it brings the focus back to what is ultimately considered important and of value to a person. Using the example of a person recovering from trauma, some of the questions presented get to the heart of the 'absent but implicit':

- What does this pain speak to in terms of important beliefs about life that have been subjugated or violated?
- What might these tears testify to about what it is that is held precious?
- What important understandings of the world have been insulted, degraded, transgressed or trodden on?'

(Carey et al. 2009: 321)

These questions fit well with trauma theories, which suggest that it is the shattering of world-views that causes the distress of traumatic life events (Janoff-Bulman 1992). These questions begin to build a narrative connection back to these core assumptions and world-views.

Asking future-focused questions

Story-telling approaches have strongly emphasised the ways in which problem stories hold us back from optimal functioning and relating. Asking questions about the maintenance of a problem (for example, 'How will you feel if you are still living like this in five years' time?') can challenge a person to think about change in the present by confronting the future realities. Sometimes it is this realisation that motivates change: the thought that unless something happens, problems will remain or be exacerbated rather than diminished in the future.

One of the best-known questions of solution-focused work is the so-called miracle question. Steve de Shazer (1994: 95) developed the miracle question. In its long form, it unfolds as follows: 'Suppose that tonight after you go to sleep a miracle happens and the problems that brought you to therapy are solved immediately. But since you were sleeping at the time you cannot know that this miracle has happened.'

This statement invites the person to think about the complete resolution of their problem. Although very few problems people bring to any social work or therapeutic context can actually be resolved this quickly, the statement proposes a future reality: what the absence of the problem would look like. The miracle question is then asked, followed by an important external reality check on the change that would be brought about: 'Once you wake up tomorrow morning, how will you discover that a miracle has happened? Without your telling them, how will other people know that a miracle has happened?' (de Shazer 1994: 95)

In this type of questioning, people are being invited to think very differently about the possibilities for change. The question not only leads to a lot of thinking about what change will look like, but also helps people to think about what goals need to be set to achieve the change. It asks for both internal and external recognition of change in relation to a particular problem. The question taps into people's strengths by asking them to think positively about a new story they can begin to tell themselves.

We now bring these ideas together in a case example: Sarah talks about her work with a client, Rosie, in Alice Springs in the Northern Territory of Australia. She describes how narrative approaches help Rosie to understand her strengths and her circumstances differently.

Case example: Narrative approaches

Rosie is a 30-year-old Arrernte woman with three children who lives in a town camp on the outskirts of Alice Springs. Rosie presented to the community centre with a request to call the police because her husband had become violent. It was decided that Rosie and her children would stay with another family that night. A Domestic Violence Order existed between Rosie and her husband, which stated that she and her husband were not to be together when they were drinking.

After the police left, this social worker talked with Rosie, who spoke about having been engaged with a drug and alcohol program previously and, although considering it again, reported, 'I feel weak, like I can't stop drinking. It is everywhere in my life.' Two days later, the women's shelter contacted this worker to advise that Rosie had been badly hurt by her partner the previous evening, had sought refuge at the shelter and would be staying there with her children for the next week. Visiting family later that week, Rosie came to the community centre to contact Legal Aid in relation to the domestic violence incident. On the wall of the community centre, there is an Indigenous painting poster, a picture model representing the stages of change.

Talking with this worker, Rosie said she had never been aware of this story of the cycle of change, and the worker reiterated the universal pattern. Rosie attempted to identify where she sat in the cycle of change, first about her drinking and then considering some of her relationship issues. She saw that the picture example could represent some cycles in her life, an insight facilitated by the visual, tangible aspect of the poster. Rosie identified that she was not alone in the process, that other people also went through these phases, and that many people experienced this changeable wheel of life. By physically drawing a circle on the poster, she could name where she was today and validate her present circumstances and emotions. Thus the visual approach not only broke down barriers of language but was also useful in that it allowed Rosie to understand her part within a cycle of change and helped her to externalise her awareness and solidify some of the chaos in her life with new-found insight. Identifying with the picture story and seeing the steps within it gave Rosie a useful tool for understanding and approaching the alcohol and domestic violence issues in her life. The constructive benefit of drawing herself into the change story for Rosie came both from identifying where she was at present and from the insight that there could be movement away from the 'I can't' feeling.

Discussing what made her stronger, she started talking about going bush. This sparked memories of times with her sister when they were younger, dancing and singing. Reflecting on this brought her back to a connection with happier, healthier relationships. She then identified where she was in the stage of change cycle at the times of these memories. Rosie realised that she had forgotten some of these moments, which reminded her of times before domestic violence and grog issues were in her life. She attributed forgetting these things from the past to some of the traumas in her present life. She also said that her life did not always revolve around drinking, and that there was a time when she did not drink. She talked about family gatherings that had happy drinking without fighting and had lots of story-telling. Rosie remembered not drinking during her pregnancies, and how she was strong about this even when there were difficulties in her life and people encouraging her to share a drink. She even remembered her aunty telling her she was a strong person because she did not follow others.

We acknowledged these moments in her life as proof of her strength of spirit. We also reflected that she was strong also in the present, realistically reauthoring her current thoughts of self. This highlighted her resilience and competence, both in her past and in her present, as we talked about the strong things she did now for herself and her children. We talked about her strength of character in not accepting violent behaviour in her life, and seeking assistance by using such resources as the police, the community centre and the women's shelter, and her use and knowledge of her legal rights. Further proof of her strength as an Aboriginal woman was seen in her three beautiful children, her being a fantastic mother among many obstacles, her dedication as a talented painter and her bonds of kinship and culture, which kept her strong.

A few days later, when Rosie was present for playgroup at the centre, this worker respectfully asked for permission to write down some of the story they had spoken about. Rosie thought about it for the rest of the day and then gave permission. The next day, this worker went to Rosie's house to read to her what the worker had written of her story. She appeared very happy and said, 'It is really good that you made that story for me.' This worker replied that Rosie had made the story for herself. Rosie said she might do a painting of it and would talk about it with her children.

The process of writing and retelling Rosie's story made it tangible for her, validating her good experiences, her great qualities and ownership of her story as it had been heard and honoured. Rosie now holds her own story and self-reflection, through a process that is constructive for her health and well-being – and therefore that of her children – as opposed to some of the dominant stories that exist within Central Australia.

Story-telling theories work well across a range of social work approaches. Although they were originally developed in the context of family therapy, and continue to be used extensively in that context, they are also used to inform individual therapeutic work, community work and social work supervision.

Narrative approaches have also informed a vast number of group work and community development initiatives and interventions (Freedman & Combs 2009; Denborough et al. 2006). For example, sexual assault survivors' groups, mental health groups and work with children have all been informed by narrative understandings (Carrey 2007; Dulwich Centre Publications 1999; Montalbano-Phelps 2004). These approaches have also been critical in many interventions following trauma experiences (Denborough 2006). For example, Atkinson's *Trauma Trails* (2002) highlights the way in which narrative group work enabled a group of Aboriginal people in the Northern Territory to reconnect with their pasts and reauthor new stories of themselves in spite of their trauma histories. Similarly, narrative approaches with Holocaust survivors have provided the means to form a new narrative about survivorship and transformation (Reiter 2005).

Narrative approaches are fundamentally about building on strengths and creating stories of resilience and hope. Like other theories for practice, they also have their strengths and challenges.

Strengths and challenges

Story-telling approaches that include narrative perspectives and strengths-based practices are consistent with many current beliefs about mental health and well-being in that they recognise the importance of a sense of coherence and control in influencing our identity and sense of self. They are also fundamentally client centred. The story-telling theories have many strengths and have resonated strongly with practitioners in different practice settings. The commonly identified areas of strength are that they are solution-focused and optimistic in their orientation, their externalised context and issues of power. Perhaps inevitably, some of these perceived strengths have their challenging components.

Solution-focused and optimistic

As we have explored throughout this chapter, narrative approaches focus on short-term work and on problem-solving. They are inherently based on the notion that people want to change, and in fact have been able to change problem situations in the past at various points. Thus the focus is on positive change rather than exploring what might be perceived as inescapable negativity and oppression. The approaches enable clients to think and talk about who they would like to be and how they would like to live. They build on people's strengths and resilience rather than focusing on deficits and psychopathology.

Many therapeutic approaches to practice rely on long-term, problem-focused work. Story-telling theories stand out in contrast to these approaches, and have challenged the very foundations of our understanding of how people change. The key question is whether change can occur without a well-established depth of understanding about long-term problems, and whether the emphasis on the positive is ultimately at the expense of truly understanding the depth of despair that some people might face. These are important challenges that, to some degree, are counteracted in the growing evidence base for the effectiveness of these approaches. Short-term therapies with a solution focus have been found to be successful.

The externalised context and issues of power

Both the externalised context in which a problem is experienced and issues of power inherent in such a context are particularly relevant to narrative approaches. It could be argued that a client is no more free of the problems of power within relationships than they are with other approaches, despite the view of practitioners that they are. Some critics have raised concern about the extent to which social workers using narrative approaches impose their own views and dominant stories on their clients (Walsh 2006: 268). The determination to seek out dominant stories, and thus drive the intervention along a particular pathway, raises questions about whether it is possible for the client to drive the agenda. The practitioner can be seen to be leading the direction of practice through the nature of the almost journalistic inquiry. This raises the additional question of whether power can ever really be decentred in a therapeutic relationship when one person is help-seeking within a professional relationship creating inferiority and/or dependence on the part of the client. To counter this criticism, White developed ways of equalising relationships through feedback mechanisms that place families in positions of leadership.

While it might seem that narrative approaches are focused primarily on the inner world of the client, they are more concerned with externalised context than they might at first appear to be. At the heart of narrative therapy is a profound acknowledgement of people's context, and a focus on this context being a major part of the problem. As we have explored throughout this chapter, narrative approaches in many practice contexts are concerned as much with listening to the individual as with listening to and challenging dominant social stories. This ensures change for both people and environments: the reauthoring of dominant social and cultural narratives becomes a critical part of narrative practice. In doing so, practitioners address power explicitly within the therapeutic relationship, and strategies are used to minimise the negative influence of power inequalities.

Conclusion

In this chapter, we have looked at the core assumptions of story-telling theories and how they translate into particular approaches and skills in practice. They focus on strengths, externalising problems and finding narrative solutions that lead to a greater sense of well-being and freedom. Given the origins in post-structural and social constructionist theories, these story-telling approaches link well with mountain-moving theories, explored in the next chapter.

Useful resources

Dulwich Centre, http://www.dulwichcentre.com.au.

Saleebey, D. (ed.). 1992. *The Strengths Perspective in Social Work Practice.* New York: Longman.

White, M. & Epston, D. 1990. *Narrative Means to Therapeutic Ends.* New York: W.W. Norton.

7 Mountain-moving theories

In the last of our metaphorical distinctions, we turn to the group of theories and perspectives within social work that seek to eliminate disadvantage and empower people to realise their hopes and aspirations. Over time, these theories have been described in many ways: as activist, progressive, structuralist, political, radical, anti-oppressive and emancipatory, to name just a few. They share an important common aim to connect the personal with the political and, in doing so, to shift focus from individual blame to collective solutions across social, economic and political domains (Trevithick 2012). In this sense, they apply 'mountain-moving' effort to create a more equal society.

Mountain-moving theories stretch this effort, conceptually and practically, across individual, family, community and societal concerns. Understanding the nature of injustice and social inequality is of critical importance, and changing structures, systems and processes to increase their responsiveness is a key practical activity in reducing disadvantage. Nevertheless, as we look at the development of these theoretical ideas over time, we will see the complexity of incorporating a social action reform agenda within contemporary practice environments.

The evolution of social reform and critical social work practice

As we noted in Chapter 1, the 1970s represented a formative time in the development of the social work profession. Dominant social orders were being radically critiqued: class and social structures, patriarchy, racism and sexism were all subjected to critical scrutiny. Within social work, these ideas built on the efforts of pioneering social reformers, such as Jane Addams, and were influenced by socialist movements and political theorising – in particular, Marxism and an analysis of capitalism's social consequences (Howe 2009). These intellectual movements provided social work with a critical edge that contrasted sharply with individualised treatment approaches that focused on human deficits. According to Mendes (2009: 21), 'the radical critique contributed to changing some of the often apolitical and oppressive practices of social work. In particular, radical social work practice assumed an end to overtones of moral or personal failure, and the value of collective action to tackle structural problems'.

Both radical social work (Fook 1993), which emphasises class and economic inequality, and structural social work (Hick & Murray 2009), which adds social dimensions of disadvantage and multiple forms of oppression, provide an important critical foundation for the profession's social justice concerns. Yet translating this into action proved more complex in practice:

> It was all very well for the sociologists and political theorists to expose the true nature of liberal, capitalist economic democracies and how their systems, including state welfare services, supported the interests of the rich and powerful, but all this social theorizing left social work sympathizers feeling either guilty or helpless. (Howe 2009: 129)

It should not have been surprising that social work practitioners faced with negotiating the subtleties of both care and control practices were challenged by the dogmatism of such transformative expectations. Particularly in the context of radical social work ideals, feminist thinkers were also critical of the lack of focus on gender and gender inequality.

From a feminist perspective, the focus on class and economic inequality neglected the essential dynamics and realities of gender oppression. Although associated with and influenced by the radical tradition, feminist social work applied feminist theory in powerful ways to influence thinking and assumptions about women across social structures. A range of feminist perspectives have influenced the way in which social work has been practised over time (Orme 2009). *Liberal feminism* reinforced the importance of equality and laid the groundwork for equal opportunity for women at all levels of society. These pioneering ideas, based on notions of citizenship, democracy and rights, provided an important foundation that inspired debate and challenge from feminist thinkers to come. *Marxist feminists* introduced a class analysis as a critical component of women's oppression, something that was seen as lacking in the liberal feminist perspective. In a critical exploration of the distribution of power, the Marxist feminists lifted feminist thinking from the equality of the individual to the collective interests of women. *Socialist feminism* went on to address interpersonal and relational aspects of women's oppression created by patriarchy. Although the patriarchy is also seen as being critical to women's oppression from feminist perspectives in general, the socialist feminist perspective broadened the analysis to consider issues of sexuality and identity as well. While socialist feminism was not averse to seeking dialogue with men to address women's disadvantage and inequality, the *radical feminist* perspective was more controversial in its response. Radical feminists were early users of the term 'patriarchy' as all-encompassing in its oppression of women – and they clearly articulated the need to reject and dismantle it (Orme 2009). From a radical feminist perspective, the freedom of women depended on the elimination of patriarchy.

Although the feminist movement has been influenced by a range of ideas over time, a key contemporary influence has been postmodernism. In the same way that postmodernist ideas challenge grand narratives, they also challenged feminist thinking. In the context of *post (modern) feminism*, the very creation of a grand feminist theory was questioned and, in the end, so too was postmodern feminism itself:

> Feminists embraced postmodernism to disturb the roots of patriarchy and modernism (Rossiter 2000) but also disturbed feminism. Black women (hooks 1984), women with disabilities (Morris 1993) and older women questioned postmodern feminism defined by white, able-bodied, young, middle-class, educated women who had divested it of its political force. This has led to explorations of diversity and difference. (Orme 2009: 68)

Feminist ideologies have been influential both with respect to strengthening the critical edge of social work practice and in inspiring empowerment practices with women (Fraser & McMaster 2009). In their daily practice, social workers have operationalised feminist ideas within practice in ways that support the particular concerns of women. We will now use a case example to illustrate how feminist ideals can be integrated into practice.

Feminist approaches in practice

This case example was provided by Sam, a social worker who works at CASA House, an agency grounded in feminist theory. Violence against women is seen as a problem caused by patriarchal society and by on-going inequality and exploitation of women. We invite you to think about the ways in which Sam uses feminist approaches to help conceptualise the issues and the practice skills used.

Case example: Feminist approaches

As a child, a young woman was sexually assaulted over a number of years by her father; no one was aware of this. As an adolescent, she began to 'self-harm' and 'act out' in ways the family told her were inappropriate. She was assessed by psychiatric services and was given a number of mental health diagnoses. Despite numerous psychiatric interventions by many professionals, her life does not seem to have improved; if anything, she now 'self-harms' more often and has become isolated and distant.

The woman discloses to a social worker the sexual assault perpetrated by her father. This is unfortunately not an uncommon story. Many victim/survivors do not disclose sexual assault until many years later, despite the high incidence and prevalence of sexual assault. The majority of the time, the perpetrator is a known and trusted male.

As a social worker who has worked in the sexual assault field, I would utilise a feminist theoretic basis, which acknowledges that 'personal problems are both created and exacerbated by societal power imbalances' (Burstow 1992: 4). This entails acknowledging that sexual assault is a crime, and that it is never the victim/survivor's fault. Sexual assault is often silenced by social structures and professionals (Breckenridge & Laing 1999). Effectively supporting the woman involves maximising her control, providing her with accurate information and supporting her in the choices that she makes (Scott, Walker & Gilmore 1995: 32–3). According to Herman (1997: 156), recovery from sexual assault involves three major phases: establishing safety; remembering and mourning; and reconnecting. These are not mutually exclusive, and clients may move between the steps. Initially it is best practice initially to explore the woman's current physical safety as she may still be at risk.

When working with the woman, it is important to acknowledge the disclosure and believe the woman. It is very difficult for any person to disclose sexual assault, due to a range of factors including (but not exclusively) feelings of shame, guilt, fear, sadness, betrayal and the inability to trust due to their experience. Perpetrators often lead their victims to believe through threats or manipulation that they will not be believed or that there will be many negative consequences of a victim/survivor disclosing sexual assault (Salter 1995: 121). The importance of demonstrating belief is central to working with victim/survivors, as it means that the social worker can engage with the woman around both how she feels about herself and the impacts of sexual assault. Consequences of sexual assault may be psychological, emotional and physical, and they may affect other aspects of a woman's life, including family relationships, housing and education. Exploring these consequences is central and should be at the woman's pace in a way that is respectful and safe for her.

Self-harm has been raised as an issue. From a feminist perspective, self-harm would be acknowledged as a coping mechanism rather than a form of attention-seeking. Considering self-harm in this way can assist us to recognise the woman's resilience in surviving the sexual assault. It also opens up a space for a discussion as to when she began to self-harm, how it works for her and what it represents to her. When understood in this way, women are often interested in exploring other methods of coping, as self-harm that was at one point useful has become a problem itself.

In summary, working effectively with victim/survivors of sexual assault requires belief, an understanding of the social context and an exploration of the impacts of the sexual assault. It requires a social worker to recognise that the woman is an expert on her own life and to work from this premise. In doing so, the social work practice will be relevant to the woman and will assist her to regain control.

In keeping with the evolution of knowledge, politically progressive approaches will continue to be influenced by a range of ideas that reject earlier perspectives and trail-blaze new ones. And indeed, according to Howe (2009), the women's movement foreshadowed pioneering work within the profession that is now referred to as *critical social work*.

Critical social work as an approach has incorporated and integrated ideas from these politically progressive perspectives. By doing so, it has broadened its exploration of the diversity of power and inequality (Mendes 2009). As a practice, Allen (2009) argues that critical social work favours multiple ways of working as opposed to focusing on a particular method – for example, working with individuals, families, groups or communities. Critical social work is practised across methods, integrating key concepts, such as the interrelatedness of the personal and the political and the importance of promoting consciousness-raising within a socio-political framework. Gray and Webb (2009) note that critical social work focuses particularly on emancipatory transformation, supporting social justice and empowerment. These ideas have emerged in social work writing internationally, but they have taken hold particularly strongly in Australia, with Jan Fook's work at the forefront of these developments (see Fook 2002). Postmodernist influences are clearly evident within contemporary interpretations of critical social work practice:

> A postmodern and critical social work practice is primarily concerned with practising in ways which further a society without domination, exploitation and oppression. It will focus both on how structures dominate, but also how people construct and are constructed by changing social structures and relations, recognising that there may be multiple and diverse constructions of ostensibly similar situations. Such an understanding of social relations and structures can be used to disrupt dominant understandings and structures, and as a basis for changing these so that they are more inclusive of different interest groups. (Fook 2002: 18)

It has been suggested that this mix of theoretical perspectives – radical ideals, postmodernism and critical theory – has weakened critical social work, hindering its potential to achieve the necessary intellectual rigour of theorising (Gray & Webb 2009). Its value base, which has harnessed both social justice and postmodernist ideals, has nevertheless resonated strongly with social work theorists and practitioners, and its practical applications have found expression in narrative and strengths-based practices (see Chapter 6) and in practices supporting empowerment, anti-oppression and human rights.

Empowerment, anti-oppression and rights-based ideas

A broad strand of social work thinking since the 1980s has focused on notions of empowerment. The 'empowerment perspective' as a generic term describes alternative approaches that seek to promote social change and social justice through a variety of practice responses. It has links with a variety of other theories – for example, the ecological (Chapter 3) and strengths-based perspectives (Chapter 6) and ideas of empowerment are prioritised in many approaches, including person-centred practice (Chapter 4), task-centred practice (Chapter 2) and cognitive-behavioural approaches (Chapter 5). However, as a theory in itself, empowerment provides conceptual scaffolding from which a number of approaches have emerged – for example, anti-oppressive practices (Dominelli 2002); partnership and participatory practices that support self-determination and involvement in decision-making (Connolly 1999; Shera & Wells 1999); advocacy and consumer empowerment approaches (Beckett 2006; Healy 2005) and rights-based practice (Briskman 2014; Connolly & Ward 2008a; Ife 2001).

Empowerment has been defined as

> the capacity of individuals, groups and/or communities to take control of their circumstances, exercise power and achieve their own goals, and the process by which, individually and collectively, they are able to help themselves and others to maximise the quality of their lives. (Adams 2008: 17)

This definition captures the essential component of *self-empowerment* as opposed to somehow being *empowered* by others. This distinction is relevant to the understanding of power dynamics in practice. There are tensions in giving effect to empowerment ideals when inevitable power differences exist between the social worker and the client. Remaining alert to power dynamics within practice, and being aware of the influence professional power can have on client outcomes, are critical to what Beckett (2006: 126) calls 'power-sensitive practice'. Being sensitive to the dynamics of power requires an understanding of different types of power.

Statutory power

Social workers are often mandated with significant powers, particularly in the context of statutory practice. As we noted in Chapter 1, social workers can have power over personal liberty and freedom, and these powers can rest uncomfortably alongside professional values of social justice, anti-oppression and anti-discrimination. As Beckett notes, professional powers can be used to force people to do things they might not otherwise do, or want to do. Of course, professional power is not necessarily bad in itself. Indeed, it is important that statutory powers can be used to protect the interests of vulnerable people. But they do have coercive elements that can bring about life-changing consequences for the people involved.

Reflection: Statutory power

I remember the first time I placed a young person in a residence. She was 16 years old and had a string of increasingly serious offences. She was completely out of control. I also knew that an older man was sexually exploiting her, and I felt there was little I could do to stop it. I think it was the right thing to do, but I'll never forget the look she gave me when the judge agreed with my recommendation.

Social worker

Beckett describes two ways in which statutory powers may be used: explicitly through *direct protection*, where a social worker takes action to protect, as in the reflection example; or through a process of *protective leverage*. Protective leverage uses statutory power implicitly to encourage compliance. Here the social worker does not take direct protective action, but the client knows they could do so in the event of non-compliance. In many respects, explicit coercive power is more straightforward and transparent, and when legal steps are taken a formal process provides accountability checks and balances for actions that are taken. However, protective leverage does not have the same checks and balances, and often becomes part of a general social work approach within a statutory practice setting. Beckett (2006: 157) expresses concern about the extensive and unconscious use of protective leverage:

> I think that we are inclined to greatly underestimate the extent of our implicit powers. Social workers sometimes exercise implicit coercive powers without even realising it, imagining that they are working in a voluntary partnership with service users when in fact service users are complying with their wishes out of fear of the consequences of not doing so.

This illustrates the dangers of making assumptions about empowerment practice, and being attuned to the ways in which using implicit power in practice can be disempowering – it is oppositional to aspirations within empowerment approaches.

Legitimate power

Power that is legitimated through organisational rules and professional roles can have an important influence on resource allocation, and ultimately on client outcomes. When a social worker undertakes a professional assessment of a client's situation, whether or not the worker has statutory powers, they can wield enormous power over decision-making. This is with respect to both the resources the client may receive and the way the client may be responded to within the service or across the sector. Assessing need is not a value-free activity, and if professionals are not insightful about the nature of legitimate power and how it can be influenced by personal or professional prejudices, there are dangers that clients may be disadvantaged. This is particularly hazardous for clients if they are disliked by the social worker or they are seen as too demanding or difficult. Closely related to this is *reward power*, which is derived from the professional's ability to provide rewards. In the context of a reward system, clients may provide what they think the professional wants in order to be rewarded emotionally or practically.

Referent power

Some people have personal qualities or professional respect that provides them with a sense of natural authority that is respected and admired by others. Beckett calls this referent power – charisma that can be used to support good client outcomes. It is interesting to see how some people can achieve positive results on the basis of authoritative persuasion when others with equally good arguments find themselves challenged in achieving results. Referent power is important when supporting clients and in the context of multidisciplinary environments, where social work as a discipline may be relegated to the bottom of a professional hierarchy.

Understanding dynamics of power and how it can help or hinder work with clients is essential to the exploration of approaches that seek to empower service users. Empowerment approaches are critically concerned with power and shifting power to meet the needs and rights of clients (Leadbetter 2002). Based on notions of equality, collaboration and transparency, a strong strand in contemporary empowerment practice has involved a commitment to anti-oppressive practice.

Anti-oppressive practice

Realising social change through the eradication of injustices – or at least those injustices that are reproduced through professional practice – is a key aim of the anti-oppressive approach (Dominelli 2002). Particularly within the context of institutional settings, social work practices have the potential to be oppressive, and to create disadvantage and inequality. Anti-oppressive practice recognises this potential and strives to support those affected by structural inequalities – for example, poverty, racism and sexism. Dominelli (2002) calls anti-oppressive practice an 'old–new' paradigm, since its origins can be found in social work's early commitment to social justice and social change. Dominelli defines anti-oppressive practice as a 'form of social work practice which addresses social divisions and structural inequalities':

> anti-oppressive practice aims to provide more appropriate and sensitive services by responding to people's needs regardless of their social status. [It] embodies a person-centred philosophy, an egalitarian value system concerned with reducing the deleterious effects of structural inequalities upon people's lives; a methodology focusing on both process and outcome; and a way of structuring relationships between individuals that aim to empower users by reducing the negative effects of hierarchy. (Dominelli 2002: 6)

She has extended these ideas more recently in her exploration of 'green' social work (Dominelli 2012). 'Green' social work is defined as:

> That part of practice that intervenes to protect the environment and enhance people's well-being by integrating the interdependencies between people and their socio-cultural, economic and physical environments, and among peoples within an egalitarian framework that addresses prevailing structural inequalities and unequal distribution of power and resources. (Dominelli 2012: 8)

This focus for anti-oppressive practice moves beyond a socially situated understanding of people and their environments to an environmentally situated one. The scope of concern includes persistent socially constructed vulnerabilities in physical environments, such as pollution, poor air and water quality, and the effects of climate change (Bankoff, Frerks & Hilhorst 2004). Thus the inequalities and oppressions that arise in our physical living circumstances become the focus of anti-oppressive practice and action.

Healy (2005) summarises a number of assumptions in the anti-oppressive approach: the recognition of multiple forms of oppression and the ways in which this can be harmful; the fact that oppression emerges from unequal power differentials; and that social workers can reduce the negative impact through adopting a critically reflective response that avoids replicating disempowering dynamics. Importantly, Healy notes that a particular strength of anti-oppressive practice is that it can legitimately be adopted within statutory and interpersonal practice contexts, and does not assume that practice within these settings is destined to be intrusively oppressive.

Healy (2005) identifies a number of practice principles within the anti-oppressive approach. First, workers need to be critically self-reflective and appreciative of the way in which the self can shape practice responses (see Chapter 1). Second, workers also need to assess critically the client's experiences of inequality and oppression:

> The anti-oppressive assessment process turns social workers' attention to the critical analysis of prevailing ideologies shaping agency policies and resource allocation ... The processes of critical reflection extend also to reflection on how the language one uses in assessment is shaped by dominant ideologies that convey and sustain oppressive power relations. (Healy 2005: 184)

Empowering clients to overcome both structural and personal disadvantage is an important principle of anti-oppressive practice, as well as using the least intrusive intervention. This supports an exploration of early intervention opportunities before troubles become entrenched, requiring more intrusive and/or coercive interventions. Healy also identifies partnership work as an important principle within the anti-oppressive approach, but also notes the vexed nature of developing partnerships with clients in the context of unequal relationships. For anti-oppressive practitioners, partnership practice requires more equal sharing of power, transparency of process and involvement in decision-making. These principles are illustrated within the unfolding of anti-oppressive theory into practice (see Figure 7.1).

Partnership and participatory practices

The importance of partnership practice and commitment to power-sharing within the anti-oppressive approach are characteristics shared by participatory practice models, particularly in the context of child and family welfare. Since the 1980s, notions of partnership and family engagement have become organising constructs in child welfare practices internationally. In the United Kingdom, far-reaching legislative reform in 1989 encouraged 'an approach to child care based on negotiation with families and involving parents and children in agreed plans' (Parton, Thorpe & Wattam 1997: 34). Also in 1989, New Zealand took partnership and family engagement a number of steps further by formally enshrining family decision-making in legislation, a step that introduced family group conferencing as a means of finding solutions for children at risk (Connolly 1999).

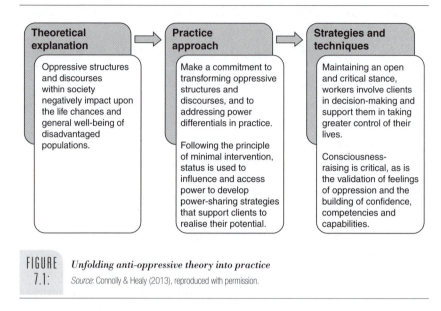

FIGURE
7.1:

Unfolding anti-oppressive theory into practice

Source: Connolly & Healy (2013), reproduced with permission.

Family group conferences (FCGs) bring together family – including extended family – in a process of decision-making for children who are assessed to be in need of care or protection. Typically, FCGs have three phases: the information-giving phase during which the family hears of the professional concerns for the child; the promotion of private family time, which enables the family to deliberate and develop solutions without the involvement of professionals; and the agree-ment phase, in which agreement is sought to the family's plan. The introduction of family decision-making was radically different from earlier practices in child welfare, whereby professionals assessed and made decisions about what should happen to children who had been notified to protective services. As illustrated by the Williams case example (Connolly 2006a: 347), the FCG is a process that pro-vides the family with the first chance of resolving the problems confronting them:

Case example: A family group conference

Janice Williams lived at home with her parents and two younger siblings. She was 12 years of age when she first came to the notice of protective services following allegations that she had been sexually abused by her father. Subsequent to the abuse disclosure, Mr Williams admitted that he had abused Janice, although social workers were concerned that he minimised the extent of the abuse and the impact it had on his daughter. He moved away from the family home, but made it clear that he felt the family should stick together and work through their problems.

Mrs Williams relied heavily on her husband for support, both in terms of the day-to-day running of the home and the emotional support he provided. When he left, she struggled to cope, and found even the most straightforward tasks virtually impossible. She was feeling increasingly depressed and, while she was supportive of Janice, she missed her husband and wanted things back the way they had been.

The Williams family had a reasonably large kinship network. Both sets of grandparents were deceased, but Mrs Williams had a younger brother who lived close by and Mr Williams had two sisters living within driving distance. Only one member of the extended family was unable to attend the FGC: Mrs Williams' older brother, who was encouraged to send a letter to the meeting in which he expressed his views.

New Zealand law provides the FGC coordinator with statutory power to exclude people from the conference if it is not in the best interests of the child. Janice was very fearful of seeing her father so soon after the abuse. Because of this, Mr Williams was excluded from the meeting; however, his views were recorded and presented to the family group as part of the information-sharing phase.

Before the FGC, the members of the extended Williams family had largely lost touch with each other, so the first part of the meeting provided an opportunity to rekindle links. Mrs Williams was uncertain how her husband's family would react to the problems raised in the FGC – particularly as her husband's letter to the FGC was so full of expressions of sorrow and distress. However, the coordinator encouraged the family members to talk about the issues confronting them, and it was clear that family members on both sides wanted to support Janice and her mother.

The family members took a long time to deliberate privately. When they finally returned to the meeting, they explained that they were troubled by Mr Williams' desire to return home, and were concerned that Mrs Williams' reliance upon her husband could create dangers for Janice. Their decisions reflected the need to both support Mrs Williams and protect Janice. They recognised the need to provide both emotional and practical support for Mrs Williams, and a plan of family support and child care was proposed. Additionally, the family requested that the social worker initiate court proceedings to secure a restraining order with respect to Mr Williams. It was acknowledged that he would find this a difficult family decision, and that he would need support to understand the position taken by the family. One of the paternal aunts took responsibility for explaining this to him and for supporting him through the process and the criminal court proceedings that were to follow.

Family engagement strategies have developed across international jurisdictions as a way of harnessing the strengths of families towards the care and protection of children, and have been identified as a practical demonstration of empowerment practice (Connolly & Healy 2013). Family engagement strategies have also found favour across cultural boundaries, particularly when cultural values support the collective care of children That said, writers have noted the challenges in implementing participatory practice, given the immense power differentials that exist within statutory child protection practice (Darlington,

Healy & Feeney 2010), and others have explored whether family group conferencing privileges the voices of children and families (Connolly & Masson 2014). Despite the challenges, recent research supporting family engagement strategies provides confidence that involving wider family in decision-making can provide good outcomes for children at risk. They are also practices that support concepts of agency, self-determination and participation – all of which are important when considering human rights-based approaches.

Rights-based practice

In recent years, considerable scholarly attention has been paid to human rights-based social work practice (Briskman 2014; Connolly & Ward 2008a; Ife 2001; Reichert 2007; Wronka 2008). Social work has a long-standing commitment to social justice and social action, both of which support a human rights agenda. Indeed Wronka (2008: 1) identifies human rights as the 'bedrock of social justice'. While attention to human rights concerns can be found in social work codes of ethics internationally, writers have also noted their lack of integration with respect to social work practice. In response, Reichert (2007: 12) argues for a new human rights paradigm for social work that gives clarity to social justice and social action concerns:

> Human rights are specific privileges and can more readily be applied to a social work situation than the often confusing notion of social or economic justice, both of which tend to bog down in needs-based theories … Human rights elevate discussions and practices beyond the needs of an individual to the rights of an individual.

In response, there has been a flurry of activity in scaffolding human rights, both in social work theorising and in practice development.

Nipperess & Briskman (2009) argue that a human rights approach is consistent with, and builds upon, a strong foundation of theorising within critical approaches to social work. In this respect, rather than rights-based thinking being under-developed, it could be seen as part of the evolution of mountain-moving ideas in social work. Rights-based ideas have been conceptualised as first-, second- and third-generation rights (Ife 2001; Nickel 2007). Connolly and Ward (2008a: 36) summarise these as follows:

> first generation rights are concerned with the protection of civil and political rights such as the right to vote, freedom of speech, and the right to a fair trial. Second generation rights refer to the economic, social and cultural entitlements of individuals, such as rights to employment, a fair wage, education

health care, and participation in the cultural life of the community. Finally, third generation rights involve rights as a collective or group level and reflect group entitlements to goods such as economic development, an unpolluted environment, and self-determination for colonized peoples.

Connolly and Ward (2008b) also explore ways in which rights can be negotiated using a life-course framework to illuminate the interaction between a human rights perspective and human needs, interdependencies, responsibilities and obligations. Using a life-course framework enables the exploration of contestable rights that intersect directly with social work practice. For example, rights and responsibilities in the context of reproductive technologies present a set of complex human rights issues. New birth technologies enable people to become parents through donor insemination – a situation in which the newborn child is biologically related only to the mother – and egg donation – whereby the child is genetically related only to the father. Over the life-course, the question of whose rights have ascendency can be acutely contestable in this area:

> Do children conceived with the assistance of reproductive technologies have a right to their identity and information about their genetic family lineage? ... Do parents have sole discretion regarding whether or not the child will be told of their conceptive history? And do donors have any rights or responsibilities beyond the birth of the child? (Connolly & Ward 2008b: 350)

Competing needs and interests within the area of new birth technologies constitute just one of many areas where legal and moral rights intersect. Typically, social workers have to negotiate human rights-based issues in areas of child and family practice, disability, health and criminal justice in the context of Indigenous concerns (Briskman 2014; Gilbert 2013; Ruwhiu 2013) and in other cultural contexts, such as working with refugees and asylum seekers (Fiske & Briskman 2013). Connolly and Ward (2008a: 180) argue that 'values and capability-building are the twin pillars of effective practice', and that rights-based analysis can help us to both negotiate these complexities and find practical ways of responding.

In recent years, practice frameworks have been developed that support rights-based ideas in specific fields of practice (e.g. see Connolly 2007 in child welfare, discussed in Chapter 2, and Ward & Connolly 2008 in criminal justice). Rights-based practice frameworks can provide ethical scaffolding for practice that goes beyond traditional approaches, and can support the core human rights values of freedom and well-being. They draw out ethical assumptions that are often implicit in models of practice, and integrate them with key motivational drivers – in particular, the human need for participation, agency and self-determination, all of which serve to promote capability-building. In order to adopt rights-based practice frameworks, however, it is necessary to understand the degree to which professional responses can equalise power differentials and give effect to mountain-moving theoretical ideas.

The democratisation of policy and practice

A common strategy characterising the mountain-moving theories discussed in this chapter has been to equalise power in practice and to create ways in which a more equal society can be created. This fundamentally involves the democratisation of services that are reflexive in terms of understanding and responding to power dynamics in policy and practice. Arnstein's (1969) 'eight rungs on the ladder of citizen participation' (see Figure 7.2) is a classic model that

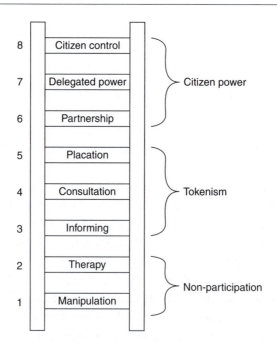

FIGURE 7.2:   *Eight rungs on the ladder of citizen participation*
Source: Arnstein (1969), reproduced with permission.

is used frequently to describe power relationships across a range of settings. Although originally developed for urban planning purposes, it provides a relatively straightforward typology that can also be easily adapted to social work processes.

The lower rungs of the ladder identify non-participatory processes, which illustrate the potential for power to be used to undermine client self-determination. Here professional power may be used, implicitly or explicitly, to drive and dominate practice processes and outcomes. Rungs 3 to 5 on the ladder identify tokenistic practices – informing, consultation, placation – that give an *impression* of participatory practice, but in fact can be seen to camouflage differentials in power. The higher rungs on the ladder, 6, 7 and 8, reflect a commitment to true citizen power, whereby partnerships are more equal and power and control is shared. The positioning of practice on the citizen participation ladder will be significantly influenced by the commitment of professionals to the democratisation of practice. The more committed the worker is, the more responsive practice will be to these ideals.

Earlier, we described family group conferencing, a process of family decision-making that has the potential to operationalise empowerment ideals. Given that it is based on assumptions of shared power, we would expect this model of practice to be positioned highly on the ladder of citizen participation. Yet research in the family group conferencing area suggests that even when models are based on aspirations of client empowerment, they have the potential to be undermined by professionally driven responses (Connolly 2006b). This reinforces the need for critical reflection in practice to interrogate the maintenance of core values and to avoid any inadvertent disempowering practices.

Of course, practitioner views are not the only perspectives that influence the democratisation of practice. Within human service organisations, a range of factors influence the degree to which notions of empowerment, equity and participation can be operationalised. Service structures, operational policy and systems influence the delivery of services, and the culture of the organisation itself can often set the tone with respect to the integration of empowerment practices (Connolly & Ward 2010). It is when institutions function in disempowering and inequitable ways that mountain-moving theories come to the fore, safeguarding the interests of clients and providing both analytical critique and practical ways of increasing service responsiveness.

Conclusion

As we have seen with other theoretical frameworks explored in previous chapters, it is clear that mountain-moving theories have evolved and developed in response to contemporary issues and concerns. They reflect a strong focus on social reform and social justice and, as a set of ideas, have provided a critical edge to social work practice over time. Like other theoretical constructs, mountain-moving theories cannot be applied uncritically or indiscriminately. Their application needs to be cognisant of social work's interpretive lenses and the need to reflect carefully upon practice, something to which we will turn in our closing chapter.

Useful resources

Allan, J., Briskman, L. & Pease, B. 2009. *Critical Social Work: Theories and Practices for a Socially Just World.* Sydney: Allen & Unwin.

Reichert, E. 2007. *Challenges in Human Rights: A Social Work Perspective.* New York: Columbia University Press.

United Nations, http://www.un.org.

8 Reflective practice and theory

Throughout this book, we have explored the ways in which we bring theory to our practice as social workers. This process is a complex and continuing one. As theoretical understandings change and develop over time, and as service systems change, we develop our understandings, practice wisdom and insights. In Chapter 1, we talked about social work's reflective interpretive lens, and we have referred to the importance of reflection in practice as we have explored theoretically informed ways of working. In recent years, the concept of reflective and reflexive practice has emerged strongly within social work discourses as the complexity of the client and worker-in-situation has been at the forefront of professional concern (Davys & Beddoe 2010; Ingram et al. 2014; Sheppard 1998). Social work as a profession has been strong in emphasising both the need for more formalised reflective practice and the opportunities that social work supervision presents to consider how practice can be improved through processes of critical reflection.

In this chapter, we look at the skills involved in critical reflection and how social work as a profession benefits from engaging in reflective and reflexive, theoretically informed practice. We also look at how supervision can be one way to support optimal practice.

Reflective and reflexive practice

The notion of social work reflexivity traces its development from two main areas: the seminal works of Schön (1983, 1987), which provide the groundwork for understanding reflective practice in action; and the sociological writings of Bourdieu (1990) and Giddens (1984). Central to Schön's work around reflective practice is the notion that professionals do not respond to complex situations using 'technical rationality' in the application of theory and technique derived from scientific knowledge to solve difficult problems. Theory can help only so much, and beyond this point the skilled practitioner uses 'professional artistry' to help them respond to unique, uncertain and conflicted situations within practice (Schön 1987: 22). This artistry, or the art of practice, can be developed by a process of action and reflection. Reinforcing the importance of reflection and mindfulness in culturally responsive supervision, Bessarab (2013: 87) notes:

> Reflection is an important process in supervision, as it can help us to understand why we do what we do, thus providing insight that can aid the process of learning … Applying mindfulness to supervision is to pay attention in a particular way to what is going on in the present moment, be accepting and non-judgemental …

The process of action and reflection is familiar to social workers, and is often used as a strategy in supervision as a worker reflects upon their work, the consequences of their intervention and how it could have been undertaken differently.

In more recent years, notions of reflective practice have been enriched by a growing interest in reflexivity and reflexive social work. While reflective practice 'refers more to a process of reflection upon professional practice which leads to practice improvement through examining (and resolving) hidden gaps between espoused thinking, and the often contradictory thinking implied in actual practice' (Askeland & Fook 2009: 290), reflexivity is a process by which the worker's thinking influences the action – which then influences the situation and subsequent interpretations of and responses to it. This enables a more sophisticated critical analysis of practice: 'the ability to locate oneself in a situation through the recognition of how actions and interpretations, social and cultural background and personal history, emotional aspects of experience, and personally held assumptions and values influence the situation' (Fook 1999: 199).

Whereas reflective practice is primarily about reflecting upon what happened – the outcome, what could have been done differently – critical reflection, or reflexive practice, adopts a more 'critical' stance, which is hinted at by Fook's definition above. The practitioner deliberately reflects on how these issues identified in reflective practice translate into power in our interactions with clients: through maintaining the status quo for people, oppressing or marginalising them further, or leading to liberating and transformative outcomes. Critical reflection or reflexive practice can be diagrammatically conceptualised as a circular process of critical action-reflection (see Figure 8.1). Within this conceptualisation, critical reflection moves beyond reflection by introducing a reflexive analysis of power and its dynamics.

The notion of social work reflexivity can also trace its history from the sociological literature, in particular the work of Bourdieu (see Bourdieu & Wacquant 1992) and Giddens (1984). According to Giddens (1984: 282): 'The knowledgeability

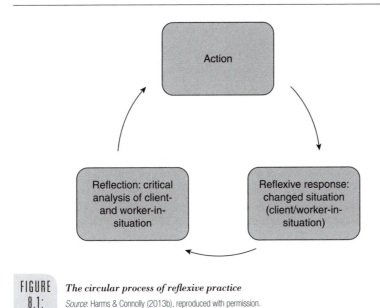

FIGURE
8.1:
The circular process of reflexive practice
Source: Harms & Connolly (2013b), reproduced with permission.

of human actors is always bounded on the one hand by the unconscious and on the other by unacknowledged conditions/unintended consequences of action.' Within this analysis, the awareness of the context of interaction also promotes the awareness of reflexivity to influence and/or control the interactional direction of the work. This is important, as it also captures the potential for unintended consequences to inadvertently influence practice adversely and unconsciously.

Fundamentally, reflective practice and critical reflection are about understanding and improving our use of self in professional practice. A reflexive process is triggered by a response to interactions within the environment. It gives rise to the concepts of transference and counter-transference that we explored in Chapter 4, and can be also seen as an everyday, normal and expected process that is inextricably related to notions of the self and the influence of the self on the work that we undertake in practice. We can understand the notion of self in at least three ways by drawing on the work of Kondrat (1999). Kondrat (1999: 468) encourages us to think about three conceptualisations:

- a *simple consciousness*, which makes our experience and memory possible
- a *reflective awareness*, which relies on a sense of self who has the experience
- a *reflexive awareness*, which is not about standing back, objectively, but knowing because 'I am on more or less familiar terms with the self'.

Increasingly, within the social work literature, writers have promoted the notion of the *reflexive practitioner* as being socially aware of this worker–client set of dynamics. Sheppard (1998: 767) captures this dynamic complexity:

> The notion of reflexivity emphasises the social worker (i) as an active thinker, one able to assess, respond and initiate action, and (ii) as a social actor, one who actually participates in the situation with which they are concerned in the conduct of their practice. Thus the reflexive practitioner, in practical terms, is one: who is aware of the socially situated relationship with their client(s), i.e. with a clear understanding of their role and purpose; who understands themselves as a participant whose actions and interactions are part of the social work process; who is capable of analysing situations and evidence, with an awareness of the way their own participation affects this process; who is able to identify the intellectual and practice processes involved in assessment and intervention; who is aware of the assumptions underlying the ways they 'make sense' of practice situations; and who is able to do so in relation to the nature and purposes of their practice.

This interrogation of the worker and client in situation has become a hallmark of reflexive practice. Our own background, and all of its familial, social and cultural assumptions, along with our professional agendas and cultural thinking, inform who we are and how we respond as practitioners.

An important space for reflecting upon and understanding the client and worker in situation is supervision, a practice to which we will return later in the chapter. Other professional checks and balances that provide us with reflective opportunities include our professional practice standards and our theories, practice conduct and interpretive lens (see Figure 8.2). These provide an ethical scaffold for professional practice.

Professional standards and their expectations

Consistency with social work's professional standards is important to the development of ethically informed practice. Professional bodies provide broad ethical guidelines for professional practice conduct that include:

- the kinds of expectations that the client should reasonably expect of the worker–client relationship
- the knowledge and competencies that are expected of a social worker
- the social worker's appropriate use of the personal self and personal attributes in practice
- transparent processes of accountability

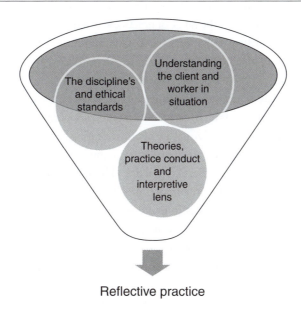

Reflective practice

FIGURE
8.2:   *Areas of reflective interrogation*

- an expectation that a social worker will be involved in macro change – the application of the social justice interpretive lens in practice
- the expectation that the social worker will use their knowledge to advocate for clients
- a commitment to ethical standards as well as a commitment to the strengthening of competencies (AASW 2013; ANZASW 2008).

Depending on the professional body, practice standards may also include more in-depth accountability expectations, including sensitivity to issues of sexism and racism, a commitment to culturally responsive practice, and the development of services that support the interest of diverse cultural groups (AASW 2013).

Theory, practice and our interpretive lenses

Throughout this book, we have drawn upon a number of theoretical perspectives that help us to understand the nature of human experience and the ways in which social work might helpfully respond. Beddoe and Egan (2009) argue that these theories also help us to reflect upon practice, sharpening our critical lens as we work with people across the range of practice settings. For example, they note the importance of critical social work perspectives informing critically reflective practice, providing insight into the ways in which people experience oppression and disadvantage at both the personal and structural levels. This critical perspective forms the basis of progressive approaches to practice explored in Chapter 7, a perspective that supports an overt commitment to social reform and change.

Understanding the pervasive nature of self-defeating beliefs (Beddoe & Egan 2009) – beliefs that we can see are drawn from cognitive theories (Chapter 5) – is also important to critically reflective practice. These insights into the subordinate positioning of roles stress the importance of remaining vigilant to the ways in which these dynamics play out in practice. This resonates with postmodernist and narrative ways of thinking, which also provide useful insights that can inform reflective practice, supporting notions of constructed realities and how language and communication play a part in constructing social contexts and realities (Chapter 6).

These are just some of the ways in which theory helps us to bring critically reflective elements to social work practice, elements in which 'links are made between personal and structural power; a commitment is made to unearth and unsettle those factors that sustain dominant power; [and exploring] ways in which personal and collective power can be used to facilitate social change' (Beddoe & Egan 2009: 419).

Returning to social work's interpretive lenses (Chapter 1), we can see the ways in which they also provide opportunities for critical reflection. Our social justice critical lens most strongly resonates with Beddoe and Egan's (2009) analysis of critically reflective theory. Testing practice against the key imperatives of the social justice lens will help to strengthen the application of critical practice and moderate elements that may work against social reform and change. Our relational lens, the ways in which we understand change in human systems and the emphasis we place on understanding cultural thinking – in essence, the importance of reflective practice – provide us with a unique disciplinary perspective supporting critical reflection in practice. These insights have also contributed to the development of critically reflective practices within supervision.

Critical reflection and supervision

The social work profession has a long-standing commitment to supervision as a means of supporting good practice. It is one of the key spaces in which we can critically reflect on practice thinking and action, and better understand what we bring to our work. Supervision has been described as 'a process occurring within a professional relationship in which one person, the supervisor, assists the other person, the supervisee, to reflect on and explore practice issues in order to develop and maintain competence in their social work practice' (Beddoe & Egan 2009: 411).

Engaging in a supervised relationship is one way of ensuring that our professional support needs are met and that we continue to learn and develop our practice skills and expertise. Although many professions have supervision as a component of their practice, social work has developed unique emphases. As Harms (2007: 102) notes:

> At its best, supervision can provide a safe learning environment; a place to test out new ideas and integrate them into practice. It can provide a place to integrate theory and practice, and the personal and the professional. Supervisees can deal with both the ongoing accumulation of work issues, as well as gain support around particular crises.

The limited research that is available in relation to the impact of supervision suggests that it is a key component of employee satisfaction and worker retention (Carroll 1996; Carroll & Gilbert 2006; Holloway & Neufeldt 1995).

Typically, supervision is provided by a more senior social worker within the agency, and happens as a regular activity in a structured format, such as an hour per week, during which time other distractions of the workplace are minimised. The process of supervision can be highly structured, with an agenda and agreed goals, or it can be a relatively unstructured, responsive space, which offers debriefing and support to workers in the context of their current workload. Supervision often occurs informally too, both in terms of timing and with regard to who provides the supervisory input.

Kadushin's (1972) writings on supervision in the 1970s form an important cornerstone for social workers' thinking about supervision. He outlines three functions of social work supervision: the administrative function, the educative function and the supportive function. These remain important to today's supervision practices.

By administrative function, supervision provides a method of accountability: typically regarding the worker's accountability to the organisation through monitoring caseload issues, but also reciprocally through monitoring workload and the worker's capacities and issues within the organisation. A skilled supervisor can help a practitioner to understand what is working well and not so well in practice, and help the worker reflect on ways forward. There are nevertheless challenges in this administrative function, and later in this chapter we will discuss the concerns of social workers about the increased surveillance role of supervision over and above its more supportive and educative functions.

The educational function or focus of supervision relates to the ways in which learning and development can occur within a relationship and across the agency setting. This may be through formal inputs, such as the provision of relevant reading or training, or through more informal means, such as modelling and observing (Trevithick 2012). Support has probably been the most distinctive function to social work. Through having a space to reflect on practice, to learn and to debrief, supervision is ideally an important source of support and encouragement (Kadushin 1972). Supervision can provide a safe place for emotional reactions to be expressed and explored, and for strategies to be shared in relation to coping with practice issues.

Elements of successful supervisory relationships

Like all relationships, many factors come into play in determining whether a supervisory relationship is a productive, enduring and trusting one. Some of the factors that have been identified as critical to the success of supervisory relationships include:

- clear expectations and goals
- commonality of practice approaches
- goodness of fit with respect to personality and learning styles
- safety and trust, given that there are often high levels of personal and professional disclosure
- organisational support, reflected in the valuing of supervision as a protected component of the work.

Supporting this, according to Bruce and Austin (2000), satisfying outcomes in supervision occur when the agency is supportive in a context where expectations are clear and transparent; where there is supervisory leadership based on competency and clarity of role; and when workers feel supported by their supervisors.

Supervision is nevertheless a political encounter, both within the immediacy of the relationship between supervisor and supervisee and, perhaps more perilously, within the wider organisational context. Numerous social workers in Australia, New Zealand and the United States have identified the way in which supervision is increasingly changing focus because of the wider 'risk society' in which social work is being practised (Noble & Irwin 2009). A 'risk society' focus has arisen in response to increasing managerialism and the perceptions that uncertainties should and can be managed. Some of the influencing trends within the context of increased managerialism are increases in risk assessment checklists and accountabilities, and far tighter oversight of practices. As Beddoe (2010: 1280) notes, this has consequences for how supervision is regarded: 'The current preoccupation with oversight of practice has arguably strengthened the mandate for supervision; however, there is concern this might threaten its integrity as a learning-focused activity.'

With increasing pressures on workplaces, protecting the place of supervision has proven more difficult in some workplace contexts. Increasing managerialism has led to increasing pressures on the accountability aspects of supervision, sometimes at the cost of the educational and support functions. As a way of ameliorating this, some social workers engage in supervision outside the workplace, and in some instances this is financially and principally supported by the agency. For many workers, this provides a safe space outside the busy environment of work and the politics of the workplace to explore their personal and professional development. Some argue, however, that this arrangement is problematic, in that the supervision can become disconnected from all three aspects considered core: education, support and administration. Thompson (2002) identifies that mediation is also an important aspect of supervision – for example, if excessively high workloads are compromising good practice standards. If this information is lost to the organisation, change within the agency cannot occur. In addition, workplace relationships are less able to be addressed through supervision.

Supervision models

Many supervision models have been designed to support supervision practice. As we noted earlier, supervisors draw upon social work theories to inform their supervisory practice. Specific models of supervision have also been developed to support specialist areas of practice – for example, in child protection (e.g. see Connolly & Morris 2011) – and we will now draw upon these ideas to illustrate the ways in which a systems analysis can inform a reflective process of supervision.

Systems-informed supervision

The systems-informed model outlined in this section has been adapted from a systemic framework used to explore practice outcomes in the context of reviewing child deaths (Connolly & Doolan 2007). It works on the basis that solutions to confounding issues in practice are more likely to be found across a range of system domains. It is often easy to assume that a lack of progress in practice relates to the client's inability to change – they are resistant, or their problems are simply too complex. The systems model of supervision suggests ways of moving beyond this one-dimensional approach – not just that we look at the client system, but also that we expand our thinking to include interfacing systems: the worker system, the agency system and the wider community system. At one time or another, most practitioners have found themselves constrained and unable to find a way to break through complex practice issues. While barriers to progress may indeed rest within the client system, the systems-informed model suggests that difficulties could just as easily be located in dynamics across the worker–client system, or the agency or wider community system. This is where a systemic analysis encourages us to consider a broader set of possibilities that includes client factors, worker factors, agency factors and community factors (see Figure 8.3). We will now consider each of these factors and the ways in which they can provide reflective practice insights.

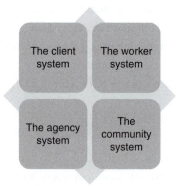

FIGURE 8.3: *A systems model of reflective practice in supervision*
Source: Connolly & Doolan (2007), adapted with permission.

The client system

A client's response to professional intervention can be influenced by a range of factors. For example, their history of professional involvement may present difficulties in creating trust within the client–worker relationship. They may have a history of trauma or may be experiencing abusive experiences in the here and now. These are factors that can inhibit a person's ability to move forward in their lives. Alternatively, there may be issues relating to the way they perceive the world: cultural thinking that constrains their ability to think more broadly about solutions, or irrational beliefs that require different approaches to resolve them. Examples of reflective questioning that enable an exploration of the client system quadrant may include:

- What has been going on for this person or family so far?
- Are there any particularly complex factors that constrain progress?
- What is the client's perception of the issues?
- Are we working at the client's pace?

The worker system

Berlin (2002) notes that we have a 'mixture of motives' when practising social work. We are expected to engage, while also maintaining a degree of distance – or at least stepping back – so that we can understand the dynamics within and across the client's system. This 'requires us to balance openness, spontaneity, and involvement with professional discipline' (Berlin 2002: 269). Parallel worker–client experiences can increase a worker's insight, or they can create reflexive responses that interfere with a worker's ability to see things clearly or to confront issues when necessary. For example, Shulman (1993: 190) notes that 'analysis of worker practice often reveals moments when workers felt like confronting a client but did not because of their own discomfort'. Prematurely shutting down difficult conversations that may have been helpful in exploring issues is an example of this. Reflective questions that help to explore the dynamics within the worker system may be:

- Do parallels exist in terms of the client's and the worker's experience?
- Is the worker sympathetic to the client's issues?
- Is there a good match of worker style, knowledge and level of skill?
- Are there factors that inhibit the worker's response?

The agency system

As we noted earlier, organisational systems and mandates can influence the way in which practice is undertaken within agencies. Beddoe and Maidment (2009: 26) note the limitations that managerialist approaches can have on advocacy efforts: 'Managerialist language associated with achieving key performance indicators, managing risk and avoiding legal liability tends now to overshadow principal social work concerns relating to addressing client oppression and poverty.' When a practice system has been subjected to efficiency drivers that reflect an 'assess and close the case as soon as possible' mode, it can become an entrenched culture of practice over time. Alternatively, the agency mandate might be misaligned with the client's concerns. For example, a worker in a Christian organisation may be inhibited in their exploration of issues relating to sexuality or a client's choices in terms of continuing with a pregnancy.

Creating opportunities for reflective dialogue and exploring the ways in which the organisation helps or hinders practice creates opportunities to do some things differently. Reflective questions might include:

- How does the organisation view the client's problem?
- How would colleagues within the agency see the way forward?
- Is there a domination of compliance targets over good practice expectations?
- Is this the right agency for this particular client – is it a good cultural fit?

The community system

Across the community system, there may be many differing views about the problems confronting the client and the ways in which the client should be responded to. Community beliefs are often reinforced by media generalisations, causing clients to feel alienated within their communities. Also, professionals across the sector may differ in their opinions about the ways in which a service or worker should best respond to the client. These differences can serve to undermine interventions – for example, if an influential professional challenges the value of counselling or professional help. Reflective questions exploring the wider community system may include:

- Are there competing ideologies that influence the client's view of the intervention?
- Who else knows about the work being done, and are they supportive of the intervention pathway?
- Are external factors influencing decision-making?

There have been many models of supervision, developed over time, that seek to support practitioners working in complex areas of practice. The systems model of supervision that we have discussed here provides a means by which factors relating to the work with clients can be reflected upon with a view to strengthening practice insight and action.

Culturally responsive supervision

The ways in which supervision may be seen as promoting and maintaining a colonising Western world-view have been raised by writers supporting culturally responsive supervision (Bessarab 2013; Elkington 2014). The monocultural lens of Western practice can be a barrier to the exploration of sensitive cultural issues and practices. From an Australian perspective, Bessarab (2013: 73) questions the use of the term itself: '"supervision" is an anathema to Aboriginal ways of working and knowing, and is itself based on a colonizing Western Enlightenment world-view that needs challenging.' She argues the need to push the boundaries in ways that will enable an Indigenous perspective to flourish. Using Indigenous ways of knowing within the supervision context provides culturally safe and effective support for Aboriginal workers, shifting supervision from a colonising process. She proposes a culturally appropriate supervision framework that focuses on key issues: sovereignty, relationships, land and beliefs (Bessarab 2013: 86):

- Sovereignty sub-elements include notions of connectedness and belonging, custodianship and Native Title, politics and child removal.
- Relationships sub-elements include notions of family and community, and issues of colonisation, as well as the obligations and reciprocal relationships.
- Land sub-elements include notions of identity and language, lore and ceremony, health, respect, authority and spirituality.
- Beliefs sub-elements include racism and class and gender positioning, the importance of context and the Stolen Generations.

Further, four pillars underpin the framework: control, power, history and social justice support. These interact with the elements and sub-elements. So, for example, control is considered in the context of sovereignty, relationships, land and beliefs, and in the sub-elements of each – for example, connectedness, family, identity/language and stolen generations.

Writers in Aotearoa New Zealand have similarly supported culturally responsive supervision processes, and in particular *Kaupapa Māori* supervision (Elkington 2014). This builds upon Professor Linda Tuhiwai Smith's seminal book *Decolonizing Methodologies* (Smith 1999), and Professor Mason Durie's critically influential *whare tapa wha* model of Māori health (1994 and 1998), discussed in Chapter 2. *Kaupapa Māori* supervision has been defined as:

> either a formal or informal relationship between members of the same culture, with the purpose being to ensure that the supervisee is practising according to the values, protocols and practices of that particular culture. It is about cultural accountability and cultural development. (Walsh-Tapiata & Webster 2004: 32)[1]

Walsh-Tapiata and Webster also mirror Durie's *whare tapa wha* model (see Chapter 2) of Māori well-being to inform a supervision model. Four quadrants are explored, across four areas of well-being, to identify life goals and work aspirations: *wairua goals* (the spiritual dimension); *tinana goals* (physical well-being); *hinengaro goals* (emotional and mental dimension); and *whānau goals* (family and extended family dimension). The exploration of the well-being dimensions helps 'to ensure safe practice and promote professional development and accountability' (Walsh-Tapiata & Webster 2004: 37).

Although a relatively recent development, culturally responsive models of supervision provide rich and vibrant opportunities to support workers in ways that strengthen cultural knowledge and practice.

Conclusion

One of the main purposes of reflective practice is to create better outcomes for clients. It provides a means through which we can both increase our awareness of our interpretive lenses, including our cultural assumptions, and explore ways of counteracting their effects if they are detrimental to the people with whom we work. This is critical for ensuring good practice outcomes, whereby the needs and rights of clients can be fully responded to rather than obscured by the views of a social worker and/or the systems in which we work. As Kondrat (1999: 468) notes, 'As individuals and as professionals, social workers' daily interactions with clients and others have consequences for maintaining or altering society's structures.' Reflection and critical reflection enable us to build a bridge between our personal and our professional selves, and to gain insight into the ways in which this integrated self influences practice. Social work is an emotionally confronting profession. We are often involved in people's lives when there is violence, distress, illness and/or despair. Our work can arouse strong physical and emotional reactions, 'such as intense sadness and distress, or anger and frustration. Some experiences can be overwhelming and evoke a sense of helplessness or powerlessness' (Harms 2007: 97). Although it is tempting to push these feelings aside, research has shown that we are far more effective practitioners when we can integrate these experiences. Engaging in processes of critical reflection enables us to build a bridge between social work theory and practice (Payne 2005), and ultimately to support the development of more creative and innovative practice responses.

Useful resources

Davys, A. & Beddoe, L. 2010. *Best Practice in Professional Supervision: A Guide for the Helping Professions.* London: Jessica Kingsley.

Scerra, N. 2011. *Models of Supervision for Aboriginal Staff: A Review of the Literature.* Social Justice Unit, Uniting Care. Research Paper #4. http:// childrenyoungpeopleandfamilies. org.au/__data/assets/pdf_ file/0004/74227/Research_Paper_ Supervision_Models_for_Aboriginal_ Staff.pdf.

Social Work Now. 2008. Supervision special issue, vol. 40 (August). http:// www.cyf.govt.nz/documents/about- us/publications/social-work-now/ social-work-now-40-aug08.pdf.

Note

1 The authors note that they have adapted this definition from CYPFS Risk Management Project, 30 June 1998, p. 11.

Concluding thoughts

As we have brought together this second edition, it is clear that social work theory is constantly evolving to meet the needs of contemporary practice. Over more than a hundred years of social work, our profession has sought to establish itself through the development of a knowledge base for practice.

As we noted in Chapter 1, the theories we have considered are not the sole purview of the social work profession. Other professional groups use them in a wide range of practice areas. We have nevertheless argued throughout the chapters of this book that, by adopting various theories, social work has integrated key professional ideas and concerns: an interpretive lens that has made them unmistakably social work theories. We have explored the way in which social work has used a relational lens to reinforce the importance of engaging with people and their concerns. Relationship-building as a foundation upon which we can more deeply understand human troubles has long been a hallmark of good social work practice. Yet we have seen times when this commitment to relationship has the potential to undermine our advocacy and social justice role. There are inevitable tensions when social workers have powers that can be used to influence clients' behaviour, either overtly or covertly. Our social justice and reflective lenses require that we consider carefully the ways in which we influence both the rights and the needs of the people with whom we work. They compel us to interrogate our practices in 'power-sensitive' ways (Beckett 2006). Our understanding of change and the importance of building on strengths is added to these interpretive lenses, providing a rich kaleidoscope that colours the theories we use in important ways. Berlin's (2002) integrative perspective, which we discussed in Chapter 5, is a good example of the way in which a social work theorist and clinician has integrated cognitive-behavioural ideas into a social work theory for practice. Berlin's social work adaptation is recognisably different from cognitive-behavioural responses applied by other disciplines. It is the social work interpretive lens that makes this difference.

As we have explored each of the theoretical perspectives, we have noted their strengths and challenges. Like any other set of ideas, social work theories are developed in particular contexts of time and place. The majority of the theories have been drawn from clinical and political movements within Anglo traditions, and many have gendered implications. In the Prelude, Shawana Andrews signals the ways in which theoretical perspectives can be colonising perspectives. This requires that we think carefully about their application in practice. It does not necessarily mean that we can assume that they are not suitable. But it does mean we need to appraise their suitability critically, and also work on developing alternative responses that enrich practice in ways that better suit cultural context, time and place. In the Foreword and Prelude to this edition, Yvonne Crichton-Hill and Shawana Andrews remind us that social workers come to the profession with diverse cultural identities. As a discipline, we need to encourage and embrace new ways of social work theorising that reflect this rich diversity.

In writing this book, we set out to capture the richness of theory development in social work over decades of theorising. Theories will continue to evolve and change, and social workers will continue to challenge them while striving to create interventions that meet the diversity of human need. In doing so, practitioners will make sure that social work's theoretical perspectives remain relevant to contemporary concerns over the next century of practice.

References

Adams, R. 2008. *Empowerment, Participation and Social Work*, 4th edn. Basingstoke: Palgrave Macmillan.

Ainsworth, M.S. 1985. Attachment: Retrospect and prospect. In *Infant–Mother Attachment: The Origins and Developmental Significance of Individual Differences in Strange Situation Behavior*, ed. M. Lamb. Hillsdale, NJ: Lawrence Erlbaum, pp. 3–27.

Aldgate, J. & McIntosh, M. 2006. *Looking After the Family: A Study of Children Looked After in Kinship Care in Scotland*. Edinburgh: Social Work Inspection Agency.

Alfred, T. 2013. Being and becoming Indigenous: Resurgence against contemporary colonialism. The Narrm Oration, University of Melbourne, 12 December. Retrieved 9 December 2014, https://www.youtube.com/watch?v=VwJNy-B3lPA.

Allen, J. 2003. Childhood attachment trauma and adulthood psychopathology. *The Menninger Clinic Lecture Series*. Melbourne: Cairnmillar Institute.

—— 2009. Doing critical social work. In *Critical Social Work: Theories and Practices for a Socially Just World*, 2nd edn, eds J. Allan, L. Briskman & B. Pease. Sydney: Allen & Unwin, pp. 70–87.

Andrews, S., Murray, N. & Torrens, C. 2012. Billibellary's Walk, The University of Melbourne. Murrup Barak Melbourne Institute of Indigenous Development. Retrieved 15 December 2014, http://www.murrupbarak.unimelb.edu.au/content/pages/billibellarys-walk.

Aotearoa New Zealand Association of Social Workers (ANZASW). 2008. *ANZASW Competency Handbook*. Christchurch: ANZASW.

Arnstein, S. 1969. A ladder of citizen participation. *Journal of the American Institute of Planners*, 35(4): 216–24.

Askeland, G. & Fook, J. 2009. Editorial: Critical reflection in social work. *European Journal of Social Work*, 12(3): 287–92.

Assman, J. 1995. Collective memory and cultural identity. *New German Critique*, 65: 125–33.

Atkinson, J. 2002. *Trauma Trails, Recreating Song Lines: The Transgenerational Effects of Trauma in Indigenous Australia*. Melbourne: Spinifex Press.

Atwool, N. 2005. Working with adults who are parenting. In *Social Work Theories in Action*, eds M. Nash, R. Munford & K. O'Donoghue. London: Jessica Kingsley, pp. 223–38.

Augusta-Scott, T. 2007. Challenging essentialist anti-oppressive discourse: Uniting against racism and sexism. In *Narrative Therapy: Making Meaning, Making Lives*, eds C. Brown & T. Augusta-Scott. Thousand Oaks, CA: Sage, pp. 211–28.

Austin, D. 1983. The Flexner myth and the history of social work. *Social Service Review*, 57(3): 357–77.

Australian Association of Social Workers (AASW). 2013. *Practice Standards*. Canberra: AASW.

—— 2014. Guideline 1.1 – Guidance on essential core curriculum content. In *AASW Education and Accreditation Standards*. Retrieved 11 April 2015, http://www.aasw.asn.au/careers-study/education-standards-accreditation.

Australian Child and Adolescent Trauma, Loss and Grief Network. 2011. Disaster and mass adversities. Retrieved 30 May 2011, http://www.earlytraumagrief.anu.edu.au/resource_hubs/disasters_children/psychological_first_aid.

Bacon, H. & Richardson, S. 2001. Attachment theory and child abuse: An overview of the literature for practitioners. *Child Abuse Review*, 10(6): 377–97.

Baird, J. & Sokol, B. (eds) 2004. *Connections Between Theory of Mind and Sociomoral Development*. San Francisco: Jossey-Bass.

Bankoff, G., Frerks, G. & Hilhorst, D. (eds). 2004. *Mapping Vulnerability: Disasters, Development and People*. London: Earthscan.

Bateson, G. 2002. *Mind and Nature: A Necessary Unity*. Toronto: Bantam Books.

Beck, A.T., Rush, A.J., Shaw, B.F. & Emery, G. 1979. *Cognitive Therapy of Depression*. New York: Guilford Press.

Beckett, C. 2006. *Essential Theory for Social Work Practice*. London: Sage.

Beddoe, L. 2010. Surveillance or reflection: Professional supervision in 'the risk society'. *British Journal of Social Work*, 40: 1279–96.

Beddoe, L. & Egan, R. 2009. Social work supervision. In *Social Work: Contexts and Practice*, 2nd edn, eds M. Connolly & L. Harms. Melbourne: Oxford University Press, pp. 410–22.

Beddoe, L. & Maidment, J. 2009. *Mapping Knowledge for Social Work Practice: Critical Intersections*. Melbourne: Cengage.

Beels, C. 2009. Some historical conditions of narrative work. *Family Process*, 48: 363–78.

Bennett, B., Green, S. & Bessarab, D. (eds). 2012. *Our Voices: Aboriginal and Torres Strait Islander Social Work*. Melbourne: Palgrave Macmillan.

Bennett, L. 2010. Lou Bennett – Indigenous Deep Listening Project. Retrieved 10 December 2014, https://www.youtube.com/watch?v=NnOSM7ZYeUI.

Berlin, S. 2002. *Clinical Social Work Practice: A Cognitive-Integrative Perspective*. New York: Oxford University Press.

Bertalanffy, L. 1968. *General System Theory: Foundations, Development, Applications*. New York: George Brazillier.

Berzoff, J., Flanagan, L. & Hertz, P. 2008. *Inside Out and Outside In: Psychodynamic Clinical Theory and Psychopathology in Contemporary Multicultural Contexts*, 2nd edn. Lanham, MD: Jason Aronson.

Bessarab, D. 2012. Yarning – A culturally safe method of Indigenous conversation. PowerPoint presentation, Aboriginal Health Education Research Unit, Centre for Health Innovation and Research Institute (CHIRI), Curtin University of Technology. Retrieved 9 December 2014, http://www.dtsc.com.au/wp-content/ … /Dementia-Yarning-Presentation-310712.pdf.

—— 2013. The supervisory yarn: Embedding Indigenous epistemology in supervision. In *Our Voices: Aboriginal and Torres Strait Islander Social Work*, eds B. Bennett, S. Green, S. Gilbert & D. Bessarab. Melbourne: Palgrave Macmillan, pp. 73–92.

Bessarab, D., Green, S., Jones, V., Stratton, K., Young, S. & Zubrycki, J. 2014. *Getting It Right – Creating Partnerships for Change: Integrating Aboriginal and Torres Strait Islander Knowledges in Social Work Education and Practice*. Teaching and Learning Framework 2014. Canberra: Office for Learning and Teaching.

Bishop, B.J., Higgins, D., Casella, F., & Contos, N. 2002. Reflections on practice: Ethics, race, and worldviews. *Journal of Community Psychology*, 30(6): 611–21.

Boulanger, G. 2012. Psychoanalytic witnessing: Professional obligation or moral imperative? *Psychoanalytic Psychology*, 29(3): 318–24.

Bourdieu, P. 1990. *Language and Symbolic Power*. Cambridge: Polity Press.

Bourdieu, P. & Wacquant, L. 1992. *An Invitation to Reflexive Sociology*. Chicago: University of Chicago Press.

Bowes, J.M. & Hayes, A. (eds) 1999. *Children, Families, and Communities: Contexts and Consequences*. Melbourne: Oxford University Press.

Bowlby, J. 1984. *Attachment*. London: Penguin.

Breckenridge, J. & Laing, L. (eds) 1999. *Challenging Silence: Innovative Responses to Sexual and Domestic Violence*. Sydney: Allen & Unwin.

Briskman, L. 2007. *Social Work with Indigenous Communities*. Sydney: Federation Press.

—— 2014. *Social Work with Indigenous Communities: A Human Rights Approach*, 2nd edn. Sydney: Federation Press.

Briskman, L. & Fiske, L. 2009. Working with refugees. In *Social Work: Contexts and Practice*, 2nd edn, eds M. Connolly & L. Harms. Melbourne: Oxford University Press, pp. 135–48.

Briskman, L., Pease, B. & Allan, J. 2009. Introducing critical theories for social work in a neo-liberal context. In *Critical Social Work: Theories and Practices for a Socially Just World*, 2nd edn, eds J. Allan, L. Briskman & B. Pease, pp. 3–14. Sydney: Allen & Unwin.

Bromfield, L.M., Higgins, J.R., Richardson, N. & Higgins, D.J. 2007. Why standard assessment processes are culturally inappropriate. Paper 3 in *Promising Practices in Out-of-Home Care for Aboriginal and Torres Strait Islander Carers and Young People: Strengths and Barriers*. Retrieved 30 May 2011, http://www.aifs.gov.au/nch/pubs/reports/promisingpractices/summarypapers/paper3.pdf.

Bronfenbrenner, U. 1979. *The Ecology of Human Development: Experiments by Nature and Design*. Cambridge, MA: Harvard University Press.

Bronson, D.E. & Thyer, B.A. 2001. Behavioral social work: Where has it been and where is it going? *Behavior Analyst Today*, 2(3): 192–5.

Brown, C. 2007. Situating knowledge and power in the therapeutic alliance. In *Narrative Therapy: Making Meaning, Making Lives*, eds C. Brown & T. Augusta-Scott. Thousand Oaks, CA: Sage, pp. 3–22.

Brown, C. & Augusta-Scott, T. (eds). 2007. *Narrative Therapy: Making Meaning, Making Lives*. Thousand Oaks, CA: Sage.

Bruce, E. & Austin, M. 2000. Social work supervision: Assessing the past and mapping the future. *Clinical Supervisor*, 19(2): 85–107.

Burchall, A. & Green, J. 2014. 'You just don't want to offend': Decolonising social work practices in remote Central Australia. Presentation to Joint World Conference on Social Work, Education and Social Development, Melbourne, July. Retrieved 6 December 2014, http://eposters.swsd2014.org/posters.

Burstow, B. 1992. *Radical Feminist Therapy: Working in the Context of Violence*. Newbury Park, CA: Sage.

Caplan, G. 1990. Loss, stress and mental health. *Community Mental Health Journal*, 26(1): 27–48.

Carey, M., Walther, S. & Russell, S. 2009. The absent but implicit: A map to support therapeutic enquiry. *Family Process*, 48: 319–31.

Carrey, N. 2007. Practicing psychiatry through a narrative lens: Working with children, youth and families. In *Narrative Therapy: Making Meaning, Making Lives*, eds C. Brown & T. Augusta-Scott. Thousand Oaks, CA: Sage, pp. 77–104.

Carroll, M. 1996. *Counselling Supervision: Theory, Skills and Practice*. London: Cassell.

Carroll, M. & Gilbert, M. 2006. *On Being a Supervisee: Creating Learning Partnerships*. London: Vukani.

Cassidy, J. & Shaver, P.R. (eds). 1999. *Handbook of Attachment: Theory, Research and Clinical Applications*. London: Guilford.

Chaffin, M. & Friedrich, B. 2004. Evidence-based treatments in child abuse and neglect. *Children and Youth Services Review*, 26: 1097–13.

Chamberlain, L. 1995. Strange attractors in patterns of family interaction. In *Chaos Theory in Psychology and the Life Sciences*, eds R. Robertson & A. Combs. Mahwah, NJ: Lawrence Erlbaum, pp. 267–74.

Charon, R. (2006), *Narrative Medicine: Honoring the Stories of Illness*. New York: Oxford University Press.

Chodorow, N. 1999. *The Power of Feelings: Personal Meaning in Psychoanalysis, Gender, and Culture*. New Haven, CT: Yale University Press.

Coates, D. 2010. Impact of childhood abuse: Biopsychosocial pathways through which adult mental health is compromised. *Australian Social Work*, 63(4): 391–403.

Connolly, M. 1999. *Effective Participatory Practice: Family Group Conferencing in Child Protection*. New York: Aldine de Gruyter.

—— 2003. Cultural components of practice: reflexive responses to diversity and difference. In *Sexual Deviance: Issues and Controversies*, eds T. Ward, D.R. Laws & S.M. Hudson. Thousand Oaks, CA: Sage, pp. 103–18.

—— 2004. Practice approaches. In *Practice Skills in Social Work and Welfare: More Than Just Common Sense*, eds J. Maidment & R. Egan. Sydney: Allen & Unwin, pp. 34–50.

—— 2006a. Upfront and personal: Confronting dynamics in the family group conference. *Family Process*, 45(3): 345–57.

—— 2006b. Fifteen years of Family Group Conferencing: Coordinators talk about their experiences in Aotearoa New Zealand. *British Journal of Social Work*, 36(4): 523–40.

—— 2007. Practice frameworks: Conceptual maps to guide interventions in child welfare. *British Journal of Social Work*, 37: 825–37.

Connolly, M., Crichton-Hill, Y. & Ward, T. 2006. *Culture and Child Protection: Reflexive Responses*. London: Jessica Kingsley.

Connolly, M. & Doolan, M. 2007. Responding to the deaths of children known to child protection agencies. *Social Policy Journal of New Zealand*, 30: 1–11.

Connolly, M. & Healy, K. 2013. Social work practice theories and frameworks. In *Social Work: Contexts and Practice*, 3rd edn, eds M. Connolly & L. Harms. Melbourne: Oxford University Press, pp. 19–33.

Connolly, M. & Masson, J. 2014. Private and public voices: Does family group conferencing privilege the voice of children and families in child welfare? *Journal of Social Welfare and Family Law*, 3(4): 403–14.

Connolly, M. & Morris, K. 2011. *Understanding Child and Family Welfare*. London: Palgrave.

Connolly, M. & Smith, R. 2010. Reforming *child welfare*. *Child Welfare*, 89(3): 9–31.

Connolly, M. & Ward, T. 2008a. *Morals, Rights and Practice in the Human Services: Effective and Fair Decision-Making in Health, Social Care and Criminal Justice*. London: Jessica Kingsley.

—— 2008b. Navigating human rights across the life course. *Child and Family Social Work*, 13(3): 348–56.

—— 2010. Supporting rights-based ideas in policy and practice. *Communities, Children and Families Australia*, 5(2): 6–15.

Cork, S. (ed.). 2010. *Resilience and Transformation: Preparing Australia for Uncertain Futures*. Melbourne: CSIRO.

Crotty, M. 1998. *The Foundations of Social Research: Meaning and Perspective in the Research Process*. Sydney: Allen & Unwin.

Darlington, Y., Healy, K. & Feeney, J.A. 2010. Challenges in implementing a participatory practice in child protection: A contingency approach. *Children and Youth Services Review*, 32(7): 1020–27.

Davys, A. & Beddoe, L. 2010. *Best Practice in Professional Supervision: A Guide for the Helping Professions*. London: Jessica Kingsley.

Denborough, D. (ed.). 2006. *Trauma: Narrative Responses to Traumatic Experience*. Adelaide: Dulwich Centre Publications.

—— 2008. *Collective Narrative Practice: Responding to Individuals, Groups, and Communities Who have Experienced Trauma*. Adelaide: Dulwich Centre Publications.

Denborough, D., Koolmatrie, C., Mununggirritj, D., Marika, D., Dhurrkay, W. & Yunupingu, M. 2006. Linking stories and initiatives: A narrative approach to working with the skills and knowledge of communities. *International Journal of Narrative Therapy and Community Work*, 2: 19–51.

Department of Health (UK) 2000. *Framework for the Assessment of Children in Need and Their Families*. London: Department of Health, Department for Education and Employment, Home Office. Retrieved 30 May 2011, http://www.dh.gov.uk/prod_consum_dh/groups/dh_digitalassets/@dh/@en/documents/digitalasset/dh_4014430.pdf.

De Shazer, S. 1994. *Words were Originally Magic*. New York: W.W. Norton.

Doel, M. 2002. Task-centred work. In *Social Work: Themes, Issues and Critical Debates*, 2nd edn, eds R. Adams, L. Dominelli & M. Payne. Basingstoke: Palgrave, pp. 191–208.

Dominelli, L. 2002. Anti-oppressive practice in context. In *Social Work: Themes, Issues and Critical Debates*, 2nd edn, eds R. Adams, L. Dominelli & M. Payne. New York: Palgrave, pp. 3–19.

—— 2012. *Green Social Work: From Environmental Crises to Environmental Justice*. Cambridge: Polity Press.

Doolan, M., Nixon, P. & Lawrence, P. 2004. *Growing Up in the Care of Relatives or Friends: Delivering Best Practice for Children in Family and Friends Care*. London: Family Rights Group.

Drisko, J. 2011. Researching clinical practice. In *Theory and Practice in Clinical Social Work*, 2nd edn, ed. J.R. Brandell. Thousand Oaks, CA: Sage, pp. 717–37.

Dulwich Centre Publications. 1999. *Narrative Therapy and Community Work: A Conference Collection*. Adelaide: Dulwich Centre Publications.

Durie, M. 1994. *Whaiora. Maori Health Development*. New York: Oxford University Press.

—— 1998. *Whaiora: Maori Health Development*, 2nd edn. Auckland: Oxford University Press.

Eagleton, T. 2000. *The Idea of Culture*. Oxford: Blackwell.

Edmunds, F. 2012. Making murals, revealing histories: Murals as an assertion of Aboriginality in Melbourne's inner north. In *Urban Representations: Cultural Expression, Identity and Politics*, eds S. Kleinert & G. Koch. Canberra: AIATSIS, pp. 21–49.

Edwards, M., Tinworth, K., Burford, G. & Pennell, J. 2007. *Family Team Meeting (FTM) Process, Outcome, and Impact Evaluation Phase II Report*. Englewood, CO: American Humane Association.

Egan, G. 2007. *The Skilled Helper: A Problem-Management and Opportunity-Development Approach to Helping*, 8th edn. Pacific Grove, CA: Brooks/Cole.

Elkington, J. 2014. A *Kaupapa Māori* supervision context – cultural and professional. *Aotearoa New Zealand Social Work*, 26 (1): 65–73.

Elliott, B. 2000. *Promoting Family Change: The Optimism Factor*. Sydney: Allen & Unwin.

Erikson, E. 1959. Identity and the life-cycle. *Psychological Issues. Monograph* 1(1): 1–171.

Falicov, C.J. 1995. Training to think culturally: A multi-dimensional comparative framework. *Family Process*, 34: 373–88.

Fanon, F. 1968. *Wretched of the Earth*. New York: Grove Press.

Fiske, L. & Briskman, L. 2013. Working with refugees. In *Social Work: Contexts and Practice*, 3rd edn, eds M. Connolly & L. Harms. Melbourne: Oxford University Press, pp. 151–62.

Flexner, A. 1915. *Is social work a profession? Proceedings of the National Conference of Charities and Correction 1915*. Chicago: Hildmann.

Fonagy, P. 2001. *Attachment Theory and Psychoanalysis*. New York: Other Press.

Fook, J. 1993. *Radical Casework: A Theory for Practice*. Sydney: Allen & Unwin.

—— 1999. Critical reflectivity in education and practice. In *Transforming Social Work Practice: Postmodern Critical Perspectives*, eds B. Pease & J. Fook. Sydney: Allen & Unwin, pp. 195–208.

—— 2002. *Social Work: Critical Theory and Practice*. London: Sage.

Fook, J. & Gardner, F. 2007. *Practising Critical Reflection: A Resource Handbook*. Maidenhead: Open University Press.

Foucault, M. 1979. Truth and power. In *Essential Works of Foucault, Volume 3: Power*, ed. J. Faubion. New York: The New Press.

Frank, A. 1995. *The Wounded Storyteller*. Chicago: University of Chicago Press.

Fraser, H. & McMaster, K. 2009. Gender, sexuality and power. In *Social Work: Contexts and Practice*, 2nd edn, eds M. Connolly & L. Harms. Melbourne: Oxford University Press, pp. 81–93.

Freedman, J. & Combs, G. 2009. Narrative ideas for consulting with communities and organizations: Ripples from the gatherings. *Family Process*, 48: 347–62.

Freud, S. 1975. *The Psychopathology of Everyday Life*, ed. J. Strachey. Ringwood: Penguin.

Friedman, B.D. & Neuman Allen, K. 2011. Systems theory. In *Theory and Practice in Clinical Social Work*, 2nd edn, ed. J.R. Brandell. Thousand Oaks, CA: Sage, pp. 3–20.

Frost, A. & Connolly, M. 2004. Reflexivity, reflection, and the change process in offender work. *Sexual Abuse: A Journal of Research and Treatment*, 16(4): 365–80.

Furlong, M. 2008. The multiple relationships between the discipline of social work and the contributions of Michael White. *Australian Social Work*, 61(4): 403–20.

Gambrill, E. 1995. Behavioral social work: Past, present, and future. *Research on Social Work Practice*, 5: 460–84.

Garland, E. 2013. Mindfulness research in social work: Conceptual and methodological recommendations. *Social Work Research*, 37(4): 439–48.

Gergen, K. 1985. The social constructionist movement in modern psychology. *American Psychologist*, 40(3): 266–75.

Germain, C. 1991. *Human Behavior in the Social Environment: An Ecological View*. New York: Columbia University Press.

Germain, C. & Bloom, M. 1999. *Human Behavior in the Social Environment: An Ecological View*, 2nd edn. New York: Columbia University Press, pp. 7–40.

Gibbons, J. 2001. Effective practice: Social work's long history of concern about outcomes. *Australian Social Work*, 54(3): 3–13.

Gibney, P. 2003. *The Pragmatics of Therapeutic Practice*. Melbourne: Psychoz.

Giddens, A. 1984. *The Constitution of Society: Outline of the Theory of Structuration*. Los Angeles: University of California Press.

Gilbert, S. 2013. Aboriginal issues in context. In *Social Work: Contexts and Practice*, 3rd edn, eds M. Connolly & L. Harms. Melbourne: Oxford University Press, pp. 111–23.

Goldstein, E. 1995. *Ego Psychology and Social Work Practice*, 2nd edn, Sydney: Free Press.

Goleman, D. 2005. *Emotional Intelligence*. New York: Bantam Books.

—— 2006. *Social Intelligence: The New Science of Human Relationships*. London: Hutchinson.

Gordon, C. (ed.). 1980. *Power/Knowledge: Selected Interviews and Other Writings by Michel Foucault*. New York: Pantheon Books.

Gould, N. 2006. An inclusive approach to knowledge for mental health social work practice and policy. *British Journal of Social Work*, 36: 109–25.

Granvold, D.K. 2011. Cognitive-behavioral therapy with adults. In *Theory and Practice in Clinical Social Work*, 2nd edn, ed. J.R. Brandell. Thousand Oaks, CA: Sage, pp. 179–212.

Gray, M. & McDonald, C. 2006. Pursuing good practice? The limits of evidence-based practice. *Journal of Social Work*, 6(1): 7–20.

Gray, M. & Webb, S.A. 2009. Critical social work. In *Social Work Theories and Methods*, eds M. Gray & S.A. Webb. London: Sage, pp. 76–85.

Green, D. & McDermott, F. 2010. Social work from inside and between complex systems: Perspectives on person-in-environment for today's social work. *British Journal of Social Work*, 40(8): 2414–30.

Green, S. & Baldry, E. 2008. Building Indigenous Australian social work. *Australian Social Work*, 61(4): 389–402.

Gunderson, K., Cahn, K. & Wirth, J. 2003. The Washington State long-term outcome study. *Protecting Children*, 18(1&2): 42–7.

Harms, L. 2007. *Working with People*. Melbourne: Oxford University Press.

—— 2010. *Understanding Human Development: A Multidimensional Approach*, 2nd edn. Melbourne: Oxford University Press.

Harms, L. & Connolly, M. 2013a. The art and science of social work. In *Social Work: Contexts and Practice*, 3rd edn, eds M. Connolly & L. Harms. Melbourne: Oxford University Press, pp. 3–18.

—— 2013b. Trans-Tasman reflections. In *Social Work: Contexts and Practice*, 3rd edn, eds M. Connolly & L. Harms. Melbourne: Oxford University Press, pp. 408–12.

Hart, M. 2010. Indigenous worldviews, knowledge, and research: The development of an Indigenous research paradigm. *Journal of Indigenous Voices in Social Work*, 1(1): 1–16.

Hayes, S. 2004. Acceptance and commitment to therapy, relational frame theory, and the third wave of behavioural and cognitive therapies. *Behaviour Therapy*, 35: 639–65.

Healy, K. 2005. *Social Work Theories in Context: Creating Frameworks for Practice*. Basingstoke: Palgrave Macmillan.

Hemingway, M. 2012. Community control: Aboriginal self-determination and Australian settler democracy: A history of the Victorian Aboriginal Health Service. PhD thesis, University of Melbourne.

Hepworth, D., Rooney, R. & Larsen, J. A. 2002. *Direct Social Work Practice: Theory and Skills*, 6th edn. Pacific Grove, CA: Brooks/Cole.

Herman, J. 1997. *Trauma and Recovery: The Aftermath of Violence – From Domestic Abuse to Political Power*. New York: Basic Books.

Hick, S.F. & Murray, K. 2009. Structural social work. In *Social Work Theories and Methods*, eds M. Gray & S.A. Webb. London: Sage, pp. 86–97.

HM Government. 2015. *Working Together to Safeguard Children*. London: HM Government.

Holland, S. 2004. *Child and Family Assessment in Social Work Practice*. London: Sage.

Holloway, E. & Neufeldt, S. 1995. Supervision: Its contributions to treatment efficacy. *Journal of Consulting and Clinical Psychology*, 63(2): 207–13.

hooks, b. 1984. *Feminist Theory: From Margin to Centre*. New York: South End Press.

Horvath, A.O. & Symonds, B.D. 1991. Relation between working alliance and outcome in psychotherapy: A meta-analysis. *Journal of Counselling Psychology*, 38: 139–49.

Howe, D. 1995. *Attachment Theory for Social Work Practice*. London: Macmillan.

—— 2009. *A Brief Introduction to Social Work Theory*. Basingstoke: Palgrave Macmillan.

Hudson, B.L. & McDonald, G. 1986. *Behavioural Social Work: An Introduction*. London: Macmillan.

Hudson, C. 2000. At the edge of chaos: A new paradigm for social work? *Journal of Social Work Education*, 36(2): 215–30.

Hutchison, E. (ed.) 1999. *Dimensions of Human Behavior: Person and Environment*. Thousand Oaks, CA: Pine Forge Press.

—— (2003), *Dimensions of Human Behavior: The Changing Life Course*, 2nd edn, Thousand Oaks, CA: Sage.

Ife, J. 2001. *Human Rights and Social Work: Towards Rights-based Practice*, Melbourne: Cambridge University Press.

Ingram, R., Fenton, J., Hodson, A. & Jindal-Snape, D. 2014. *Reflective Social Work Practice*. Basingstoke: Palgrave Macmillan.

Janoff-Bulman, R. 1992. *Shattered Assumptions: Towards a New Psychology of Trauma*. New York: Free Press.

Jordan, B. 2004. Emancipatory social work? Opportunity or oxymoron. *British Journal of Social Work*, 34: 5–19.

Kabat-Zinn, J. 2013. *Full Catastrophe Living: Using the Wisdom of your Body and Mind to Face Stress, Pain and Illness*, rev. edn. New York: Bantam Books.

Kadushin, A. 1972. *The Social Work Interview*. New York: Columbia University Press.

Kashdan, T. & Ciarrochi, J. 2013. *Mindfulness, Acceptance and Positive Psychology: The Seven Foundations of Wellbeing*. Oakland, CA: New Harbinger.

Kayser, K. 2011. Couple therapy. In *Theory and Practice in Clinical Social Work*, 2nd edn, ed. J.R. Brandell. Thousand Oaks, CA: Sage, pp. 259–88.

Kazantzis, N., Reinecke, M.A. & Freeman, A. 2010. *Cognitive and Behavioral Theories in Clinical Practice*. New York: Guilford Press.

Keenan, T. & Ward, T. 2003. Developmental antecedents of sexual offending. In *Sexual Deviance: Issues and Controversies*, eds T. Ward, D.R. Laws & S.M. Hudson. Thousand Oaks, CA: Sage, pp. 119–34.

Kemp, S., Whittaker, J. & Tracy, E. 1997. *Person-Environment Practice: The Social Ecology of Interpersonal Helping*. New York: Aldine de Gruyter.

Kleinman, A., Das, V. & Lock, M. (eds). 1997. *Social Suffering*. Berkeley, CA: University of California Press.

Koch, M., Hilt, L., Jenkins, L. & Dunn, T. 2006. Family group conferencing: 45 children – a 12 month study. Paper presented at the World Forum: Future Directions in Child Welfare, Vancouver, British Columbia, November.

Kondrat, D.C. 2010. The strengths perspective. In *An Introduction to Applying Social Work Theories and Methods*, ed. B. Teater, chapter 3, pp. 39–53. Maidenhead, UK: Open University Press.

Kondrat, M.E. 1999. Who is the 'self' in self-aware? Professional self-awareness from a critical theory perspective. *Social Service Review*, 73(4): 451–77.

Koole, S. 2009. The psychology of emotion regulation: An integrative review. *Cognition and Emotion*, 23(1): 4–41.

Kovach, M. 2010. Conversational method in Indigenous research. *First Peoples Child and Family Review*, 5(1): 40–8.

Kunoth-Monks, R. 2014. '*I am not the problem*', speech, *Q&A*, ABC Television, 9 October.

Lambert, M. & Barley, D. 2001. Research summary on the therapeutic relationship and psychotherapy outcome. *Psychotherapy*, 38(4): 357–61.

Langer, E., Blank, A. & Chanowitz, B. 1978. The mindlessness of ostensibly thoughtful action: The role of 'placebic' information in interpersonal interaction. *Journal of Personality and Social Psychology*, 36(6): 635–42.

Laub, D. & Auerhahn, N. 1993. Knowing and not knowing massive psychic trauma: Forms of traumatic memory. *International Journal of Psycho-Analysis*, 74: 287–302.

Leadbetter, M. 2002. Empowerment and advocacy. In *Social Work: Themes, Issues and Critical Debates*, eds R. Adams, L. Dominelli & M. Payne, 2nd edn. Basingstoke: Palgrave Macmillan, pp. 200–8.

Lee, M. & Greene, G.J. (1999). A social constructivist framework for integrating cross-cultural issues in teaching clinical social work. *Journal of Social Work Education*, 35(1): 21–37.

Lee, M.Y., Ng, S.-M., Leung, P. & Chan, C. 2009. *Integrative Body–Mind–Spirit Social Work: An Empirically Based Approach to Assessment and Treatment*. New York: Oxford University Press.

Leiden University Institute for History. 2014. Memory, concepts and theory. *Tales of the Revolt*. Retrieved 9 December 2014, http://www.hum.leiden.edu/history/talesoftherevolt/approach/approach-1.html,

Leighninger, L. 1987. *Social Work: Search for Identity*. New York: Greenwood Press.

Lishman, J. 2002. Personal and professional development. In *Social Work: Themes, Issues and Critical Debates*, 2nd edn, eds R. Adams, L. Dominelli &. M. Payne. Basingstoke: Palgrave, pp. 95–108.

Lonne, B., Parton, N., Thomson, J. & Harries, M. 2009. *Reforming Child Protection*. Oxford: Routledge.

Lyth, I.M. 1988. *Selected Essays*. London: Free Association Books.

Mafile'o, T. 2013. Pasifika social work. In *Social Work: Contexts and Practice*, 3rd edn, eds M. Connolly & L. Harms. Melbourne: Oxford University Press, pp. 138–50.

Mandell, D. 2007. Use of self: Contexts and dimensions. In *Revisiting the Use of Self: Questioning Professional Identities*, ed. D. Mandell. Toronto: Canadian Scholars' Press, pp. 1–19.

Marshall, W.L., Serran, G.A., Fernandez, Y.M., Mulloy, R., Mann, R.E. & Thornton, D. 2003. Therapist characteristics in the treatment of sexual offenders: tentative data on their relationship with indices of behaviour change. *Journal of Sexual Aggression*, 9: 25–30.

McKee, M. 2003. Excavating our frames of mind: The key to dialogue and collaboration. *Social Work*, 48(3): 401–8.

McKeown, K. 2000. *Supporting Families: A Guide to What Works in Family Support Services for Vulnerable Families*. Unpublished report. Dublin: Department of Health and Children.

McPhie, L. & Chaffey, C. 1999. The journey of a lifetime: Group work with young women who have experienced sexual assault. In *Extending Narrative Therapy: A Collection of Practice-based Papers*, ed. Dulwich Centre. Adelaide: Dulwich Centre Publications.

McQueen, C. & Hobbs, C. 2014. Working with parents: Using narrative therapy to work towards genuine partnership. *Educational and Child Psychology*, 31(4): 9–17.

Melbourne Museum. 2014. *Coranderrk Petition*. Retrieved 16 December 2014, http://museumvictoria.com.au/melbournemuseum/whatson/current-exhibitions/melbournestory/favourite-objects/coranderrk-petition.

Mendes, P. 2009. Tracing the origins of critical social work practice. In *Critical Social Work: Theories and Practices for a Socially Just World*, 2nd edn, eds J. Allan, L. Briskman & B. Pease. Sydney: Allen & Unwin, pp. 17–29.

Mennen, F.E. & O'Keefe, M. 2005. Informed decisions in child welfare: The use of attachment theory. *Children and Youth Services Review*, 27: 577–93.

Miehls, D. 2011. Neurobiology and clinical social work. In *Theory and Practice in Clinical Social Work*, 2nd edn, ed. J.R. Brandell. Thousand Oaks, CA: Sage, pp. 81–98.

Mikhailova, O. & Nol, J. 2011. Clinical social work with depressed clients. In *Theory and Practice in Clinical Social Work*, 2nd edn, ed. J.R. Brandell. Thousand Oaks, CA: Sage, pp. 471–500.

Miller, S. Hubble, M., Chow, D. & Seidel, J. 2014. The outcome of psychotherapy: Yesterday, today and tomorrow. *Psychotherapy in Australia*, 20(3): 64–75.

Miller, S., Hubble, M. & Duncan, B. (eds). 1996. *Handbook of Solution-focused Brief Therapy*. San Francisco: Jossey-Bass.

Minuchin, S. & Fishman, H. 1981. *Family Therapy Techniques*. Cambridge, MA: Harvard University Press.

Montalbano-Phelps, L. 2004. *Taking Narrative Risk: The Empowerment of Abuse Survivors*. Dallas, TX: University Press of America.

Moore, T. 2004. *Dark Nights of the Soul: A Guide to Finding Your Way Through Life's Ordeals.* London: Piatkus Books.

Morris, J. 1993. *Independent Lives: Community Care and Disabled People.* Basingstoke: Macmillan.

Morris, K. 2007. Camden family group conference service: An evaluation of service use and outcomes. Retrieved 30 May 2011, http://www.frg.org.uk/pdfs/Camden%20FGC%20Service.pdf.

Mullaly, B. 2002. *Challenging Oppression: A Critical Social Work Approach.* Ontario: Oxford University Press.

Munford, R. & Sanders, J. 1999. *Supporting Families.* Palmerston North, NZ: Dunmore Press.

Murphy, D., Archard, P.J., Regel, S. & Joseph, S. 2013. A survey of specialized traumatic stress services in the United Kingdom. *Journal of Psychiatric and Mental Health Nursing,* 20(5): 433–41.

Nakata, M. 2007. The cultural interface. *The Australian Journal of Indigenous Education,* 36(Supplement): 7–14.

Nathan, L., Wilson, N.J. & Hillman, D. 2003. *Te Whakakotahitanga: An Evaluation of the Te Piriti Special Treatment Programme.* Retrieved 30 May 2011, http://www.corrections.govt.nz/_data/assets/pdf_file/0005/176954/tewhaka.pdf.

National Aboriginal Community Controlled Health Organisation (NACCHO). 2014. Aboriginal health. http://www.naccho.org.au/aboriginal-health/definitions.

National Inquiry into the Separation of Aboriginal and Torres Strait Islander Children from Their Families. 1997. *Bringing Them Home: Report of the National Inquiry into the Separation of Aboriginal and Torres Strait Islander Children from Their Families.* Sydney: Human Rights and Equal Opportunity Commission.

Nelson-Jones, R. 2006. *Theory and Practice of Counselling and Therapy,* 4th edn. Thousand Oaks, CA: Sage.

Nickel, J.W. 2007. *Making Sense of Human Rights,* 2nd edn. Oxford: Blackwell.

Nipperess, S. & Briskman, L. 2009. Promoting a human rights perspective on critical social work. In *Critical Social Work Theories and Practices for a Socially Just World,* 2nd edn, eds J. Allan, L. Briskman & B. Pease. Sydney: Allen & Unwin, pp. 58–69.

Noble, C. & Irwin, J. 2009. Social work supervision: An exploration of the current challenges in a rapidly changing social, economic and political environment. *Journal of Social Work,* 9(3): 345–58.

Norlin, J., Chess, W., Dale, O. & Smith, R. 2003. *Human Behavior and the Social Environment: Social Systems Theory,* 4th edn. Boston: Allyn & Bacon.

O'Connell, B. 1998. *Solution-focused Therapy.* London: Sage.

Orme, J. 2009. Feminist social work. In M. Gray & S.A. Webb (eds), *Social Work Theories and Methods.* London: Sage.

Owen, I. 1999. Exploring the similarities and differences between person-centred and psychodynamic therapy. *British Journal of Guidance and Counselling,* 27(2): 165–78.

Paradies, Y.C. 2006. Beyond black and white: Essentialism, hybridity and indigeneity. *Journal of Sociology,* 42(4): 355–67.

Parliament of Australia. 2014. *Defining Aboriginality in Australia.* Retrieved 11 December 2014, http://www.aph.gov.au/About_Parliament/Parliamentary_Departments/Parliamentary_Library/Publications_Archive/CIB/cib0203/03Cib10,

Parton, N., Thorpe, D. & Wattam, C. 1997. *Child Protection: Risk and the Moral Order.* London: Macmillan.

Patterson, J. & Garwick, A. 1994. Levels of meaning in family stress theory. *Family Process,* 33(3): 287–304.

—— 2005. Systemic and ecological approaches. *Modern Social Work Theory,* 3rd edn. Chicago: Lyceum Books, pp. 108–20.

Payne, M. 2005. *Modern Social Work Theory.* Basingstoke: Palgrave Macmillan.

Pemberton, A. & Locke, R. 1971. Towards a radical critique of social work and welfare ideology. *Australian Journal of Social Issues*, 6(2): 95–107.

Pennebaker, J. (ed.) 1995. *Emotion, Disclosure and Health*. Washington, DC: American Psychological Society.

Pennell, J. & Burford, G. 2000. Family group decision-making: Protecting children and women. *Child Welfare*, 79(2): 131–58.

Perlman, H.H. 1957. *Social Casework: A Problem-solving Process*. Chicago: Chicago University Press.

Phillipson, J. 2002. Supervision and being supervised. In *Critical Practice in Social Work*, eds R. Adams, L. Dominelli & M. Payne. New York: Palgrave, pp. 244–51.

Pithers, W.D., Marques, J.K., Gibat, C.C. & Marlatt, G.A. 1983. Relapse prevention with sexual aggressors: A self-control model of treatment and maintenance of change. In *The Sexual Aggressor: Current Perspectives on Treatment*, eds J.G. Greer & I.R. Stuart. New York: Van Nostrand Reinhold, pp. 214–39.

Plath, D. 2009. Evidence-based practice. In *Social Work Theories and Methods*, eds M. Gray & S. Webb. London: Sage, pp. 173–83.

Ramsden, I. & O'Brien, L. 2000. Defining cultural safety and transcultural nursing. Letter to the editor. *Kai Tiaki: Nursing New Zealand*, 6(8): 4.

Raphael, B. & Swan, P. 1998. The mental health of Aboriginal and Torres Strait Islander people. *International Journal of Mental Health*, 26(3): 9–22.

Rapp, C.A. 1998. *The Strengths Model: Case Management with People Suffering from Severe and Persistent Mental Illness*. New York: Oxford University Press.

Reichert, E. 2007. *Challenges in Human Rights: A Social Work Perspective*. New York: Columbia University Press.

Reid, W. & Epstein, L. 1972. *Task-centered Casework*. New York: Columbia University Press.

Reid, W.J. & Shyne, A. 1969. *Brief and Extended Casework*. New York: Columbia University Press.

Reiter, A. 2005. *Narrating the Holocaust*. London: Continuum.

Richmond, M. 1917. *Social Diagnosis*. New York: Russell Sage Foundation.

Robertson, R. 1995. Chaos theory and the relationship between psychology and science. In *Chaos Theory in Psychology and the Life Sciences*, eds R. Robertson & A. Combs. Mahwah, NJ: Lawrence Erlbaum, pp. 3–16.

Rogers, C. 1965. *Client-centered Therapy: Its Current Practice Implications and Theory*. Boston: Houghton Mifflin.

—— 1980. *A Way of Being*. Boston: Houghton Mifflin.

Rossiter, A. 2000. The post-modern feminist condition: New conditions for social work. In *Research in Social Work: Post-modern Feminist Perspectives*, eds B. Fawcett, B. Featherstone, J. Fook & A. Rossiter. London: Routledge.

Roth, A. & Fonagy, P. 1996. *What Works for Whom: A Critical Review of Psychotherapy Research*. New York: Guilford Press.

Rubin, D., Downes, K., O'Reilly, A., Mekonnen, R., Luan, X. & Localio, R. (2008). Impact of kinship care on behavioral well-being for children in out-of-home care. *Archives of Pediatric and Adolescent Medicine*, 162(6): 550–6.

Ruwhiu, L. 2013. Indigenous issues in Aotearoa New Zealand. In *Social Work: Contexts and Practice*, 3rd edn, eds M. Connolly & L. Harms. Melbourne: Oxford University Press, pp. 124–37.

Sackett, D., Rosenberg, W., Muir Gray, J., Haynes, R. & Richardson, W. 1996. Evidence-based medicine: what it is and what it isn't. *British Medical Journal*, 312(7023): 71–2.

Said, E. 1978. *Orientalism*. New York: Vintage Books.

Saleebey, D. (ed.) 1997. *The Strengths Perspective in Social Work Practice*. New York: Longman.

Salter, A.C. 1995. *Transforming Trauma: A Guide to Understanding and Treating Adult Survivors of Child Sexual Abuse*. London: Sage.

Sandler, J. 1985. *The Analysis of Defense: The Ego and the Mechanisms of Defense Revisited*. New York: International Universities Press.

Schön, D. 1983. *The Reflective Practitioner*. London: Temple Smith.

—— 1987. *Educating the Reflective Practitioner: Towards a New Design for Teaching and Learning in the Professions*. San Francisco: Jossey-Bass.

Schore, A. 2002. Dysregulation of the right brain: A fundamental mechanism of traumatic attachment and the psychopathogenesis of posttraumatic stress disorder. *Australian and New Zealand Journal of Psychiatry*, 36: 9–30.

Scott, D., Walker, L. & Gilmore, K. 1995. *Breaking the Silence: A Guide to Supporting Adult Victim/Survivors of Sexual Assault*, 2nd edn. Melbourne: CASA House.

Sennett, R. 2003. *Respect in a World of Inequality*. New York: W.W. Norton.

Sheehan, R. 2013. Social work and the law. In *Social Work: Contexts and Practice*, 2nd edn, eds M. Connolly & L. Harms. Melbourne: Oxford University Press, pp. 334–44.

Sheldon, B. 1995. *Cognitive-Behavioural Therapy: Research, Practice and Philosophy*. London: Tavistock.

Sheldon, B. & Macdonald, G. 2009. *A Textbook of Social Work*. London: Routledge.

Sheppard, M. 1998. Practice validity, reflexivity and knowledge for social work. *British Journal of Social Work*, 28(5): 763–81.

Shera, W. & Wells, L.M. (eds) 1999. *Empowerment Practice in Social Work: Developing Richer Conceptual Foundations*. Toronto: Canadian Scholars' Press.

Shonkoff, J. & Phillips, D. (eds). 2000. *From Neurons to Neighbourhoods: The Science of Early Childhood Development*. Washington, DC: National Academy Press.

Shulman, L. 1993. *Interactional Supervision*. Washington, DC: NASW Press.

Skenridge, P. & Lennie, I. 1978. Social work: The wolf in sheep's clothing. *Arena*, 51: 47–92.

Smith, L.T. 2003. *Decolonizing Methodologies: Research and Indigenous Peoples*. Dunedin, NZ: University of Otago Press.

Spitzer, R. 1981. The diagnostic status of homosexuality in DSM-III: A reformulation of the issues. *American Journal of Psychiatry*, 138: 210–15.

Staples, L. 1990. Powerful ideas about empowerment. *Administration in Social Work*, 14: 29–42.

Sternberg, E. 2010. *Healing Spaces: The Science of Place and Well-being*. Cambridge, MA: Belknap Press.

Stone, S., Berzin, S., Taylor, S. & Austin, M. 2008. Human behavior and the social environment: Exploring conceptual foundations. In *Comprehensive Handbook of Social Work and Social Welfare: Human Behavior in the Social Environment*, vol. 2, ed. B. Thyer. New York: John Wiley & Sons.

Strom-Gottfried, K. 2002a. Multidimensional assessment. In *Direct Social Work Practice: Theory and Skills*, 6th edn, eds D.H. Hepworth, R.H. Rooney & J.A. Larsen, Pacific Grove, CA: Brooks/Cole, pp. 187–217.

—— 2002b. Assessing intrapersonal and environmental systems. In *Direct Social Work Practice: Theory and Skills*, 6th edn, eds. D.H. Hepworth, R.H. Rooney & J.A. Larsen. Pacific Grove CA: Brooks/Cole, pp. 219–58.

Teater, B. 2010. *An Introduction to Applying Social Work Theories and Methods*. Maidenhead: Open University Press.

Thoburn, J. 2007. *Globalisation and Child Welfare: Some Lessons from a Cross-National Study of Children in Out-of-Home Care*. Norwich: University of East Anglia, School of Social Work and Psychosocial Studies.

Thompson, N. 2002. *People Skills*, 2nd edn. New York: Palgrave Macmillan.

—— 2003. *Promoting Equality: Challenging Discrimination and Oppression*, 2nd edn. Basingstoke: Palgrave.

—— 2006. *Anti-Discriminatory Practice*. Basingstoke: Palgrave Macmillan.

Thorne, B. 1997. Person-centred counselling. In *The Blackwell Companion to Social Work*, ed. M. Davies, pp. 177–84. Oxford: Blackwell.

Thyer, B.A. & Myers, L.L. 2011. Behavioural and cognitive theories. In *Theory and Practice in Clinical Social Work*, 2nd edn, ed. J.R. Brandell. Thousand Oaks, CA: Sage, pp. 21–40.

Titcomb, A. & LeCroy, C. 2005. Outcomes of Arizona's family group decision making program. *Protecting Children*, 19(4): 47–53.

Trevithick, P. 1998. *Feminism and Psychotherapy: Reflections on Contemporary Theories and Practices*. London: Sage.

—— 2012. *Social Work Skills and Knowledge: A Practice Handbook*, 3rd edn. Milton Keyes: Open University Press.

Trotter, C. 2004. *Helping Abused Children and Their Families*. Sydney: Allen & Unwin.

Tumarkin, M. 2005. *Traumascapes: The Power and Fate of Places Transformed by Tragedy*. Melbourne: Melbourne University Press.

Turnell, A. & Edwards, S. 1999. *Signs of Safety: A Solution and Safety Oriented Approach to Child Protection Casework*. New York: W.W. Norton.

Ungunmerr-Baumann, M.R. 2002. *Dadirri: Inner Deep Listening and Quiet Still Awareness*. Daly River: Emmaus Productions.

Vaillant, G. 1993. *The Wisdom of the Ego*, Cambridge, MA: Harvard University Press.

—— 2002. *Ageing Well: Surprising Guideposts to a Happier Life from the Landmark Harvard Study of Adult Development*. Melbourne: Scribe.

Wacquant, L. 1998. Pierre Bourdieu. In *Key Sociological Thinkers*, ed. R. Stones. New York: New York University Press.

Wakefield, J. 1996a. Does social work need the eco-systems perspective? Part 1: Is the perspective clinically useful? *Social Service Review*, March: 1–31.

—— 1996b. Does social work need the eco-systems perspective? Part 2: Does the perspective save social work from incoherence? *Social Service Review*, March: 183–213.

Walsh, F. 1998. *Strengthening Family Resilience*. New York: Guilford Press.

Walsh, J. 2006. *Theories for Direct Social Work Practice*. Belmont, CA: Thompson Brooks/Cole.

Walsh, R. & Shapiro, S. 2006. The meeting of meditative disciplines and Western psychology. *American Psychologist*, 61: 227–39.

Walsh-Tapiata, W. & Webster, J. 2004. *Te Mahere*: The supervision plan. In *The Proceedings of the Te Rau Tipu Māori Mental Health Child and Adolescent Workforce Conference*, ed. T. Waetford. Palmerston North, NZ: Massey University, pp. 31–38. Retrieved 20 November 2014, http://www.matatini.co.nz/sites/default/files/resources/publications/tipu_ conference.pdf.

Ward, T. 2002. Good lives and the rehabilitation of sex offenders: problems and promises. *Aggression and Violent Behavior*, 7: 1–17.

Ward, T. & Connolly, M. 2008. A human rights-based practice framework for sex offenders. *Journal of Sexual Aggression*, 14(2): 87–98.

Watson, S. 2005. Attachment theory and social work. In *Social Work Theories in Action*, eds M. Nash, R. Munford & K. O'Donoghue. London: Jessica Kingsley, pp. 208–22.

Watzlawick, P., Weakland, J. & Fisch, R. 1974. *Change: Principles of Problem Formation and Problem Resolution*. New York: W.W. Norton.

Webber, M. & Nathan, J. 2010. Challenges and opportunities for psychosocial practice in mental health. In *Reflective Practice in Mental Health: Advanced Psychosocial Practice with Children, Adolescents and Adults*, eds M. Webber & J. Nathan. London: Jessica Kingsley, pp. 254–62.

Wheeler, C.E. & Johnson, S. 2003. Evaluating family group decision making: The Santa Clara example. *Protecting Children*, 18(1&2): 65–9.

White, M. 2007. *Maps of Narrative Practice*. New York: W.W. Norton.

White, M. & Epston, D. 1990. *Narrative Means to Therapeutic Ends*. New York: W.W. Norton.

Wingard, B. & Lester, J. 2001. *Telling Our Stories in Ways That Make Us Stronger*. Adelaide: Dulwich Centre Publications.

Wolpe, J. 1990. *The Practice of Behaviour Therapy*, 4th edn. New York: Pergamon Press.

Wronka, J. 2008. *Human Rights and Social Justice: Social Action and Service for the Helping and Health Professions*. Thousand Oaks, CA: Sage.

Index